# Agriculture, Trade, and the Environment: Discovering and Measuring the Critical Linkages

# Agriculture, Trade, and the Environment: Discovering and Measuring the Critical Linkages

edited by
## Maury E. Bredahl, Nicole Ballenger, John C. Dunmore, and Terry L. Roe

WestviewPress
*A Division of* HarperCollins*Publishers*

Copyright © 1996 by Westview Press, Inc., A Division of HarperCollins Publishers, Inc., except for Chapters 3, 5, 6, and 15, which are works of the U.S. Government

Published in 1996 in the United States of America by Westview Press, Inc., 5500 Central Avenue, Boulder, Colorado 80301-2877, and in the United Kingdom by Westview Press, 12 Hid's Copse Road, Cumnor Hill, Oxford OX2 9JJ

A CIP catalog record for this book is available from the Library of Congress.
ISBN 0-8133-8896-1 (HC)

The paper used in this publication meets the requirements of the American National Standard for Permanence of Paper for Printed Library Materials Z39.48-1984.

10    9    8    7    6    5    4    3    2    1

# Contents

# Preface

The International Agricultural Trade Research Consortium (IATRC) is a group of 160 economists from 16 countries who are interested in fostering research relating to international trade of agricultural products and commodities and providing a forum for the exchange of ideas. Each summer the IATRC sponsors a symposium on a topic relating to trade and trade policy from which proceedings are published. A list of past symposia and related publications may be obtained from Laura Bipes, IATRC Executive Director, Department of Applied Economics, University of Minnesota, St. Paul, MN 55108.

The financial support of the Economic Research Service, the Foreign Agricultural Service and the Cooperative State Research Service of the U. S. Department of Agriculture, Agriculture Canada, and U.S. Agency for International Development and MUCIA, under the auspices of the Environmental and Natural Resources Policy and Training Project, made the conference and this book possible.

The editors acknowledge the help of Laura Bipes of the University of Minnesota for arranging the symposium. A special thanks to Denise Gray of the Economic Research Service for her diligent and timely review of many of the chapters and for suggestions on organization. Cynthia Barnes, Jody Pestle and Judith Harrison provided expert technical and grammatical editing. Finally, Anne Roehlke is thanked for preparing the camera-ready copy of this book, with grace, wisdom, dedication, and a greatly appreciated sense of humor.

*Maury E. Bredahl*
*Nicole Ballenger*
*John C. Dunmore*
*Terry L. Roe*

# PART ONE

# Introduction

# 1

# Introduction

*Maury E. Bredahl, Nicole Ballenger and John C. Dunmore*

Most of the chapters in this book were presented at a symposium sponsored by the International Agricultural Trade Research Consortium: Agriculture, Trade and the Environment: Understanding and Measuring the Critical Linkages. Additional chapters were invited to provide more complete coverage of the broad range of topics in this area.

The symposium grew from the perceived opportunity to contribute to the debate on the interaction of trade and the environment, with a special emphasis on agricultural trade and the interaction of food and agricultural production with the environment. The goals of the symposium, and this book, were:

- to explore the important policy issues in the trade and environment debate, the perspectives of different interest groups, and the evolving roles of international institutions such as the World Trade Organization and NAFTA;
- to focus the trade and environment debate on agricultural and natural resource issues;
- to assess the state of knowledge in the economics profession regarding two sets of critical linkages: between agricultural trade liberalization and natural resources and the environment, and between environmental policy and agricultural trade and competitiveness;
- and to identify a research agenda for agricultural economists, particularly trade consortium members.

Reflecting that agenda, the book is divided into four parts. The first explores the emerging critical linkages of trade, international institutions and the environment. The second develops the conceptual linkages between trade, renewable resources and international environmental goods.

The third part presents a variety of measurements of the critical linkages. Measurements range from the global effects of trade liberalization on the environment to the decidedly micro-level analysis of the impacts of trade policies on agricultural production and environmental quality in the Andes. Other chapters attempt to measure the impacts of environmental regulations on the competitiveness of agricultural production in the developed countries. The final part of the book attempts to identify research issues and the needs for future research.

The chapters in Section II of this book are about the interest groups and political forces that are shaping the trade and environment debate, and thereby reshaping the institutions and rules of international trade. These chapters also turn to economics to ask: what is known generally about the conceptual and empirical linkages between trade and the environment; and to ask what can economics contribute to resolving the more critical issues?

Bhagwati opens in Chapter 2 by acknowledging that trade and environment issues became important in shaping the final outcome of the Uruguay Round and the implementation of the World Trade Organization. Pointing to the economics literature, which finds a positive correlation between income growth (stimulated by freer trade) and the demand for environmental protection, and the initial empirical evidence regarding the impacts of agricultural trade liberalization on the environment, he concludes there is no inherent reason that the two great objectives of environmental protection and freer trade cannot both be pursued. Bhagwati also reasons the institution of the GATT can and will accommodate some legitimate concerns raised by environmentalists.

Bhagwati discusses "competitiveness and harmonization" issues, particularly the concern of countries with high environmental standards for the competitiveness of their industries. While making the case for the validity of diverse preferences and, thus, differing standards and tax rates, Bhagwati also acknowledges that political market failures can lead to lower-than-optimal levels of environmental protection in these countries with lower standards. He indicates a possible practical solution of requiring multinational firms to follow "home" rules and preferences.

A later section of the chapter discusses "values-related issues," which include objections to the ways in which goods are produced—such as catching tuna in a manner that harms dolphins or trapping fur-bearing animals in steel leg-hold traps. Bhagwati again argues in favor of preserving a diversity of production and processing methods (PPMs)—and suggests that allowing general objections to PPMs based on value judgements could lead to serious trouble for international trade. However, striking a practical note, he suggests that specific pernicious practices could be outlawed based upon international consensus. He also suggests that environmental interests should be better represented in the GATT's dispute settlement process in order to provide more balance. Overall, he believes the GATT is on the right track and that many environmental objectives can be accommodated without real difficulty.

In the third chapter, Gruenspecht also reviews the evidence regarding trade and environment linkages. In the second section of his chapter, he discusses the politics that have demanded the two issues be linked. In the last section, he reflects on the environmental implications of the Uruguay Round. According to Gruenspecht, the evidence does not support the view that current environmental regulations affect competitiveness to any significant degree. There is evidence, however, that the trade liberalization—through its well-recognized impact on economic growth—enhances the demand for environmental protections generally. An important exception is carbon dioxide emissions, which increase with income.

According to Gruenspecht, the potential loss of specific, identifiable jobs (not the impact on jobs in the aggregate), motivates the concern with both trade liberalization and environmental regulation, and thus provides the political demand for linkage. The call for international harmonization of environmental standards, as one example, reflects the environmentalists' interest in removing political objections to their agenda from vulnerable labor and industry groups. Gruenspecht also notes that some environmental interest groups oppose trade liberalization for strategic reasons even when their own internal analyses show net environmental gains; the reasons are to get better deals or to raise their influence in the WTO.

In reflecting on the outcome of the Uruguay Round, Gruenspecht sees increased latitude for environmental policy actions, particularly through changes to the sanitary and phytosanitary code, the technical barriers to trade code, and the agreement on subsidies and countervailing measures. He foresees increases in the use of environmental policy as a form of protection, and that trade liberalization losers will align themselves with environmental interests.

In the fourth chapter, Ambassador Smith poses the daunting challenges facing negotiators of a "Green Round." "If we think we endured agonies in agriculture just from a trade viewpoint," he writes, "imagine what torture we have in store when the traders and the environmentalists lock horns over agriculture in the Green Round. If the trading system survives, it will be akin to a miracle." Concerned by this potential, Smith has been bringing the traders and the environmentalists together in a "pretrench" effort to find common ground. He believes the first challenge is to design a trading system that to the greatest degree possible takes into account environmental impacts. (He believes this can be done because many free traders are at heart sympathetic to environmental concerns.) Thus, environmental impact statements are not uncalled for; likewise, environmental measures should require a "trade impact statement." In other words, politicians and citizens should know the benefits and costs of both trade and environmental measures. Smith argues that economists can contribute significantly by computing non-market values for external—or environmental—costs.

Another major challenge to the traders and the environmentalists is to reach an agreement on the use of trade tools to enforce environmental rules. Smith believes that the trading system has an obligation to the world's citizens not to condone the ruthless spoiling of the planet. However, he argues, trade policy offers the only current means of enforcing multinational environmental agreements; and thus there must also be other forms of penalties if the trading system is to survive. The issue of whether environmental subsidies will be countervailable poses another serious challenge to the Green Round negotiators. Lastly, Smith argues that the traders and the environmentalists must both "weed out the extremists" if a consensus is to be reached.

In Chapter 5, Charnovitz introduces the "ecolonomy," a planetary system in which the economy and the environment are symbiotic systems. The first section of the chapter discusses the connections between economic and environmental policy making, and the need for closer linkages at all levels of government. Charnovitz notes that the new generation of market-oriented environmental policies is an example of how a closer connection between economics and the environment can yield better outcomes. Despite the potential for collaboration, the goals of economists and environmentalists are fundamentally different, he states.

In the second section Charnovitz turns to rules for the ecolonomy. He makes the point that even if nations did not trade at all they would need environmental agreements so long as they share the planet. The existence of trade complicates environmental policy because consuming nations do not regulate the production of what they consume, which interferes with their ability "to engage in social costs internalization, life cycle analysis, and sustainable development," weakening the ability of governments to engage in environmental regulation. Thus, trade strengthens the case for better international environmental governance.

In the last section, Charnovitz makes the case for a global environmental organization (GEO) rather than a "greener" WTO, because the WTO mandate is already broad and demanding enough. A GEO would devise environmental standards for serious issues; conduct negotiating rounds; reconcile international environmental disputes; and improve the delivery of environmental technical assistance. Environmental non-government organizations would be represented alongside governments and businesses at the GEO.

Ballenger and Krissoff turn from GATT (and the Uruguay and "Green" Rounds) to NAFTA (and its environmental provisions and side agreement). They first review the environmental provisions and terms of the side agreement. They make the point that there has been little economic analysis of the environmental agreements because the provisions are difficult to interpret and much less specific than the trade provisions (which have been analyzed quite thoroughly). Ballenger and Krissoff suggest, however, that the environmental components may, over the long run, have a greater impact than the reductions in trade barriers. This is, in part, because they create a "living" document. They establish new institutional structures and rules—that promote environmental cooperation and facilitate public challenge—and thus have the potential to generate a continuing evolution of environmental policy change.

In the next section of the chapter, they report the results of interviews with environmental and farm groups that had an interest in NAFTA. They found that environmental and farm groups shared an interest in the sanitary and phytosanitary provisions: both groups were concerned that the agreement would result in easier entry into the United States for Mexican food and agricultural products that do not currently meet U.S. health and safety standards. Some farm and some environmental groups (particularly those that ultimately opposed NAFTA) also shared an interest in the impacts of trade liberalization on smaller family farms and sustainable agriculture in the U.S., and environmental organizations expressed concern with the impacts on Mexico's small-scale, subsistence producers. Both groups felt that the PPM debate, not being resolved in the NAFTA, is likely to become very important for agriculture.

Despite statements of shared interests and concerns, environmental groups felt they knew too little about agriculture (or how it related to their issues) and farm groups were not very involved in the discussions or negotiations surrounding the environmental provisions.

The chapters of Part III turn to the critical linkages of trade, renewable resources and international environmental goods. The thrust of Chapter 7 by Heal is the management of international environmental goods. Examples of such goods include climate change from the emission of carbon dioxide, depletion of the ozone layer, and acid rain and the international movement of environmental pollutants. Heal develops a model of efficient carbon dioxide abatement characterized by trade in private goods and emission permits. Surprisingly, trade in goods coupled with international trade of emission permits does not lead to an efficient outcome. Rather, additional lump-sum transfers are needed to reach an economically efficient point.

Heal then applies the framework of trading emission permits to the joint implementation introduced at the Rio Convention on Climate Change. Joint implementation is reasoned to be an inadequate precursor to trading of emission permits, but it is an approach that might be justified if there is a clear migration to a more multilateral and organized market for permits.

Chichilnisky focuses on the linkage of property rights, trade, and resource dynamics in Chapter 8. A traditional model of trade is modified in two important ways. First, one of the inputs in production is an environmental resource, i.e., it is renewable and exhaustible. The second is the assumption of differing regimes for property rights in the two regions. Chichilnisky concludes that the difference in property rights is sufficient to explain differing trade patterns between two regions with the same endowments, preferences and technologies. The logic is extended to trade between the North and the South, with the conclusion that property rights improvements in the South could mitigate the economic source of resource overuse (prices which are below social costs).

Diao and Roe develop a general-equilibrium model, where health is an argument of the utility function, to consider trade impacts of three types of pollution: local-disembodied (local air pollution), global-disembodied (pollution that migrates to other regions), and embodied pollution (associated with consumption of the good). The model is complex, and meaningful results can be arrived at only with a number of assumptions about the relative size of certain effects.

The results show that an optimal tax can, in principle, improve each country's welfare if the country is small in the world market. However, for a large country or region, changes in the terms of trade may cause one country to be made better off at the expense of the other. Then, a Pareto improvement can only be reached by an optimal tax with compensation, which suggests that some form of compensatory payment may be required to encourage the other country to pursue abatement policies. Under cooperative behavior, both countries can improve their welfare by jointly imposing a pollution control tax with a necessarily compensatory transfer.

For the case of embodied pollution, the optimal tax for the exporting country not only depends on its own marginal welfare loss of pollution, but also on the losses the country's exports caused on consumers in the importing country. Further, if only the polluting input is taxed, then its after tax rental rate falls if this input is intensively used. Hence the effectiveness of this instrument to lower the embodied pollutants is limited and can even be negative. Instead, a tax on the polluting input in combination with a subsidy to the non-polluting input can reduce pollution and improve a country's welfare if the country is small in the world market.

Whalley, in Chapter 10, surveys the quantitative dimensions of linkages between trade and the environment emerging from economy wide modeling. Preliminary findings from five studies are summarized. Whalley concludes that many of the proposed environmentally motivated trade actions have surprising little consequence for the global system. Conversely, environmentally motivated policies, such as carbon taxes, have major impacts on global production and trade patterns.

The policy debate surrounding the trade and environment nexus will increasingly demand informed answers to the questions: (1) How do environmental policies affect agricultural trade and competitiveness; and (2) How will trade and policy reform, and accompanying economic growth, affect environmental quality. Section IV reviews various attempts at quantifying the trade and environment linkage. Accurate empirical estimates of the trade and competitiveness consequences of environmental policy and regulation, or the environmental consequences of trade and policy reform are difficult to obtain. While the authors review a multitude of specific constraints to obtaining accurate empirical estimates, most fall into the generic class of "aggregation problems"—the difficulty in linking site-specific environmental and resource adjustments with trade or policy adjustments occurring at a nation's border.

Chapters by Blom (13), Gardner (14), and Leuck and Haley (15) consider agriculture related environmental policies in the United States (Gardner) and Europe (Blom, and Haley and Leuck) and derive implications for the balance of agricultural trade and competition in the global marketplace. They conclude that environmental policies can and do influence the level and composition of trade, as well as the competitive positions of countries, industries, and firms. However, they also conclude that the direction and magnitude of the effect of environmental regulation on costs of production, prices, and trade competitiveness in agriculture could vary on the basis of several factors, thus it is difficult to make generalizations. For example, Gardner points to the stringency of the environmental measure as one significant factor. The stringency of the regulation or environmental measure (a complete ban versus a tax, for example) would have a differential effect on production costs.

Another factor may be the narrowness of application—to a specific commodity or geographic area—of an environmental measure. Trade competitiveness is determined at the national border. Leuck and Haley point out that environmental regulation targeted at a particular geographic site or environmental problem may result in geographically diverse costs, and resource and production adjustments. Price and trade competitiveness at the national border may be only slightly affected.

One other factor is the availability, or lack thereof, of alternative low-cost or cost-reducing production techniques. One of the major factors underlying the differences in the magnitude of the trade effects of European environmental regulation between the chapter by Blom and that of Leuck and Haley is the assumption made with respect to the potential availability of alternative low-cost livestock production and management techniques.

Lucas, Anderson and Strutt, and Antle, et al., consider trade-related policy reform and approaches to measuring the associated changes in production practices and linkages to environmental change. Lucas takes a broad approach and investigates the linkage of a country's economic growth strategy, including its trade orientation, to environmental change and polluting activities. Antle and Anderson leave no doubt that trade policy reforms, like other market or policy changes, will likely have both positive and negative consequences for natural resources and the environment. The Antle and Anderson chapters offer contrasting approaches and directions that may be taken to quantifying and measuring the trade and environment linkage—aggregating up to a "damage function" from very location-specific environmental studies versus the use of a more stylized "damage function" to measure the environmental damage associated with trade and policy reform.

The final part of the book, consisting of three chapters, turns to research needs and priorities. Ervin and Keller set the tone for the section by noting that "research that has already been done . . . is theoretical, incomplete, and lacks sufficient empirical content." They pose three questions that should be the focus of research. First, can existing national programs adequately address any negative environmental effects of expanded agricultural trade? Second, how much do environmental policies adversely affect trade? Third, how should transboundary or global environmental problems be addressed—through trade or other measures? In addition, they raise the issue of the introduction of harmful nonindigenous species.

Nelson, in Chapter 18, raises two issues that are akin to those raised by Ervin and Keller. First, how do changes in environmental policies affect trade flows, and, second, how do changes in trade policies affect the environment. Nelson calls for more direct analysis of the consequences of trade policies, for incorporation of the spatial nature of the environment, and for great attention to data needs.

In the final chapter of the book, Wessells reflects on the extent to which the symposium met its goals and objectives, and then concludes that definition of a research agenda is far from simple.

# PART TWO

# Discovering the Critical Linkages: Trade, International Institutions and the Environment

# 2

# Trade and the Environment: Exploring the Critical Linkages[1]

*Jagdish Bhagwati*

### Introduction

The issue of the critical linkage of trade and the environment has become quite important as the Uruguay Round winds its way through ratification by parliaments and the U.S. Congress. A joint coalition of environmental and labor groups has raised important issues in the ratification process and in the implementation of the World Trade Organization (WTO). The labor groups are borrowing a leaf from the environmental side and are trying to introduce labor standard requirements on the part of the other countries as a precondition for market access. These groups will liven up the proceedings, but will also obfuscate many legitimate issues. There will be continuing attacks on GATT and the WTO in the name of national sovereignty.

It is imperative to identify linkages and to assess their respective importance. Although there are some gratuitously inappropriate issues, which can be dismissed by rational, discerning individuals, there are some substantive issues that will have to be resolved. Problems can be anticipated in adjusting the WTO to the increased concerns about environmental issues.

Why do conflicts arise between two areas that both seem to be desirable—environmental protection and freer trade? Freer trade brings about more efficiency, more economic growth, and therefore more tax revenues (within any given tax structure). As incomes expand, there are also more resources to do other things of value for society, such as reducing poverty through public health programs and increasing environmental protection. In principle, there should be no substantial conflicts between these two objectives, and if there are, it should be possible to accommodate and resolve them in the standard trade-off sense. There is no good reason for environmental protection and freer trade, two admirable and desirable objectives, to be incompatible.

There are some very genuine difficulties that we perhaps may never be able to resolve. One issue, addressed only briefly here, is philosophical in nature. That is, many environmentalists tend to think philosophically in terms of nature having its own autonomy. Conversely, most economists are in the tradition of thinking that nature can be used for man's ends. That's a fundamental conflict. If you read Hausman or Wordsworth, you will get a sense, through poetry, of the feeling of nature's autonomy.

Most of the tradition which defines the economist's training, aside from it being a Benthamite tradition, is philosophically one in which nature is subservient to man. On some levels, economists and environmentalists are talking past one another; the two simply are not trained to think alike.

Another philosophical difference, much more easily resolved, is the notion that somehow trade automatically will degrade the environment. The GATT report—and in particular, Kym Anderson's work on agriculture—pointed out very clearly that this was not a necessary outcome. In fact, the lengthy sections of the report that looked at these linkages showed that agricultural liberalization would be more likely to foster environmental preservation than to hurt it.

There is no prescribed outcome based on the relationship between environmental degradation or enhancement, and trade liberalization or economic growth generally; it depends on the parameters and the issues, and the specific problems at hand. Some think that economics provides absolute parametric answers to questions of this nature, but it does not. It is comforting to know, however, that in agricultural liberalization—which is an important component of the liberalization in the Uruguay Round—the best estimates do in fact show a complementary relationship.

Critical linkages are addressed in the following section, with emphasis on specific areas requiring systematic examination.

## Exploring the Linkages

The first set of international linkages encompasses what would be described as *domestically-orientated pollution problems* or *environmental problems*. These are problems that fall only within one nation's domestic jurisdiction, such as the pollution of a lake or river. The pollution does not "spill over" into another country in any other than a psychological sense. If, on the other hand, the discharge is into waters that flow into a second country, then there is an impact "downstream," and the second country would be likely to object. Only in the latter case is the pollution (environment) "international" in scope, and international cooperation can become necessary.

The second (or "international") scenario is important to economists only because it is an uncompensated externality (or it can be labeled an externality for short, and considered uncompensated by definition). If there were a pollution market that charged one country for polluting another, then even though it is an international problem, an equitable resolution would be implemented. It is only when the market fails because of jurisdictional differences that the transborder externality comes into play.

Let's return to the first case—that of no transboundary spillovers. We might ask, "Why should we worry about the first scenario at all? Why is that of any importance?" This case is, in fact, the basis for the competitiveness issues. If the polluters are not charged, then an uncompensated market externality exists within your own system or jurisdiction. As a result, firms may become more competitive in the polluting industry (than if a polluter-pays principle were applied), and that competitiveness implication can become a major bone of contention. Thus, this case becomes an international issue despite the jurisdictional containment of the pollution problem.

### Competitiveness and Harmonization Issues

Let us examine first the class of problems arising from countries with high standards objecting to the lower standards of other countries. Advanced countries are more rigorous than developing countries in terms of environmental standards for specific types of industries. The advanced-country producers complain, "Look, the developing countries don't have these standards; therefore, it's leading to a competitiveness implication for us." This is exactly the nature of the argument used for harmonizing labor standards, too. So there is a parallel between these two arguments. Although it is much more obvious in the case of labor standards, it is becoming increasingly apparent in relation to environmental standards as well.

This is the issue at the heart of some of the "green and blue" legislation which has been introduced in the United States. The legislation proposes that if the other country's standards are lower in relation to U.S. "blue collar" (labor) standards or U.S. "green" (environmental) standards, then the United States should be allowed to take a trade action, such as imposing a countervailing duty, applying the U.S. anti-dumping law, putting a tariff in place, or simply prohibiting imports. The essence of the proposed legislation is that the other countries, by having lower "green" and "blue" standards, are implicitly subsidizing their products and thereby indulging in illegitimate and unfair competition. In the policy jargon of these cases, the environmental side is termed "eco-dumping," and the labor side is called "social-dumping."

How does an economist analyze this issue? There are some basic propositions on which economists should agree. For example, the polluter-pays principle ought to be exercised. However, even if that is agreed, the emerging tax rates will be very different because they will reflect, for example, the value placed on a particular type of pollution in a particular jurisdiction. If Lake Michigan is being polluted, the residents in that area may negatively value that pollution more than residents in the jurisdiction near a different lake. So it's perfectly possible that even if the polluter must pay, how much he or she will have to pay will depend on how the externality is valued. Even expecting the same standard, and applying the polluter-pays principle, the tax rates that would emerge might be very different in varying locations. Therefore, the diversity of standards observed within the same industry across countries, even with the same commitment to the environment, may be very apparent.

Economists would say that diversity is legitimate and to be expected. Objecting to another country having a different standard or tax is objecting to a natural diversity, just like objecting to another country having more labor or having different weather or different conditions of work or different styles of work. Unfortunately, the vast majority of environmentalists make the mistake of jumping from the polluter-pays principle to identical tax rates, and then arguing that it isn't fair that one industry should carry more of a tax burden than another.

Even if two countries have the same utility function in the aggregate, the specific compositions of environmental preferences may be very different. To take a straightforward example: Mexico may have the same utility function on environment and income as the United States, but may prefer to address clean water, since dysentery is a much greater concern in Mexico. The U.S. may prefer to emphasize clean air, because the U.S. already has clean water as part of its initial conditions. Thus, the U.S. will be focusing more on removing lead from gasoline, and Mexico might prefer to devote its resources to cleaning up the water. This situation would also lead to different standards within industries across the two countries.

It is my opinion that if higher-standard countries insist on identical tax rates or pollution rates in the same industry across countries, they are taking us down the wrong road. Unfortunately, this issue is currently an important battleground, and its outcome is one that very much concerns developing countries because of the possibilities of countervailing duty actions.

Another question is: if a country is not following the polluter-pays principle, and has a sub-optimal tax, or has a sub-optimally low standard within its own preference function, should we then countervail simply because that country is not following an optimal policy? Not being a Chicago-trained economist, I believe there are many imperfections in the world. That being the case, looking at any country, you will see—instead of a bunch of wise men and women—massive market failures. I would revert therefore to the economists' view that no matter what the other guys are doing, free trade is sensible. If I want to worry about specific environmental policies, I would use other instruments to educate, persuade and so on, to get them to change things in the direction which I think they ought to go.

One final fallacy is that high-standard countries will automatically gain if a country with a lower standard were to raise its standards. This notion appears to result from a confusion between absolute and comparative cost or absolute and comparative advantage. For example, suppose the minimum wage in Mexico were raised as part of the NAFTA agreement. Then, comparing U.S. textiles with Mexican textiles, Mexico's labor cost increases. So the U.S. wins in terms of textile competition. But that minimum wage will be raised across the board in Mexico, affecting numerous industries. So, in fact, the effect of an across-the-board minimum wage increase may be to hurt the U.S. textile industry, not to help it. Yet every industry thinks in terms of just an absolute comparison.

In harmonization questions, it is industry-specific issues that drive the debate. Of course, if the standard being imposed is confined to just one industry, then the comparative and the absolute cost advantage analysis would go together. But economists typically must work out what the net effect on comparative advantage of different industries will be as a result of getting a country to raise its environmental standards in a generic or more broad-based way.

One other point to be considered is that if you make the general assumption that a developing country's standards are legitimately derived and reflect some kind of optimality or some kind of legitimate diversity—if we then get them to revise their standards upward to reflect ours, then in fact they are moving away from their optimal situation. In other words, at the same time that you may not in fact benefit from changing another country's standards upward, you are certainly hurting the other party. This runs contrary to the whole WTO concept, which is premised on the principle of mutual benefits through trade.

### Political Market Failure

Here is where the final problem appears. Many environmentalists would point out that these preferences are not legitimately expressed by these countries. There may be a failure of political markets, as in the case of a dictatorship. Or a country's citizens and consumers may not be free to protest about the environment. This is indeed a key issue. So far, it has been assumed that preferences are legitimately translated into policies. Taking as examples Eastern Europe and the Soviet Union, obviously there were complete market failures both economically and politically. In these instances, environmental preferences of any kind could not possibly be translated into policy actions. People who had been hurt by pollution could not really interact with or get governments to do anything.

In recent years, however, political market failure is not a major problem because, fortunately, democracy is much more widespread. Of course, there is no perfect democracy, even in the United States and Canada. But so long as there is the possibility of NGO activity, dissemination of consumer information, and the freedom to associate for such purposes, the outcome is more or less democratic. Collective choices do not necessarily reflect individual preferences, but on this point everybody and every country are in the same circumstances. Additionally, if you really worry about democracy, or democracy is not as good as you think it ought to be, then you ought to attempt to affect the democratic process itself. To presume that if the country had a democratic process, then its people would choose my standards is itself a gratuitous assumption.

These issues are not going to go away. There are powerful motivations, particularly with respect to harmonizing labor standards, which are being fed by this great concern that poorer countries are in competition with us, creating paupers in our midst by depressing real wages of unskilled workers. Clearly this concern comes from a fear of these impacts. This is why many labor unions have suddenly turned more moralistic in regard to spreading labor standards around the world. Most of them see this as an indirect way of raising the cost of labor. Blame cannot be placed on a confusion between absolute and comparative costs in this case—for the unions clearly see this as a way of protecting their own industries and jobs. One of the ideas that I have proposed is a new OECD code specifying that domestic firms operating abroad (in Malaysia or elsewhere) must follow our standards. Legally speaking, if they are our firms and our citizens, that could be done. Alternatively, what if Canadian firms were allowed to follow Malaysian standards, and U.S. firms had to follow U.S. standards? With the implementation of this OECD code, the potential for a lack of horizontal equity would be greatly reduced. Such an approach is only second best, since it still runs into the diversity problem, but it would supply some sort of political response to what is, in fact, a politically very salient demand. Rational argument doesn't always win, and so it may be necessary to make some gestures. The best gesture may be to tell your own firms that operate multinationally to follow "home" rules and preferences.

## Value-Related Linkages

In this section, value-related environmental issues will be examined—such as the tuna-dolphin case. These issues are tricky. For example, if the Netherlands wants to restrict imports of tropical timber (rain forest timber), how is that handled? That's a value-related intervention. Objections to production and processing methods, like the way an animal is caught (for example, with a steel leg-hold trap) or fish are harvested (for example, with purse seine nets that entrap dolphins), may also be based on values. The GATT has looked at these kinds of value-related issues and concluded that objecting to production and processing standards of other countries (lower standards, as it were) on the basis of values is a "slippery slope."

As an aside, it should be noted that the hormone-fed beef case is a slightly different issue, though it looks much the same on the surface. The objection to hormone-fed beef was not that the process was amoral (i.e., that animals were being treated cruelly); rather, Europeans were saying that the product (the beef) was contaminated and that it would be harmful to human health. There was, however, no scientific basis for the concern, so the issue was one of a science test, not of values. There could, of course, be objections based on values to the way cattle are raised. For example, it could be said that cattle should not be kept in pens, that they should be free to roam.

Allowing diversity among production and process methods is extremely important. Even within one country, every process in every plant is different. Thus, allowing general objections to processes could lead to serious trouble for international trade. A solution might be to focus on outlawing specific practices on which there might be a multilateral consensus. Do we take the "easy way"—capturing our own government through, say, the Marine Mammal Protection Act, and then unilaterally suspending Mexico's right to export tuna? Or do we do the hard work, and get a multilateral consensus that saving dolphins is more important than getting more productivity with the use of purse seine nets?

Returning for a moment to the tuna-dolphin case, the GATT report made clear that the U.S. is not required to import the tuna; it only says that if the U.S. suspends Mexico's trading rights, then it must pay. And payment doesn't mean hard cash; it just means opening up another trade concession for the one being closed. Now, since we'll never have free trade, at least not in my lifetime, there ought to be some concession you can make. To me that is a perfectly acceptable solution, although some may ask "Why should I pay for my principles?" Some environmentalists don't like paying for their principles, but I think that is an unreasonable position. This is actually what happened in the beef hormone case. The Europeans did not want to take it to a science test. They simply allowed the United States to retaliate; in other words, they paid for their beliefs. Those duties are still in place in the United States. The Europeans never took the case to GATT dispute settlement because they would have lost.

## GATT Principles and the Environment

The GATT does, however, stipulate three things. First, it says a contracting party of the GATT should be able to challenge the *bona fide* nature of a regulation. In other words, is the intended effect truly an environmental or social objective, or actually protectionism? This seems reasonable. There are many examples, like the Ontario Beer case, that support this point. The current case involving the U.S. CAFE standards falls into this area. There is a rule that every vehicle manufacturer who supplies the U.S. market must have a balanced fleet, in the sense that on average its vehicles sold should meet certain mileage requirements. Thus, if you are exporting only Mercedes Benzes to the United States, then obviously you do not meet that average because you have no small cars with which to balance the large ones, and therefore you have to pay a substantial fine. The Europeans have gone to court to challenge the U.S. rule, saying this is really protectionism. If the United States loses, it is likely to react the way it did to the tuna-dolphin case, arguing that the decision interferes with U.S. sovereignty with respect to its national values.

The second GATT principle is a more controversial one: Meeting an environmental or social objective should be done in the least trade-disruptive way. This is difficult; it's very hard to find exact, identical outcomes with two alternative ways of reaching them. This is perhaps an area where the environmentalist does have a legitimate objection to the existing procedures. In this context, "existing procedures" means that people who are in the trade community sit on the panels and decide on these issues. There are no environmentalists on the panels, and when trade-offs are involved, it is assumed that those who are interested in trade will assign a higher value to the trade disruption being minimized and less value to the environmental objective being satisfied. A solution would be to have more environmentalists involved in these dispute settlement cases.

The GATT's third principle is the science test. Of course, everyone knows that science is not as clean as we would like it to be. But if there were no science test, it would result in many more hormone-fed beef cases. The main value of the principles laid out by the GATT is the relative stability of expectations for those wanting to invest in trade.

Overall, the GATT appears to be on the right track and many of the changes that need to be made to accommodate environmental objectives can be accomplished without real difficulty. There is, however, the transboundary concern—a big problem that encompasses two issues. One is "free riders," i.e., a multilateral agreement among a subset of GATT members or WTO members arriving at a protocol like the Montreal, but there are some countries that haven't signed. What should be done about the trading rights of these countries? They really should not be allowed to free ride; otherwise, the very purpose of the agreement is compromised. If there is just a small subset of countries that have signed, then it looks less multilateral and becomes more of a unilateral action—in which case there should be some concern about why these countries are not coming on board.

If countries are not coming on board because of some scientific reason, then it might be prudent to "fix" the GATT in such a way that those who have scientific objections cannot be forced into compliance through trade sanctions by these countries. However, objections based on equity aspects might be another reason for not joining. For example, preventing Brazil from cutting down rain forests might be the cheapest way to reduce ozone depletion, whereas the U.S. and Canada and other OECD countries may choose to do *nothing* because it's very expensive for them to do *something*. So they may impose on Brazil, through a multilateral agreement, all the cost of adjusting to an ozone reduction. Although that may be the most efficient solution in terms of opportunity costs or social costs, it also leaves Brazil with the entire bill. In some ways, it's like free trade. Free trade is good for everybody, but the distribution implications are different.

Distribution implications are different from the efficient outcomes. The developing countries have been worried that they'll begin getting the "short end of the stick." But the developed countries, on issues like the Montreal Protocol, have really been quite responsive, even providing transfer payments. It appears that there is a lot of give and take and understanding among countries of the difference between equity and efficiency. Overall, the desire to agree on these things is in itself so great that no really serious problems should be anticipated *vis-à-vis* the GATT.

## Concluding Comment

In sum, there are many policy issues in the intersection of trade and the environment which can be worked out. Sadly, there are some bad solutions likely to be put in place—like the eco-dumping and social-dumping laws, which should be challenged. Unfortunately, many of the environmental groups and some of the politicians are deeply committed to these approaches. We will see more battles ahead.

## Note

1. This chapter is an edited transcript of the keynote address presented at the start of the Trade and Environment Conference.

# 3

---

# Trade and Environment:
# A Tale of Two Paradigms

*Howard Gruenspecht*

### Introduction

Environmentalists and some political leaders are making a strong effort to inject environmental concerns into the development of trade policies and related institutions. Yet, the available literature generally suggests that trade liberalization furthers rather than damages environmental values, and that domestic environmental programs aimed at reducing emissions to air, water, and land do not have a major influence on trade flows and competitiveness.

This chapter examines the motivation for the interest in coordination of trade and environment policies during the public debate surrounding the North American Free Trade Agreement (NAFTA) and the Uruguay Round agreement to strengthen and extend the General Agreement on Tariffs and Trade (GATT). The chapter is divided into four sections. The first reviews evidence regarding the effects of trade liberalization and economic growth on environmental quality and the effects of domestic environmental policy on trade flows. The second considers the domestic and international political forces that create demand for a linkage between trade and environment policy. For many interests, such as environmental groups that oppose trade liberalization that is itself environmentally neutral or beneficial, strategic considerations in a political process involving multiple decisions over time can be more important than any substantive tie in driving a desire for policy coordination. The final two sections briefly assess the environmental implications of the Uruguay

Round agreement and the likely positions of various groups in future discussions surrounding these issues.

## Substantive Relationships Between Trade
## Liberalization and Environmental Quality

According to the U.S. Environmental Protection Agency (EPA), environmental protection expenditures in the United States in 1990 totaled $115 billion, or slightly less than 2 percent of gross domestic output (U.S. EPA 1990). With implementation of the 1990 Clean Air Act and the phase-in of more stringent requirements for solid waste disposal and underground storage tanks under the Resource Conservation and Recovery Act and the Clean Water Act, environmental expenditures are projected to rise to 2.6 percent of the gross domestic product (GDP) by the year 2000.

Figure 3.1 arrays a representative set of environmental issues on a spectrum ranging from fully global to purely domestic. While global and offshore issues are receiving increased public attention, virtually all current U.S. environmental costs are associated with pursuit of environmental programs that address purely domestic issues.[1] Even under the assumption that substantial efforts are initiated to mitigate anthropogenic greenhouse gas emissions that may change the earth's climate, the lion's share of environmental costs will continue to result from policies to address environmental issues that arise on a subcontinental scale.

**FIGURE 3.1  Spectrum of Environmental Issues**

---

GLOBAL
 - Stratospheric Ozone Depletion
 - Greenhouse Warming

COMMON PROPERTY
 - Migratory Species Protection

OFFSHORE
 - Endangered Species
 - Rainforest Preservation
 - Air Quality, Water Quality, Toxics, Pesticides, and Waste Disposal in Foreign Countries

TRANSBOUNDARY
 - Acid Rain in Europe, U.S./Canada Great Lakes and Air Quality, U.S./Mexico Border Issues

DOMESTIC
 - Air Quality, Water Quality, Toxics, Pesticides, and Waste Disposal
 - Species and Habitat Protection Within National Borders

---

## Impact of Environmental Programs on Competitiveness

Impacts of environmental programs on the cost structure or productivity of businesses might be reflected in effects on trade in pollution-intensive goods, on net exports, or on plant siting decisions. Empirical analyses of these effects have been hampered by limited data on differences in environmental programs. Data problems are particularly acute with respect to information on program implementation, which can be a major determinant of both the environmental and cost impacts of laws and regulations.

Low and Yeats (1992) track trade flows in product categories where U.S. pollution control and abatement expenditures are high. (They implicitly presume that standards affecting these industries are either lower or nonexistent in developing countries.) They find that the share of pollution-intensive goods in total trade declined slightly over the 1965-1988 period, with North America's share falling by one-third, and the share originating in Southeast Asia more than doubling. While this pattern is consistent with the hypothesis that environmental regulations affect trade patterns, the analysis does not explicitly address environmental costs or control for other influences that could explain these trade patterns. For example, the declining share of pollution-intensive goods in world trade could reflect income-inelastic demand for such goods during a period of rapidly growing world income, rather than a loss in comparative advantage by developed country exporters. Also, since increased manufacturing is a natural stage in the development process, changes in regional shares of pollution-intensive trade must be placed in the context of overall manufacturing and trade trends before any inference regarding the driving role of environmental regulations can be drawn.

Grossman and Krueger (1992) consider the impact of environmental regulation on the composition of value-added generated in Mexico's malquiladora sector and the composition of U.S.-Mexico trade. Notwithstanding claims by Ross Perot and others regarding the importance of Mexico's status as a "pollution haven" as a motivation for past (and presumably future) locational decisions, Grossman and Krueger find no evidence that either value-added or U.S. imports from Mexico are disproportionately skewed towards pollution-intensive industries.

Kalt (1988) examines the relationship between environmental regulation and the level of net exports of U.S. industries. He estimates both level and first-difference forms, finding a statistically significant relationship. Jaffe et al. (1993) raise several questions regarding Kalt's results, notably the fact that results appear to be stronger when the chemical industry, which is subject to very stringent environmental requirements, is excluded from the sample. Jaffe et al. also cite Wheeler and Mody's (1992) finding that corporate tax rates do not affect siting decisions as evidence that environmental regulations, which affect direct costs in a similar fashion, are unlikely to play a significant role in siting decisions. Differences in the stringency of environmental regulation applied across jurisdictions within the United States provide a further opportunity to examine the role of environmental regulation as a factor in siting decisions. Bartik (1988) finds no evidence that considerable differences across states in environmental requirements (with federal minimum standards as a floor) and enforcement resources have had a significant impact on siting. However, the U.S. General Accounting Office (1991) reports that owners and managers of furniture firms in the Los Angeles area consider environmental regulations as an important determinant of their relocation decisions.

Porter (1991) provides a completely different perspective on the nature of the relationship between environmental regulation and competitiveness. In his view, which is supported by anecdotal rather than empirical evidence, environmental regulation improves competitiveness by spurring affected firms to adopt improved products and production methods. Given the perceived worldwide trend towards increased environmental protection, Porter also argues that environmental policy leadership provides local firms with competitive advantages in foreign markets whose governments are environmental policy followers.

Direct comparisons of national environmental policies and costs are another potential source of insight into the competitiveness issue. Ideally, such comparisons would focus on differences in actual environmental practices rather than differences in laws, since enforcement and interpretation are critical determinants of impacts on industry, but little information is available. Even where allowable practices differ substantially across countries, many multinational firms have corporate policies that mandate "world class" levels of environmental protection in their facilities, irrespective of their location. For such companies, locational decisions are insensitive to national environmental policies.

The Organization for Economic Cooperation and Development (OECD 1991), which uses a different measurement approach than U.S. government agencies, reports that pollution control expenditures account for roughly 1.5 percent of national output in most large member countries. While there are differences of up to several tenths of a percent across major countries, these are far smaller than differences in other policy areas that affect relative costs, such as energy policies, employment security, social insurance, and health care systems. [Many of the most pollution-intensive industries (e.g., steel, paper, chemicals, and refining) are also very energy intensive.] For example, industrial energy costs differ substantially within the OECD area, with a large cost advantage for North America relative to Western Europe and Japan. Health care costs are 14 percent of U.S. national output, as compared to an average of 9 percent in the rest of the

OECD. Against this backdrop, the focus on environmental policies as a main source of competitiveness concerns appears to be misplaced.

While the current evidence does not support the view that environmental regulations have large competitiveness impacts, such impacts could arise in the future, particularly if major actions, such as steps to reduce emissions of greenhouse gases, were taken on a globally uncoordinated basis. Results regarding the impact of environmental regulation on siting decisions can also be sensitive to the design of environmental programs. The trend towards increased use of market mechanisms, such as tradable pollution rights or emissions fees, in environmental regulation is likely to raise locational sensitivity even as it lowers overall compliance costs. In contrast to the "use it or lose it" situation facing operators of existing plants under conventional command-and-control regulation, tradable rights give firms the opportunity to "cash in" their pollution endowments via relocation.

## Impact of Trade Liberalization on Environmental Quality

Trade liberalization affects environmental quality primarily through its impact on the level of economic activity. Although trade liberalization may have adverse impacts on particular economic sectors, it is widely accepted that a reduction in trade barriers stimulates overall economic activity in both developed and developing countries. Indeed, projected economic growth benefits are often cited as the primary motivation for trade liberalization on both a regional and a global scale.

The implications of economic growth for environmental quality are more controversial. Some environmentalists adopt the position that the expansion of economic activity necessarily damages environmental quality by pushing us closer to (or further beyond) the boundary of sustainability. The pursuit of economic growth only diverts attention from their focus on meeting basic human needs (not wants) via a redistribution of wealth and income. While anti-growth activists recognize the political infeasibility of implementing a no-growth prescription, opposition to trade liberalization and other growth-enhancing policies may be pursued as an indirect means of slowing growth.

From an alternative perspective that recognizes the prominent role of human aspirations and behavior in determining environmental performance, the case can be made that economic growth has a positive effect on environmental quality. In the U.S., for example, the 70 percent growth in real output in the two decades following the first Earth Day in 1970—which also marks the creation of the Environmental Protection Agency and the passage of landmark clean air legislation—has been accompanied by significant reductions in emissions levels of most key pollutants. Between 1970 and 1990, emissions of sulfur oxides, reactive volatile organic compounds, carbon monoxide, suspended particulates, and lead fell by 26 percent, 36 percent, 46 percent, 61 percent, and 97 percent, respectively. Among the six criteria pollutants, only nitrogen oxide emissions increased, and by just 2 percent (Council on Environmental Quality 1992). This environmental progress, and the future gains that will occur pursuant to the 1990 Clean Air Act amendments, would be unlikely to win popular support against the backdrop of a stagnant economy.

The role of income growth as a source of increased demand for environmental protection is also evident in developing countries. The *World Development Report* (World Bank 1992) reports empirical relationships between income levels and key indicators of environmental quality. Urban airshed concentrations of particulate matter, of sulfur dioxide, and the percentage of urban population without access to adequate sanitation or safe water supplies decline as per capita income increases. In contrast, municipal waste per capita and carbon dioxide emissions per capita are positively related to per capita income. Reports on additional indicators of environmental quality (World Resources Institute 1992) generally support the notion that overall indicators of environmental impact or quality (deforestation, emissions loadings, etc.) improve with rising per capita income. A notable exception to the generally positive impact of income growth on environmental indicators is the case of carbon dioxide emissions, which are directly associated with fossil energy use.

## Trade and Environment: The (Political) Ties that Bind

The substantive relationships outlined above belie the notion of an inherent conflict between trade liberalization and environmental progress. While the strongest support for trade liberalization is likely to come from interests who place a high value on economic growth, increased economic growth is also likely to advance environmental interests. While Porter's (1991) argument that environmental protection actually contributes to cost reduction and productivity enhancement reflects an extreme view, the literature reviewed in the previous section provides no basis for placing environmental regulation high on the "hit list" of those seeking to improve the relative competitiveness of domestic production. Against this background of compatibility, if not harmony, on the substantive level, the emergence of the trade/environment policy nexus as an area of contention can best be explained as arising from a systematic divergence between the political and substantive linkages.

### *The Political Primacy of Jobs and Economic Growth*

Notwithstanding the attention accorded to issues surrounding the sustainability of growth and development in international environmental fora, economic growth as conventionally defined remains the primary preoccupation of the voting public and national governments in democratic countries.

Recognizing the primacy of economic issues in the political process, advocates for any cause have an incentive to cast their case in terms of economic impacts whether or not there is a strong substantive link. Economic impacts are characterized not in terms of growth rates, productivity indices, or real wages, but in terms that nearly every voter can directly relate to: jobs created and job losses avoided.

Trade policymakers have a long experience in dealing with jobs concerns. Despite solid evidence that trade liberalization itself stimulates economic growth and net employment, the potency of the jobs argument is reflected in the incorporation of trade adjustment assistance packages in domestic legislation implementing trade liberalization packages beginning in the 1960s. The demonstrated adverse effect of environmental regulation on economic growth and productivity improvement as measured by conventional accounts (see, for example, Denison 1985; Jorgenson and Wilcoxen 1992) has made the employment question a particularly sensitive issue in the formulation of domestic environmental policies. As in the case of trade policy, the focus is less on aggregate employment levels or real wages than on avoiding the loss of identifiable jobs.

Avoidance of job losses affecting identifiable individuals has played a major role in shaping the basic structure of environmental regulation in the United States. The fear that low environmental standards would be used by individual states as a competitive weapon to retain and attract industrial facilities was a major motivation for federal environmental programs. The system of national "new source performance standards," applied without regard to the need for emissions reductions to meet ambient air and water quality objectives, is one direct manifestation of job-related concerns. Another is the bias that subjects new facilities to much more stringent emission control requirements than existing facilities. If existing facilities are regulated at all, regulators routinely seek to minimize cost burdens on economically marginal facilities to prevent job losses. In effect, activities generating the least social surplus are permitted to pollute the most.

The strong aversion to the loss of identifiable jobs is clearly illustrated by provisions in the 1977 Clean Air Act amendments relating to the control of sulfur dioxide emissions from electric power plants. Recognizing that adoption of a performance standard limiting the sulfur emission rate would favor increased use of low-sulfur coal and a loss of mining jobs in high-sulfur coal regions, an alliance of clean air and dirty coal interests successfully pushed instead for adoption of a percentage removal standard that applied independently of the sulfur content of the coal (Ackerman and Hassler 1981). In effect, Congress chose to ignore the inherent advantages of cleaner coal in a standard ostensibly designed to reduce emissions from coal combustion. When Congress returned to this issue in 1990, the jobs issue again dominated discussions. Senate floor debate was stalled by the concerns of a single senator that a proposed market-based tradable permit system that would cut emissions from existing power plants by over 50 percent might lead to a shift of approximately 2,000 mining jobs from high-sulfur to low-sulfur areas within his state. The debate was able to move forward after six weeks on a one-vote margin only, with inclusion of a generous compensation scheme for potential job losers.

Notwithstanding the lack of evidence of major trade and investment effects from existing environmental regulations, potential job losses, rather than the relationship between the costs and benefits of proposed provisions, became the focal point of opposition to new or tighter standards in a wide variety of areas as the 1990 Clean Air Act amendments were debated. While there may be no actual "race to the bottom" among states or countries in establishing environmental standards (Revesz 1992; Stewart 1993), concerns related to potential competitiveness impacts clearly exert a major political drag on efforts to reach new heights in the level of domestic environmental standards. Calls for international harmonization of environmental standards at a high level, or border adjustments to compensate for differences in standards, reflect environmentalists' interest in removing a politically potent objection to their domestic policy agenda.

### Takings and Unfunded Mandates

Tight limits on discretionary federal spending, including the "pay as you go" requirement that any policy requiring new on-budget outlays be explicitly offset by spending reductions or revenue increases, have shifted the attention of an activist Congress towards initiatives whose costs are borne directly by affected parties, including environmental regulation.

Recently, concern over the growth in the costs imposed on private citizens and state and local governments to meet requirements imposed by the federal government, labeled respectively as "regulatory takings" and "unfunded mandates," has resulted in proposals that these parties should be required to comply with federal dictates only to the extent that on-budget resources are provided to offset costs incurred. Given the current budget situation, environmental advocates view these proposals as a serious threat to their agenda, since it places their agenda in direct competition with other spending programs for scarce budgetary resources. Environmental groups have identified proposals to require compensation for "takings" and "unfunded mandates" as two-thirds of an "unholy trinity" that must be stopped, even at the cost of delaying reauthorization of core environmental statutes or elevating the Environmental Protection Agency to Cabinet status. A proposal to require formal risk assessment for environmental regulations is the third member of the trinity. The political strength of the trinity was demonstrated most recently in the defeat, by a forty-vote margin, of a "closed rule" that would have precluded consideration of trinity amendments during House floor debate on the EPA Cabinet elevation bill.

The questions of who pays, and how payments are structured, are even more sensitive in the context of global environmental concerns such as global warming, where efficient mitigation policy may require action by countries at different stages of development. There is no international analogue to the domestic legislative process that can impose mandates directly on activities in developing countries. Moreover, developing countries are generally unwilling to divert their own resources to address concerns that have a low priority relative to development itself and other, more pressing, environmental issues such as basic water and sanitation needs. Absent funding support from industrialized countries, developing countries may resist commitments to undertake significant emissions mitigation steps.

Increased official transfers to pursue a combined agenda of global environmental protection and development provide common ground for environmentalists and developing countries. However, popularly-elected governments in industrialized countries that are already highly sensitized to the spending cuts or tax increases necessary to provide on-budget funding of domestic environmental protection are unlikely to fund new large-scale programs outside their national borders.

Two alternatives to official transfers are available. The first is to earmark a portion of the anticipated economic gains from trade liberalization for environmental purposes by requiring enhanced environmental commitments as a precondition for liberalization. Such a strategy was evident in the U.S. debate over NAFTA, where higher spending on border environmental issues from both the U.S. and Mexican governments, as well as a side agreement with additional environmental provisions, were extracted as the price required to win the support of some environmental groups.

The second approach is joint implementation (JI). JI focuses direct obligations to address global environmental issues on developed countries, but then seeks both cost reduction and developing country participation by allowing industrialized countries to meet all or part of their obligations through support of emissions reduction projects in developing countries. The ability to operate outside of the government budget process in cases where obligations in industrialized countries are passed as unfunded mandates to the private sector is a major potential advantage of JI—in effect, finessing the barrier to unfunded international mandates.

However, JI may not be viewed as a fully satisfactory approach by either industrial interests or environmentalists. The former may view JI as a means of implementing programs that could otherwise be completely avoided. The latter may object to the perceived loss of ancillary local environmental improvements and a reduction in the incentive to develop "clean and green" technologies as compared to a regime in which the same goals must be met through internal actions alone. Developing countries may also have doubts about being drawn into environmental solutions that address problems caused by others, particularly if the solution involves limitations on emissions that might be associated with the pursuit of their economic development objectives.

### The Political Process as a Repeated Game

The political process involves multiple decisions made over an extended time horizon. Within this context, interest group positions will reflect an interest in maximizing future influence as well as a substantive assessment of the immediate issue to be decided. Where these two factors favor different positions, it can be rational to play a decisive role in the defeat of a policy proposal that is preferred on substantive grounds. For example, an environmental group whose internal analysis recognizes NAFTA as having net environmental benefits—as compared to a NAFTA-defeat scenario in which slower income growth and antagonism in the U.S.-Mexico relationship result in lower environmental quality throughout Mexico and especially in the border region—may nonetheless oppose the agreement to force an even better deal, or raise its influence as a decisive participant in the GATT debate.

## The Uruguay Round: Trade and Environment Implications

The Uruguay Round agreements bend significantly in the direction of greater accommodation of national environmental policies that may distort trade. While the basic GATT exceptions under Article XX, allowing for national environmental policies inconsistent with general GATT obligations, are unchanged,[2] several revisions in the codes relating to sanitary and phytosanitary standards (SPS), technical barriers to trade (TBT), and the agreement on subsidies and countervailing measures appear to provide increased latitude for environmental policy actions affecting code signatories.

Most important for agricultural issues, the SPS code weakens the current interpretation that "necessary" actions taken under Article XX(b) be "least trade restrictive." Instead, SPS actions that restrict trade can be justified provided there are no "reasonably available alternatives" to the measure in question.

The TBT code specifies that actions not be more trade restrictive than necessary to fulfill a legitimate objective, taking account of the risks that non-fulfillment would create. The vagueness of the legitimacy criterion and the emphasis on avoiding risks of non-fulfillment appear to widen the latitude for acceptable policy action. Moreover, the new code language allows for regulations that specify "product characteristics or their related processes and production methods." Looking behind the characteristics of the product itself to methods of production is a high priority for environmentalists.

Finally, the agreement on subsidies and countervailing measures for the first time includes a provision that government subsidization of the capital costs of environmental compliance are not to be subject to countervailing actions. The safe harbor for environmental subsidies, despite an explicit and largely unenforceable injunction that they are not to be used for investments that lower manufacturing costs, reflects a willingness to significantly weaken GATT disciplines to accommodate environmental concerns.

The nearly uniform opposition of environmental interests to GATT despite such adjustments reflects a combination of strategic positioning and concerns regarding non-environmental provisions of the agreement. Changes in dispute settlement procedures that prevent individual countries from blocking GATT Panel decisions are most often cited as a key substantive problem, since parties faced with findings that their environmental or other practices are not consistent with GATT obligations will have to revise them or compensate affected parties.

On a broader level, opposition to trade liberalization reflects a general unease with the implications of a more open economy. From this perspective, any agreement that improves the "rules of the road" for trade and investment and makes it easier to organize commerce that transcends the reach of national policies is undesirable, even if there is no direct adverse environmental impact. However, since the GATT negotiations are as much a symptom as a cause of expanding scope of commerce, which has been driven by forces such as economic and political reforms and improvements in communications technologies, it may be impossible to stem the tide of globalization even if a particular liberalization agreement can be stopped.

### Looking Forward

Notwithstanding the low probability that speculation regarding the future will be validated as events unfold, the perspectives presented above suggest several likely developments at the intersection of trade and environment issues.

First, the use of environmental programs as a form of protection against foreign competition is likely to increase. This trend is already evident within the European Union, where the availability of other tariff and nontariff barriers to trade has been sharply circumscribed. The Uruguay Round agreement, which incorporates changes that provide greater latitude for domestic environmental policy actions that can disadvantage foreign suppliers even as opportunities to impose other types of impediments to trade are narrowed, will have a similar effect.

The net impact of the decision to accommodate increased latitude for environmental policy in the GATT is unclear. The benefits of increased latitude for domestic environmental policy and environmental subsidies must be weighed against the potential costs of reduced access to foreign markets whose governments avail themselves of new opportunities for GATT-legal trade distortion. (The United States, which has no programs to subsidize environmental compliance costs, is likely to be a net loser from the safe harbor provision in the new subsidies code.) Experience with provisions that allow for unilateral anti-dumping policies—which were fiercely protected by the United States in the Tokyo Round, but are now increasingly used by an ever-growing list of countries to impede import competition—illustrates the possibility that assessments of net advantage are subject to rapid change.

Second, domestic interests who perceive themselves as economic losers from trade liberalization will continue to seek alliances with environmental interests to stop or weaken liberalization initiatives. From their perspective, alliances with environmentalists on trade that do not limit their flexibility to differ in other areas are a no-lose proposition. Environmentalists, in contrast, face a harder decision in making common cause with those who perceive themselves as economic losers from trade liberalization. Alliances with protectionists will be most attractive to those who focus on environmental issues within U.S. borders. The perceived defusing of competitiveness concerns, that results from either the failure of trade liberalization or the enactment of "environmental equalization" schemes, removes a powerful political argument against the adoption of more stringent environmental policies.

Environmentalists concerned with global environmental issues face a more difficult choice. Here, the need to promote developing country participation is a primary concern. A strategy that seeks to divert a portion of the projected economic gains from trade liberalization to environmental purposes requires a careful hand. Environmentalists who accept the premise that economic growth makes a net contribution to improved environmental outcomes must weigh the risk of killing the goose that lays the green eggs if their demands for special environmental provisions are excessive.

Third, the trend away from unilateralism in addressing environmental issues outside of national borders will continue. In a world where competition among industrialized countries is keen, unilateralism, whether motivated by environmental or human rights objectives, is increasingly recognized as a self-defeating approach. The recent decision by the United States to extend most favored nation treatment to China, as well as Austria's hasty recision of a policy designed to prevent tropical deforestation, reflect the practical pitfalls of using unilateral trade actions to address issues beyond one's borders. Changes in the GATT dispute settlement rules will only help to tip the balance further away from unilateralism.

Fourth, the issues of "who decides" and "who pays" will remain inextricably linked in discussions of international environmental issues. The content of multilateral environmental agreements will continue to be directly linked to treatment of the "who pays" issue. Conventions that carry their own financing provisions, like the Montreal Protocol to the Vienna Convention on Ozone Depleting Substances, can incorporate significant commitments affecting a wide spectrum of developed and developing countries. In cases where agreements do not incorporate financing mechanisms, significant commitments will be limited to industrialized countries, with reliance on joint implementation and related schemes to engage the rest of the world.

Efforts to intervene in environmental policy within foreign countries will continue to be driven by environmental altruism, a desire to reduce political drag on higher standards at home, and competitiveness concerns (however misguided). Stiff opposition to establishment of worldwide standards for production and process methods that fail to respect national sovereignty or reflect differing conditions may channel interventionists towards the more modest objective of promoting enforcement of internally established goals and standards. NAFTA already establishes a trilateral environmental commission that provides a forum for raising concerns about discrepancies between stated and actual environmental practice. The "Blue and Green" 301 proposal, sponsored by House Democratic Leader Richard Gephardt, proposes to extend this approach by implementing countervailing duties calculated to offset any cost advantage to foreign producers that may result from incomplete enforcement of foreign environmental standards. It is unclear how such proposals will address situations where environmental legislation reflects national aspirations rather than realistic objectives, resulting in regular violations of the "letter of the law."

Finally, the political linkage of trade and environment could significantly retard future efforts towards trade liberalization. Even without the environment factor, the duration of recent negotiating rounds has lengthened with the increased complexity of the issues addressed and effective opposition from liberalization "losers" that has effectively counterbalanced the lukewarm support of the larger, but diffuse set of potential beneficiaries.

Adding environment to the agenda complicates the negotiating process in several ways. First, attempts to earmark a major portion of the projected economic gains from trade liberalization for environmental purposes may reduce net private gains below the level required to overcome the inertia of the political process. Second, a process that involves the cooperation of two distinct policy communities on an ongoing basis is likely to be cumbersome. Differences in terms of art and frames of reference within and across national delegations will compound difficulties arising from differences in positions. Third, the environment and trade agenda is diffuse, encompassing some matters that primarily affect relationships among industrialized countries and others with North/South overtones. It will be difficult to address this diffuse agenda in a small group setting, where the most rapid negotiating progress is usually made.

## Notes

1. The costs associated with the phaseout of halogenated compounds (CFCs and HFCs) that are implicated in stratospheric ozone depletion are an important exception. However, major domestic CFC and HFC producers, who are also the leading providers of substitutes that can be sold at higher profits in less competitive markets, have been strong supporters of the phaseout. The reduction in sulfur dioxide emissions from existing power plants mandated by the 1990 Clean Air Act reflects transboundary interests of Canada to a very minor extent.

2. Article XX(b) provides for actions necessary to protect human, animal, or plant life or health, while Article XX(g) allows for policies relating to the conservation of exhaustible natural resources if such measures are made effective in conjunction with restrictions on domestic production or consumption. The Article XX chapeau requires that exceptions not be applied in a manner that would constitute a means of arbitrary or unjustified description or as a disguised restriction on international trade.

## References

Ackerman, B., and W. Hassler. *Clean Coal/Dirty Air.* New Haven, CT: Yale University Press, 1981.

Bartik, T.J. "The Effects of Environmental Regulation on Business Location in the United States." *Growth and Change* 19, no. 3(1988):22–44.

Council on Environmental Quality. *Environmental Quality: 23rd Annual Report of the Council on Environmental Quality.* Washington, DC, 1992.

Denison, E. *Trends in American Economic Growth, 1929–1982.* Washington, DC: The Brookings Institution, 1985.

Grossman, G.M., and A.B. Krueger. "Environmental Impacts of a North American Free Trade Agreement." Discussion Paper (revised), Woodrow Wilson School, Princeton University, Princeton, NJ, 1992.

Jaffe, A.B., S.R. Peterson, P.R. Portney, and R.N. Stavins. "Environmental Regulations and the Competitiveness of U.S. Industry." Research Report, The Economics Resource Group, Cambridge, MA, 1993.

Jorgenson, D.W., and P.J. Wilcoxen. "Impact of Environmental Legislation on U.S. Economic Growth, Investment, and Capital Costs." In *U.S. Environmental Policy and Economic Growth: How Do We Fare?* Washington, DC: American Council for Capital Formation, 1992.

Kalt, J.P. "The Impact of Domestic Environmental Regulatory Policies on U.S. International Competitiveness." In *International Competitiveness*, M.A. Spence and H.A. Hazard, eds. Cambridge, MA: Harper and Row, 1988.

Low, P., and A. Yeats. "Do `Dirty' Industries Migrate?" In *International Trade and the Environment*, P. Low, ed. Washington, DC: The World Bank, 1992.

Organization for Economic Cooperation and Development (OECD). "Environmental Costs and Industrial Competitiveness." Publication No. DSTI/IND(91)46, OECD, Paris, 1991.

Porter, M.E. "America's Green Strategy." *Scientific American* 264, no. 4(April 1991):168.

Revesz, R.L. "Rehabilitating Interstate Competition: Rethinking the `Race-to-the-Bottom' Rationale for Federal Environmental Regulation." *New York University Law Review* 67(December 1992):1210–54.

Stewart, R.B. "Environmental Regulation and International Competitiveness." *Yale Law Journal* 102(June 1993):2039–106.

U.S. Environmental Protection Agency. "Environmental Investments: The Costs of a Clean Environment." EPA Staff Report, Washington, DC, 1990.

U.S. General Accounting Office, 1991. "U.S.-Mexico Trade: Some Wood Furniture Firms Relocated from the Los Angeles Area to Mexico." Publication No. GAO/NSIAD-91-191, Washington, DC, 1991.

Wheeler, D., and A. Mody. "International Investment Location Decisions: The Case of U.S. Firms." *Journal of International Economics* 33(1992):57–76.

The World Bank. *World Development Report 1992: Development and the Environment.* Washington, DC: The World Bank, 1992.

World Resources Institute. *World Resources, 1992–93: A Guide to the Global Environment.* New York: Oxford University Press, 1992.

# 4

---

# GATT From the Trenches

*Ambassador Michael B. Smith*

About four years ago, environmental activists in California succeeded in placing on a referendum what became known as Proposition 65. In essence, that proposition would have established a sanitary and phytosanitary regime unparalleled in the world. Under the proposed referendum, the State of California could have arbitrarily, and without any required adherence to what is accepted as "sound science," imposed sanitary and phytosanitary requirements on a wide range of agricultural products intended for trade within the state.

Among the "experts" identified as commissioners for implementing this new regime were Jane Fonda and Tom Hayden, whose status as eminent scientific experts on what is good for "ordinary folks" is certainly questionable. Happily, for once, the people of California voted with their heads and defeated Proposition 65. At approximately the same time, the now famous "Tuna/Dolphin Case" was winding its way through the labyrinths of the GATT; about a year later, the GATT released its controversial decision on tuna/dolphin. The combination of Proposition 65 and the tuna/dolphin issue is the beginning of what I believe to be the hottest and the most difficult challenge facing the GATT, the WTO, and the world trading systems. These two issues are raised here because I was asked to talk about "GATT from the Trenches" (or perhaps more accurately, "GATT in the Trenches").

When I was the American Ambassador to the GATT, in the relatively calm days during and immediately following the Tokyo Round, all we had to worry about was implementing the Tokyo Round and preparing for a new round. That latter assignment involved getting such "easy subjects" on the agenda as services, intellectual property, and investment. It only took us four years to accomplish this! I say that with an exclamation point, because they were an obviously very arduous four years.

That new round is now history. The Uruguay Round has been ratified by the big powers, and most importantly, by the United States. One would presume, after such an arduous four years of preparation and seven years of negotiations, that the trade leaders of the world would sit back awhile, take a break, and let the results of the Uruguay Round permeate the system. This is not the case.

Already there are clarion calls for a new round, a so-called "Green Round," where trade and the environment will be negotiated. If that isn't daunting enough, it is the trade lawyers of the world who are calling for that new round. The Green Round also would take on the question of competition policy—which is, in a nutshell, the harmonization of the world's anti-trust laws. It is difficult to imagine a single subject which would so warm the hearts of the fifth estate (which is what I call the lawyers) as competition policy. Imagine, if you will, the American Bar Association descending en masse on Geneva to argue the case for harmonization of anti-trust law with trade law. The poor "trade gurus" would be overwhelmed, and the carefully constructed trade system, built up over forty-five years, would soon be subject to the judicial arguments and blandishments of advocates, solicitors, and attorneys from around the world.

Members of the International Agricultural Trade Research Consortium (IATRC) have seen firsthand the agonies of the agricultural trade negotiations. The Blair House Agreement, for example, stood the test of time for all of two months until the French and Mickey Kantor decided to undo it. In my view, the results of the agricultural negotiations and Uruguay Round are mediocre at best. The world lost a great opportunity to strike a blow for agricultural trade freedom.

Yet, if we think that we endured agonies in agriculture just from a trade viewpoint, imagine what torture we have in store when the traders and the environmentalists lock horns over agriculture in the Green Round. It will be akin to a miracle if the trading system survives.

Take, for example, the thorny issue of production and process methods. The founding fathers of the GATT system recognized early on that rules governing production and process would be difficult, if not impossible, to negotiate. So, the existing GATT rules are relatively silent about processes and leave the trade disciplines largely to final-product problems. In other words, the rules address the finished product—not how it was produced. But to have meaningful environmental disciplines internationally, rules on processes are critical—and the process is a key element of agricultural production. Yet how does one negotiate on inputs, whether they be upstream or downstream?

We in the developed world may have stricter environmental standards regarding the use of pesticides, for example, because we don't face food privation, by and large. Although this sounds arrogant, developed countries can afford to be tougher. In Africa, the luxury of that choice may not be possible; pesticides we wouldn't tolerate here may be crucial there to prevent famine. Who is to judge this?—the traders? the environmentalists? Jane Fonda? the United Nations?

In the United States, an example is provided by the age-old battle between the centralists and the federalists. Under the U.S. Constitution, powers not specifically given to the federal government belong to the states. Generally speaking, these state powers include the right to set environmental standards. For example, California can enact more rigorous standards than those established by the federal government. This might be beneficial for Californians, but suppose you represent a foreign company trying to trade with the United States. You are immediately faced with an economic dilemma: are you obliged to comply with the standards of the federal government *plus* those of the State of California? Or do you avail yourself of your implicit GATT rights, and claim that you only have to meet the U.S. national standards, and leave it to "Uncle Sam" to enforce your rights?

The preceding is, in essence, what Proposition 65 was about. Yet the federal government was very cautious of intervening, given the politics involved. As a "GATTologist," I would submit that state standards must give way to national standards. As a pragmatist, however, I would not fight the point, because I would probably lose in the political arena. Hence, when viewing emerging issues "from the trenches" of the GATT, it is necessary to be ever-conscious of the tug-of-war between what is right from a trade perspective and what is actually attainable.

When we decided in 1982 to put sanitary and phytosanitary standards on the agenda of the new Round as part of the agricultural group, we did so because we felt then that such standards, if abused, would become yet another form of disguised protectionism. We had seen the problem of chilled beef with the European Union. Unfortunately, however, we overlooked our own problem of federal versus state rights—and that came back to haunt us.

Today, the problem in standards is not so much about protectionism pure and simple; rather, the concern is whether it's better to have a lower, but common, set of standards or to let each nation-state adopt its own standards—with the hope that trade between nations will not be unduly impeded. Scratch an environmentalist, and underneath you will generally find a nationalist—in the sense that the environmentalist believes that his/her country's standards are inviolate, even if someone else's trade rights are violated. Scratch a trader, and he/she will try to insist on the multilateral negotiated approach—even though the trader is a bit uneasy about potentially lowering environmental standards which are known to be beneficial to the common good. This exemplifies the dilemma of the Tuna/Dolphin Case. Legally, the people who decided that case in Geneva were correct, but morally perhaps, they were not.

For the past five years, as a private-sector trade practitioner, I have been attempting to bring the traders and the environmentalists together in a "pre-trench" effort to find common ground. With the assistance of Steve Charnovitz, Bruce Gardner, C. Ford Runge, and others, I have been seeking this common ground based on two fundamental principles: (1) that traders are, at heart, environmentalists (they feel as sympathetic toward Flipper the Dolphin as anybody else); and (2) that carried to an extreme, the international crusade of the environmentalists can end up hurting everyone. As a "trenchman," I believe that getting the two sides together, away from governments, and having frank discussions about the problems of trade and the environment, is a critical precursor to any governmental attempts to negotiate agreements on trade and the environment.

Hence, I was asked to chair the Council on Foreign Relations work group on trade and the environment, and also the EPA private-sector work group on GATT, trade, and the environment. At the very least, it appears there is today in the United States a greater mutual understanding and appreciation of the difficulties involved between the two camps than there was, about five years ago. This partial success should not obscure the fundamental contradictions that are involved: on one hand, liberalizing world trade, and on the other, protecting the environment.

Let me posit two points which, I believe, illustrate the dilemma. By definition, liberalized trade means, *inter alia*, letting the most efficient producers of goods and services take advantage of their competitive edge. In other words, liberalized trade means the most efficient allocation of resources, almost regardless of the environmental considerations. Environmental protection, on the other hand, implies at the very least that one is more concerned with the environmental implications of the use of resources than with the most efficient use of those resources.

Traders will argue that a rising tide lifts all boats; that is, as countries become more prosperous, they will do more to protect the environment. This may be true in the long run, but in the short run, we may do such damage to the environment that there will be no long run.

Environmentalists, for their part, will argue that we live on only one planet, with finite resources, and that we can't continue our practices of global degradation. The politicians, while pledging some allegiance to this viewpoint, generally will vote in favor of jobs over endangered snail darters, when major economic dislocations would result from an environmental measure.

Hence, the challenge is to design a trade system which, to the greatest degree possible, takes into account the environmental impact. Toward this end, environmental impact statements are *not* uncalled for. Equally, however, environmental measures should be subjected to a "trade impact statement." Politicians ought to know the benefits and costs of either trade or environmental measures. We, as an electorate, should insist on it. Second, the traders and the environmentalists are going to have to come to agreement about what is termed the "internalization of costs." The environmentalists make a valid point when they claim that many goods and services placed on the market do not reflect the true cost, i.e., *inter alia*, the environmental cost. To date, there is precious little knowledge about how to compute internalized costs, but if consumers are to be given a true choice in the market, it is logical and appropriate that the market price include price internalization. The people at the GATT (or the WTO) are not equipped to handle the theoretical calculations for internalization of costs. Their job would be simply to design rules to take such a discipline into account. Clearly, the entire subject of internalization of costs is a matter ripe for academic study.

Third, the traders and the environmentalists are going to have to reach some sort of understanding regarding enforcement, i.e., using trade tools to enforce environmental rules. Just as a single nation cannot be the world's policeman for every transgression, the WTO cannot act as the policeman for the environment. At the same time, the trading system does have an obligation to the world's citizens not to condone the ruthless spoiling of the planet. At present, virtually the only recourse nations can use for environmental enforcement is through trade. That will ultimately doom the trade system. There also needs to be political and cultural penalties. Just as an army does not rely on only one weapon, so, too, should nations have a variety of weapons in their enforcement arsenal.

Related to this issue is, of course, the conflict between the developed and the developing world over trade and the environment. A number of developing countries fear (with some reason) that the developed world's new-found love of the environment is nothing more than another form of Western protectionism. This is witnessed by the difficulties of the Montreal Protocol a number of years ago and, more recently, the fights within GATT over the revitalization of its Trade and Environment

Committee. It is my prediction that the developed countries will have to pay a pretty penny in terms of trade concessions to get the developing world to agree to any GATT (WTO) accords on the environment.

Finally, both traders and environmentalists need to weed out the extremists within their ranks. Those free traders who state that whales have a certain market value, and hence are "fair game" for exploitation, are just as hurtful to the trade cause as are those environmentalists to the environmental cause when they would have us revert to eating berries and foregoing air conditioning. Candidly stated, the "tree hugger" and the "smokestack lover" are not useful in bringing us to some sort of consensus. The whole issue of green subsidies clearly needs to be addressed.

There is a movement afoot supporting the view that industries should be subsidized if they do the "right thing" environmentally. Take, for example, a steel factory in Germany which is somewhat outmoded in its production facilities. It applies to either the German Federal Government or to one of the German landaus, and receives a subsidy for modernization—under the guise that it is going to be upgraded to an environmentally-correct facility. Under current U.S. law, whether it is environmentally correct, politically correct, or otherwise, that subsidy is countervailable. Indeed, in most other countries that subscribe to the GATT, such a subsidy is countervailable. Politically, however, it would be very difficult for the Clinton Administration (or any other administration) to propose opposition via a countervailing duty case against this German company—because this company is trying to help clean up the atmosphere. Yet, from the perspective of a U.S. steel company, this is viewed as an inequity: the German steel company now has an improved competitive advantage because it got a better facility under the guise of environmental cleanup. Thus green subsidies represent a compelling issue which the next Green Round is going to have to address—and it may present a difficult challenge.

The introduction of the environment into the trade agenda, *perforce*, means compromise. In GATT, agreements were reached by consensus. Consensus implies give and take. The people in the trenches need assurance that this concept of compromise is fully supported by their political overseers back home. That suggests, in turn, that the political authorities would be willing to face down the extremists, be they environmentalists or traders. If the political officials aren't willing to do so, then chaos will reign in Geneva—and ultimately elsewhere.

I remember very well the day I first introduced into the GATT Council the notion that intellectual property rights (IPR) were, *inter alia*, a valid trade concern. The Europeans and the developing world descended upon me with vehement opposition. How could I dare to suggest that patents, copyrights, trademarks, and the like were anything but the sole domain of the World Intellectual Property Organization (WIPO)? Well, I made my arguments, continued to make them for four years, and was rewarded in Punta del Este when the GATT agreed to take on this issue as part of the Uruguay Round.

It took a lot of time and a lot of compromise. The Uruguay Round has not built an IPR paradise—yet. The same will hold true for trade and the environment. There is no question that the issue needs negotiation, and this burden will fall on the men and women at Geneva. The key to success will be patient examination of the issues and difficulties involved, thereby lessening the potential for political undermining.

In closing, I return to a central theme. I believe all traders are environmentalists at heart. I hope that all environmentalists are traders at heart. It is indisputable that we share two common goals: the preservation of the planet, and the raising of the standard of living for all the planet's inhabitants, human and otherwise.

# 5

# Competitiveness, Harmonization, and the Global Ecolonomy

*Steve Charnovitz*

## Introduction

The debate over the linkage of trade and the environment has provided a new window for understanding the exigencies of these dual goals. By encouraging both communities to defend their precepts to the other, the debate has clarified the synergies as well as the incompatibilities. The advent of the World Trade Organization (WTO) is focusing attention on the benefits (and inadequacies) of international rules.

The GATT Secretariat (1994) is optimistic about the Uruguay Round and its impact on the environment. It states, "The conclusion of the Uruguay Round represents an achievement in multilateral policy coordination, and should help to raise expectations of similar successes in the environment field" (p. 2). This is an interesting judgment given the lengthiness of the negotiations, the disappointing amount of liberalization achieved, and the new rules that will limit the application of environmental trade measures [e.g., technical barriers to trade (TBT) and sanitary/phytosanitary standards (SPS)]. Still, the sentiment is basically correct. The world community needs to embark on environmental negotiations commensurate in intensity to the Uruguay Round.

### What is the Ecolonomy?

In recent years, it has become increasingly apparent that the world economy and the global environment are connected. The 1990 Bergen Ministerial Declaration on Sustainable Development pointed out the "symbiotic nature of economy and the environment" (U.N. Economic

Commission for Europe, para. 13). The Rio Declaration on Environment
and Development of 1992 declared: "In order to achieve sustainable
development, environmental protection shall constitute an integral part
of the development process and cannot be considered in isolation from
it" (Principle 4, 31 ILM, 874).

There are many economic issues that are far more domestic than
international. There are also environmental issues that are more domestic
than international. Some economic issues have no serious environmental
implications, and some environmental issues have small implications for
the economy. Nevertheless, the world economy and the global environment are, to a large and probably ever-increasing extent, two sides of the
same coin. I have termed this planetary coin the *ecolonomy*.

This chapter presents an overview of the key issues in the debate and
makes some recommendations for policy changes. Four major sections
comprise the remainder of this chapter, providing discussion on: (1) the
key problems in our ecolonomy, (2) the need for international rules, (3)
the need for better international institutions, and (4) some areas where
caution is advised.

### Dysfunctions in the Ecolonomy

Understanding the ecolonomy does not require new analytical models.
What is needed is a good blend of economics (especially resource
economics) and science. One can start with equilibrium in economics and
in nature, and then examine how various perturbations such as pollution
or overabsorption can produce negative results. One can measure the
impact of environmental change in economic terms and the cost of
economic development in environmental terms. (This requires better
national income accounting to reflect the environmental dimension.) Many
of the insights of political economy regarding the failure of economic
policy are also applicable to environmental policy.

Of course, there are already many connections between economic and
environmental policymaking in some countries. It may be appropriate to
continue utilizing separate government bureaus and officials dealing with
these issues because of the need for specialized skills. But closer linkages
are needed at all levels of government, especially in international
institutions such as the GATT, which until now have been very insular.
Closer linkages can help reduce the high economic costs of poor environmental policies and the high environmental costs of poor economic
policies.

The new generation of environmental policies, which are market-
friendly, are an example of how a closer connection between economics
and environment can yield better outcomes. The importance of property

rights is also something that has become clearer as former communist countries struggle to upgrade their economies and as developing countries attempt to use their natural resources wisely, including their biodiversity.[1] In view of the high unemployment in industrial countries, it is becoming increasingly apparent that we should be shifting from taxes on employment to taxes on pollution and resource extraction.[2] Population control is a concern of both economics and environment.

In considering the connections between environmental and economic policies, it is important not to lose sight of some fundamental differences. The economic goal is growth, production, and consumption. The environmental goal is the maintenance of the ecosystem and, where necessary, environmental restoration. The difference between the two is *not* that economists embrace change and environmentalists oppose it. Only a dead ecosystem fails to evolve. The difference is that while economists focus on increasing outputs and reducing inputs, environmentalists focus on the rates of change and on the need for balance. Environmentalists also tend to have long time horizons (and implicitly low discount rates).

### Trade and Environment Conflicts

Increasing trade and safeguarding the environment are not generally inconsistent objectives. But there are two potentials for conflict that need attention. First, international trade permits countries to specialize, which alters patterns of production. When the impact of this induced production is extrajurisdictional, that is, affecting other countries or the global commons, one can say that trade affects the environment. For example, there might be an increase in the use of ozone-depleting chemicals or of pesticides harmful to birds. When trade leads to the use of exhaustible resources, such as minerals, this may limit options for the future.

The changing patterns of production stemming from trade can have extensive effects on the development of poor countries. There is no reason why the effects of industrialization or agricultural mechanization need to be negative. The benefits of such growth for the economy and the environment will depend on the quality of governmental regulation and planning.

Insofar as industrial countries desire to promote the development of poor countries and tax their own citizens to pay for this, then the environmental policies of poor countries are a legitimate concern. If these environmental policies undercut development, then donor countries may be wasting their money.

A second potential for conflict involves competitiveness. International trade can boost the competitiveness of industries by expanding potential markets, thereby achieving economies of scale.[3] Trade can also wipe out prior market dominance.

Differences in environmental regulation between countries can affect the cost of production and thereby change patterns of comparative advantage and disadvantage.[4] Some of these differences may be viewed as making international trade unfair. Such unfairness claims should sometimes be rejected (for example, when there is little environmental connection between countries), but many such claims will be justified in a global ecolonomy. This is particularly so when competitiveness pressure puts a drag on necessary environmental regulation.

In the face of the ecological, development, and competitiveness problems brought about by international trade, the appropriate policy responses include international disciplines and intergovernmental cooperative activities.[5] For example, disciplines are needed to deal with global environmental problems that require a harmonized response (e.g., ozone protection). Cooperation is needed to assure that one country s policy does not cancel out another s. All governments need better policies on trade and better policies on the environment.

We should also recognize that international rules on the use of trade measures (e.g., GATT rules) can interfere with national social regulation. As James E. Meade (1975) once noted:

> ... it is not possible for the developed countries to bind themselves to a strict and effective free-trade code...and at the same time to retain complete freedom of action to intervene in their national economies (by taxes, subsidies, or other means) to encourage or discourage any particular line of consumption or production on social grounds (p.141).

Many environmentalists believe that the GATT has gone too far in recent adjudication and in the Uruguay Round toward supervision of national environmental laws. If that were all GATT was doing, there would be less controversy. But the GATT Secretariat and some GATT members have also suggested that international environmental treaties have to conform to international trade rules. The GATT Committee on Environmental Measures met for two years, but was unable to agree whether the Conference on Trade in Endangered Species (CITES), the Montreal Protocol, and the Basel Convention should be deemed GATT-legal.

## Rules for the Ecolonomy

There are some treaties about production [e.g., International Labor Organization (ILO) conventions] and about commerce (e.g., CITES). But for the most part, economic and environmental decisions remain national (or subnational). When should such decisions become international?

## Environmental Effects of Trade

There are few environmental effects of trade per se. Most of the environmental concerns involving trade are really concerns about production rather than trade. If production presents a transborder environmental problem, then it deserves attention, whether the good is consumed domestically or exported. It is interesting to note that international labor conventions have always recognized this and are not limited to export sectors. Nevertheless, since trade is inherently international, it may be less controversial to characterize proposed multilateral regulation as rules about trade than as rules about domestic production.

The main environmental effects related to trade are: (1) importation of waste; (2) overuse of renewable resources (including humans); and (3) pollution caused by production stimulated by foreign demand. These effects are exacerbated by the large differences in wealth between poor and rich countries (Stone 1993, p. 111). For example, landowners or governments can be induced to accept industrial country waste for disposal. When the waste is lethal, the morality of such trades becomes questionable.[6] The recent action by the Basel Convention to ban waste trade between Organization for Economic Cooperation and Development (OECD) and non-OECD countries provides one solution to this problem (though it may need some fine tuning).

## Regulatory Motives

Governments use regulations (and some taxes) as instruments for changing production and/or consumption. For example, a regulation might ban the production of cosmetics tested on animals or ban the consumption of narcotics. When such regulations (or taxes) apply to imported goods, parallel trade measures can be used at the border. For instance, a regulation might ban CFCs in domestically-produced or imported products.

The GATT Secretariat and both GATT Dolphin panels have suggested that a critical distinction in the trade and environment debate is whether a regulation seeks to influence foreign producer behavior. Yet making such a distinction is difficult because production and consumption are interrelated. (There is an interchangeability between the regulation of production and consumption. If one bans production, there is nothing to consume. If one bans consumption, producers will stop production.) This author has not found any way to draw this line consistently. For example, a ban on the sale of dolphin-unsafe tuna aims to change production as well as consumption. The same is true for a ban on the sale of meat produced with hormones.

Motives are often difficult to judge. Since regulations can influence production or consumption, it seems likely that many regulations will do both. Thus, a regulation applied to an import may influence foreign production and consumption as well as domestic production and consumption.

One can validly distinguish between trade measures that reflect domestic regulation and trade measures that apply only to imports.[7] But it is interesting to note that the GATT permits many trade measures in the latter category. A tariff, for example, applies only to imports. The GATT also permits trade measures that seek to influence foreign production, such as anti-dumping and countervailing duties. Thus, it would seem difficult to argue that the GATT, as a matter of principle, does not permit countries to use trade measures to influence activities in other countries.

### Complex Exchanges

It is sometimes suggested that trade should be solely about exchange—that no other baggage (such as human rights) should intrude. One can certainly imagine such value-free trades. But if individuals *want* to incorporate issues relating to values in their negotiations, then such issues become part of the free market. To illustrate, if someone wants to buy running shoes made without prison labor, such tastes become part of the transaction. If a group of individuals wants to boycott Norwegian products until that government stops its citizens from hunting whales, then such preferences would seem as valid as any other.

Depending on the extent of popular support, individuals might want to employ government help for their cause. The simplest intervention would be government action to assure that labels on goods are accurate. For example, if the producer of the running shoes advertises that they were not made with forced labor or child labor, one can imagine a government agency assuring the accuracy of that claim. The GATT Dolphin I panel found that a U.S. law requiring such truth in labeling was GATT-consistent.

A more complex intervention would be government action to ban the sale of goods produced in a way that the "public" finds objectionable. For instance, a government might forbid the sale of dolphin-unsafe tuna (as the United States does). Some commentators object to such a law as "coercing" foreign fishermen to change their practices. But the commentators often miss the fact that this economic coercion pales next to the legal coercion directed at domestic fishermen on how to fish or at domestic consumers on what to eat. It is true that foreign citizens may not participate in such rulemaking (although they increasingly have lobbyists). But many domestic citizens do not participate either (or may participate but lose). A foreign fisherman who dislikes the dolphin-unsafe regulation is no more injured than a domestic consumer (perhaps a dolphin hater) who dislikes it.

All government regulations are "coercive" to some extent. A requirement that automobiles have catalytic converters coerces foreign producers to install them. In considering whether there should be limits to such coercive regulations, it is useful to distinguish among three types of environmental trade measures: (1) defiled items, (2) production practices, and (3) government policy.[8] Defiled item standards aim at the product itself—such as no cosmetics tested on animals. (This can be viewed as an agreement between the buyer and the producer.) Production practice standards focus on how all such products are made—for example, no tuna caught from industries that use dolphin-unsafe techniques. Government policy standards aim at how a government regulates the production—for example, no fur caught with leg-hold traps. The coercion of the latter two categories might be viewed as more onerous than the first. It should also be noted that the latter two categories are not standards (applying equally to domestic production). They can only be import bans.

## Trade and International Rulemaking

When an overlap of interests occurs among countries, as often occurs in an ecolonomy, then international cooperation and rulemaking is needed. Treaties can be used to commit governments to take certain actions (e.g., the Wellington Convention on driftnets). Treaties can also be used to commit governments not to take certain actions (e.g., GATT rules against discrimination).

Trade accentuates the need for such rulemaking. In a country that didn t trade, it would be easy for the government to regulate both production and consumption. But the more a country engages in trade, the greater the percentage of its consumption that comes from imports. In a highly specialized (and efficient) ecolonomy, each country would export nearly all of its production and import its consumptive needs. (It might be noted that most individuals in industrial countries do this now.) There is nothing troublesome about this from an economic perspective. But from an environmental perspective, it may prove troublesome, as consuming nations do not regulate the production of what they consume. This interferes with the ability of a nation to engage in social cost internalization, life cycle analysis, and sustainable development.

Nevertheless, one should not misunderstand this problem. Even if nations did not trade at all, they would still need environmental agreements so long as they shared the same planet. Although trade does not create additional environmental problems, it does magnify problems, as the GATT Secretariat (1994) has noted. Trade also weakens the ability of governments to engage in effective environmental regulation. This is not meant to be an argument against trade. Trade is desirable for economic reasons. But trade strengthens the case for attaining better international environmental governance.

### Setting the Level

One key task of environmental governance is to determine the appropriate level for a problem to be addressed, i.e, global, regional, or local. Many commentators have suggested a principle of subsidiary—that problems should be handled at the "lowest" possible level. Others argue that subsidiary may be a distraction from determining the optimal level.

For any particular issue, there may be more than one response, and therefore more than one level. That is, some aspects may require harmonized international standards, while for other aspects, minimum standards will suffice. Still other aspects might be dealt with through coordination. Labels might also be used.

In some circumstances, the best level may not be regulation at all, but rather a code of conduct for corporations. This will allow investors to insist upon responsible action without running up against difficult legal and psychological problems of extraterritoriality.

It is sometimes suggested that while product standards (e.g., pesticide-free wine) may be imposed unilaterally by governments, process standards (e.g., dolphin-safe tuna) should be imposed only multilaterally.[9] This view is untenable.[10] First, it is becoming increasingly difficult to distinguish between product and process standards (Charnovitz 1993). Second, the regulation of services involves both. Third, the critical environmental issues in the future are likely to be process-oriented rather than product-oriented. Thus, while it would certainly be desirable if multilateral agreements on process could be obtained, it would be counterproductive to rule out unilateral measures in the meantime. As David Wirth (1992) has noted, "The international system as currently structured invites the proliferation of holdouts, free riders, laggards, scofflaws, and defectors."

## Improving International Organizations

Throughout the past century, our perception of the "internationality" of many economic and conservation issues has evolved. A common response has been to create international organizations to devise rules and/or to encourage cooperation. Within its narrow purview,[11] the GATT has become more successful both in rulemaking and in cooperation. The ILO, with a much broader purview, has become less successful in recent decades. The United Nations Environmental Program (UNEP) has had only modest success.

### Creating a Global Environmental Organization

Even though we live in an ecolonomy, it is probably better to have specialized institutions rather than general ones. But while we have a GATT (soon to be WTO) and an ILO, we lack any comparable institution for the environment. Some environmental groups would like to green the WTO and turn it into an environmental institution. But this would be unwise, since combating protectionism is a full-time job.

Instead, we need to create a Global Environmental Organization (GEO).[12] The GEO could fulfill the following functions:

> Devise environmental standards for critical issues.
> Conduct environmental negotiating "rounds" which seek to group together issues involving trade-offs between North and South.
> Conciliate environmental disputes between countries.
> Improve the delivery of environmental technical assistance.

It may seem inconsistent to advocate a new international organization for the environment at the same time that one points out the interrelationship between environmental and economic issues. But this is a pragmatic stance. Organizations with broad mandates do not perform as well as those with narrow ones. The way to deal with the interrelationships is to insist that international organizations coordinate more with each other. (The recent proposal for a U.N. Economic Security Council merits consideration.)

It may also be useful to begin exploring direct regulation (and taxation) of multinational corporations by an international institution. In the absence of such regulation, there will be more conflicts of legal jurisdiction and a declining effectiveness of regulation. This will require new concepts of "sovereignty."

### Role of Interest Groups

Elsewhere I have advocated that the GEO be organized on a tripartite basis (like the ILO) with representatives from businesses, governments, and environmental non-government organizations (NGOs).[13] The participation of NGOs is also important for existing institutions, not organized on tripartite lines, such as the GATT. Many countries have resisted this idea in the GATT on the grounds that NGOs should filter their ideas through their governments. But this traditional model is becoming increasingly obsolete for several reasons.

First, as more issues require collective action, international organizations will become a more important site for decision making. To exclude NGOs is to weaken their effectiveness. Second, NGOs are increasingly becoming multinational. As a result, an NGO can no longer lobby its government, since it has none (or several). Third, the government-only approach is not suited for the complex decision making required for global issues (particularly since governments do not perfectly reflect well-informed public opinion). We need "virtual" negotiations involving all the key players at once.

## Cautionary Notes

As we improve our capacity for global decision making through institutions like the WTO, we should exercise caution in three areas. First, we should preserve national (and subnational) sovereignty when possible. Nations should not be told to lower their environmental standards unnecessarily or to raise them unnecessarily.

Second, we should recognize that international trade has a homogenizing effect on culture and community. In some cases, it may be appropriate to sacrifice some economic gain in order to retain these values. For instance, there are good arguments for preserving traditional family farms.

Third, the inevitable participation of NGOs has a downside. It can lead to "Demosclerosis," a malady that we suffer from greatly in the United States. Thus, any system of governance will need periodic reinvention. As Joan Robinson (1962) commented, "Social life will always present mankind with a choice of evils. No metaphysical solution that can ever be formulated will seem satisfactory for long."

In conclusion, the trade and environment debate is providing a useful impetus for improving both international environmental governance and national decision making. By recognizing the ecolonomy, we can link policies more constructively as we seek both sustainable growth and sustainable employment.

## Notes

1. For a good discussion of property rights and environmental resources, see Chichilnisky (1994).

2. For additional information on this subject, see European Commission (1994), especially chapter 10.

3. Thus, promoting exports is useful because it allows nations to specialize more. It is not mercantilism to be export-oriented or to promote exports. One crosses the line into mercantilism when one combines an export orientation with an *anti*-import orientation. Ideally, a country would promote exports and imports.

4. The effects so far have been very small. See Sorsa (1994).

5. For an early discussion of the need for an international economic authority, see Fisher (1945, p. 351).

6. Although voluntary exchanges should carry a presumption of legitimacy, there are many instances where government paternalism will override objectionable transactions.

7. Sometimes trade measures may support domestic measures. For example, a country seeking to regulate the harvesting of lobsters might apply equivalent controls to foreign lobsters because of the possibility of substitution. This approach is also used for look-alike species.

8. For further discussion, see Charnovitz (1993).

9. For example, see Vossenaar and Jha (1994), and OECD Secretariat (1994).

10. A better characterization might be production-related, use-related, transport-related, and disposal-related.

11. GATT is mainly about abstention or mutual de-escalation. This is conceptually a far easier task than that faced by UNEP or the ILO.

12. For a thoughtful proposal for a World Environmental Organization, see Runge (1994, pp. 100-07).

13. For example, see Charnovitz (1993, pp. 283-85).

## References

Bergen Ministerial Declaration on Sustainable Development U.N. Economic Commission for Europe, May, 1990.

Charnovitz, S. "Environmental Harmonization and Trade Policy." In *Trade and the Environment*, D. Zaelke, P. Orbuch, and Robert F. Housman., eds., pp. 283–85. Washington, DC: Island Press, 1993.

—————. "The Regulation of Environmental Standards by International Trade Agreements." *International Environment Reporter* 16, no. 17(August 1993):631–35.

—————. "A Taxonomy of Environmental Trade Measures." *Georgetown International Environmental Law Review* VI(Winter 1993):1-46.

Chichilnisky, G. "North-South Trade and the Global Environment." *The American Economic Review* 84, no. 4(September 1994):851–74.

European Commission. *Growth, Competitiveness, Employment: The Challenges and Ways Forward into the 21st Century*. White Paper, Brussels, 1994.

Fisher, A.G.B. *Economic Progress and Social Security*. London: MacMillan & Co., 1945.

GATT Secretariat. "Report to the Second Meeting of the Commission on Sustainable Development." Geneva, May 1994.

Meade, J.E. *The Intelligent Radical's Guide to Economic Policy*. London: George Allen & Unwin, Ltd., 1975.

OECD Secretariat. "Note to Members of the Joint Session on Trade and Environment." Paris, COM/TD/ENV(94)39, 1994.

Rio Declaration on Environment and Development, Principle 4, International Legal Materials, 31(1992):874.

Robinson, J. *Economic Philosophy*. Chicago: Aldine Publishing, 1962.

Runge, C.F. *Free Trade, Protected Environment*. New York: Council on Foreign Relations, 1994.

Sorsa, P. "Competitiveness and Environmental Standards." Working Paper No. 1249, The World Bank, Washington, DC, February 1994.

Stone, C.D. *The Gnat Is Older than Man*. Princeton, NJ: Princeton University Press, 1993.

Vossenaar, R., and V. Jha. "Environmentally Based Process and Production Method Standards: Some Implications for Developing Countries." UNCTAD, Geneva, April 1994.

Wirth, D. "The International Trade Regime and the Municipal Law of Federal States: How Close a Fit?" *Washington and Lee Law Review* 49 (Fall 1992):1389–1401.

# 6

# Environmental Side Agreements: Will They Take Center Stage?

*Nicole Ballenger and Barry Krissoff*

## Introduction

Over the past few years, members of our profession have analyzed the effects on agriculture of the North American Free Trade Agreement (NAFTA). Almost all such efforts have focused on the removal of tariffs, quotas, and nontariff barriers such as import license requirements in a single or multiple agricultural commodity framework or in an applied general equilibrium framework. Studies tend to agree that with NAFTA, the United States will increase its exports to Mexico of grains and oilseeds, and increase its two-way trade in livestock, meat, and horticultural products (U.S. Department of Agriculture 1992; Grennes and Krissoff 1993; Burfisher, Robinson, and Thierfelder 1992).

A few studies have taken the additional steps of attempting to assess the effect of liberalized agricultural trade in North America on input use and environmental factors. Abler and Pick (1993) assess the environmental impact of increased horticulture production in the Mexican state of Sinaloa. Their empirical results indicate that tomato, pepper, and cucumber production would only marginally increase in chemical intensity relative to alternative uses of the land and would remain less chemical intensive than in the competing U.S. state of Florida.

In another paper, Newman (1991) addresses the issue of U.S. food safety following the NAFTA. In particular, he examines increases in U.S. fruit and vegetable imports from Mexico following trade reform. He finds that there may be some questions regarding the adequacy of food safety monitoring, but that pesticide residue violations for agricultural imports from Mexico are similar to violations for U.S. production.

Most analyses, like the studies mentioned above, emphasize the impacts of NAFTA's *trade policy* reforms. For the most part, agricultural economists have been reticent to examine NAFTA's environmental provisions, and maybe for good reason.[1] The environmental provisions are often vague, subject to interpretation, and lacking in concrete policy prescriptions. The Japanese describe such agreements as *tama-mushi iro*, after a common Japanese beetle. The beetle, *tama-mushi*, has translucent wings that appear as different colors depending on the angle of the viewer and the sunlight.

The *tama-mushi* analogy may be appropriate. Nevertheless, it is also possible that the environmental provisions will have a more lasting influence on the agricultural sector of North America than the more concrete agricultural trade reforms. This may come about in part because the liberalization impacts are limited due to the modest magnitude of current agricultural trade barriers among the three partners. A U.S. Department of Agriculture (1992) report estimates U.S. agricultural exports will increase only 2 percent under NAFTA's trade policy reforms, due to the relatively small size of trade barriers and the large current export base.

Perhaps of more significance is that NAFTA's environmental provisions create a "living" document, whereas the reform of traditional trade barriers will be completed within fifteen years. NAFTA and its environmental side agreement establish new institutional structures and rules for promoting environmental cooperation, multilateral discussion, and public challenge that have the potential to generate a continuing evolution of environmental policy change. The promulgation of environmental policy stemming from this institutional innovation could, over the long run, have significant implications for agricultural production and markets, depending on the course it takes. Much will depend on the direction and vigor that environmental, consumer, and industry organizations bring to shaping the scope and specifics of NAFTA's environmental agenda.

Our general objective in writing this chapter was to attempt to get a "handle" on NAFTA's environmental provisions *in the context of our interest in agriculture*. In the first part, we describe the environmental provisions of NAFTA and its environmental side agreement. Next, we summarize the concerns and perceptions of environmental and commodity groups, as elicited from personal interviews, to assess how the environmental provisions might apply to agriculture. Last, we use our reading of the agreement and input from those we interviewed to suggest a research agenda at the nexus of trade, environment, and agriculture in North America.

## NAFTA and the Environmental Cooperation
## Agreement: Why Is It New and Green?

The United States, Canada, and Mexico (the parties) reached two accords which contain environmental provisions: the North American Free Trade Agreement (NAFTA) and the North American Agreement on Environmental Cooperation (NAAEC). In addition, the United States and Mexico agreed to establish a Border Environmental Cooperation Commission (BECC) and a North American Development Bank (NADBank).[2] Together, these agreements contain a wide array of provisions to encourage economic growth and to promote cooperation in improving environmental conditions throughout North America. This chapter focuses on the NAFTA and NAAEC.

### Environmental Provisions of NAFTA

Blackhurst and Subramanian (1992) write that the main challenge facing countries attempting to regulate environmental externalities within their borders is how to agree on rules that minimize commercial friction between countries. NAFTA and NAAEC appear, jointly, to attempt to accomplish this task. In the preamble to NAFTA, the three parties state their resolve to "contribute to the harmonious development and expansion of world trade ... in a manner consistent with environmental protection and conservation, ... [and to] promote sustainable development and strengthen the development and enforcement of environmental laws and regulations." Three specific environment-related concerns are discussed in the NAFTA text: (1) pollution havens; (2) human, animal, and plant health and safety; and (3) international environmental agreements.

*Pollution Havens.* Environmental, industry, and labor organizations shared concerns during the formulation of NAFTA with the impacts of differing environmental standards, thought to be more stringent in the United States and Canada than in Mexico, in the presence of a more liberalized trade and investment regime. The fear was that firms subject to more stringent environmental regulations would find it easier, in the more open trade and investment environment, to relocate to a jurisdiction with lower standards. To mitigate the opportunities for "pollution havens," the parties renounce the relaxation of environmental, health, and safety measures for the purpose of attracting investment. The NAFTA also develops procedures for compulsory consultations—but only consultations—between parties in case such a relaxation occurs.

*Sanitary and Phytosanitary and Standards-Related Provisions.* NAFTA contains provisions for the use of measures to protect food safety, animal, plant and environmental health, and other consumer interests. Provisions regarding the use of sanitary and phytosanitary (SPS) measures are found in Chapter 7 of the NAFTA treaty. SPS measures are those used to protect animals and plants from undue risk of disease and pests, and humans from dangerous organisms in food or beverages, or toxins such as food additives and contaminants. Examples of SPS measures include U.S. pesticide residue tolerances and restrictions on food additives.

A set of related provisions—those pertaining to the use of product standards-related (SR) measures—are found in NAFTA's Chapter 9. SR measures extend regulations on consumer safety, the environment, and the protection of human, plant, and animal health to encompass labeling, packaging, and product content requirements, and some technical requirements related to food safety.

The NAFTA text asserts the right of countries to choose and establish their own appropriate level of protection of human, animal, and plant life using a scientific basis. NAFTA provides recommendations for using international standards as a scientific basis and as a way of making countries' standards more similar, but explicitly states that there should be no downward reduction of standards. It also states that the individual countries may use a more stringent standard than the international one so long as there is no discrimination against the goods from another party and no disguised restriction to trade. In choosing standards stricter than international standards, each country should consider relevant risk assessment technologies, relevant production methods and practices, relevant scientific evidence, relevant ecological and environmental conditions, and relevant economic conditions. (In a good bit of *tama-mushi iro*, specifics with respect to what is "relevant" are not stated.)

NAFTA also asserts each country's right to establish, maintain, or apply SR measures that it considers appropriate in pursuing its legitimate objectives of safety, or protection of human, animal, and plant life and health. While the language on SR measures is similar to that for SPS measures, there is no obligation to consider the measure's scientific basis.

An agriculture-related example of an SR measure has recently challenged U.S-Canadian relations. Canada is considering legislation requiring generic packaging (that is, a plain white pack) for all cigarettes as a means of discouraging smoking. U.S. tobacco interests object to this action, claiming that the Canadians, under international obligations, do not have the right to discourage consumption by impairing trademarks (Trueheart 1994).[3]

NAFTA establishes SPS and SR committees to facilitate consultation in attempting to resolve such conflicts. If a mutually agreeable solution is not reached (see discussion related to dispute settlement provisions, below), then the burden of proving any inconsistency of SPS or SR measures is on the challenging party. For example, if the U.S. wanted to dispute the environmental tax placed on beer cans in Ontario, it would have to demonstrate that the tax is inconsistent with NAFTA principles.

Under NAFTA, comparability of standards is to be promoted through the application of the following principles:

- *Transparency*: The disclosure of methods used in formulating and adopting health-related measures, the dispensing of information and advance notification to the public, and the opportunity for public comment.
- *Equivalency*: The recognition that different methods may be used to achieve the same level of health protection.
- *Consistency*: Avoiding arbitrary or unjustifiable distinctions across commodities in choosing the level of risk or the adoption of SPS and SR measures.

If operationalized, these principles have the potential to assist producers and traders in selling products subject to SPS and SR measures across national borders, while benefiting consumers through increased information on product content and greater diversity of products for purchase. Thus, this is an area where NAFTA has the potential to enhance both producer and consumer welfare.

*International Environmental Agreements.* NAFTA grants priority to the trade provisions of certain international environmental agreements (IEAs). Three treaties are specifically delineated—the Convention on International Trade in Endangered Species of Wild Fauna and Flora (CITES), the Montreal Protocol on Substances that Deplete the Ozone Layer, and the Basel Convention on the Control of Transboundary Movements or Hazardous Wastes—and others could be added. The intention is to protect national measures taken under these treaties against challenges that they are inconsistent with the trade-liberalizing rules of NAFTA.

## The North American Agreement on Environmental Cooperation: Objectives and Provisions

The NAAEC goes beyond NAFTA's environmental provisions and existing IEAs in its breadth of coverage. Its scope is not limited to one or several specific environmental concerns, and environmental concerns taken up by NAAEC need not necessarily be directly related to trade. NAAEC recognizes the importance of conservation, environmental protection, and sustainable development, with an emphasis on cooperation, compliance, and enforcement of each country's *own* public policies. Thus, it attempts to reach a balance between transnational environmental aims and each government's sovereignty in managing its internal business.

*Institutional Framework.* NAAEC establishes a new framework and infrastructure, called the Commission on Environmental Cooperation (CEC), to address current and future environmental issues in the region. The NAAEC specifically commits the parties to effective enforcement of their environmental laws (local and federal) and to monitoring the environmental effects of NAFTA. The latter is primarily achieved through cooperation between the CEC and NAFTA's Free Trade Commission. The CEC is comprised of a Council (made up of Cabinet-level appointees), a Secretariat for administrative and operational support, and a Joint Public Advisory Committee (JPAC). The U.S. representative to the Council is the administrator of the Environmental Protection Agency (EPA).

The CEC can address a full range of environmental or natural resource issues through its work program and, therefore, its creation may be the most significant element of the agreement. The CEC's role is to oversee implementation of the environmental agreement, to serve as a forum for discussion, and to facilitate environmental cooperation. It has wide discretion on the areas that it can consider and for which it can develop recommendations. Its scope of inquiry includes, but is not limited to, pollution prevention techniques, environmental implications of goods throughout their life cycles, use of economic instruments for the pursuit of domestic and international environmental objectives, and eco-labeling. Thus, the CEC may examine issues related to *production processes and methods*, a potentially contentious issue between environmental and producer groups.

*National Environmental Policies and Enforcement.* The environmental side agreement spells out a number of obligations, the most notable of which is the commitment to effective enforcement of environmental laws. Each party has committed to effectively enforce its own environmental laws through appropriate government action. Such actions include: appointment and training of inspectors; monitoring compliance and investigating suspected violations; seeking assurances of voluntary compliance agreements; publicly releasing noncompliance information; initiating judicial, quasi-judicial, or administrative proceedings to seek appropriate sanctions or remedies for violations of its environmental laws and regulations (Article 5). Interested persons also have administrative, quasi-judicial, and judicial access to remedies of alleged violations of domestic environmental laws and regulations including the right to sue another for damages under that party's jurisdiction (Articles 6 and 7).

The dispute settlement procedures are purposefully cumbersome. A country complaining about another country's nonenforcement of its national environmental policies must first give official notice and then formally request a consultation with the offending country. If the countries cannot resolve their dispute involving a party's alleged persistent pattern of failure to effectively enforce an environmental law, then any country can request a meeting of the Council. The Council's primary responsibility is to correct the problems of nonenforcement. If the Council cannot successfully resolve the dispute, the Council will establish a formal dispute settlement panel on a two-thirds vote. This track though, is applicable *only to nonenforcement practices affecting trade* between the parties, or competing goods and services.

Once the panel has made a final determination that a country does not sufficiently enforce its law, a remedial enforcement plan is drawn up. If the "action" plan is not implemented, the panel may impose a monetary fine up to 0.007 percent of the total trade in goods between the parties (or $20 million currently). If the fine is not paid within six months, the complaining party may impose trade sanctions on imports from the party complained against. Trade sanctions, therefore, only come at the end of a step-by-step, time-consuming process.

*The Public's Role.* The influence of environmental organizations on the creation of NAAEC has been made possible through their discussions with U.S., Canadian, and Mexican environmental and trade agencies. For example, according to position papers prepared by the National Wildlife Federation (NWF) and their correspondences with both the Bush and Clinton administrations (through the U.S. Trade Representative's Office and EPA), NWF strongly encouraged the establishment of a committee on the environment as well as influenced the language of the agreement. Canadian and Mexican governments faced similar pressures from their domestic environmental organizations (Hudson and Prudencio 1993).

Environmental organizations may influence the potential implement-ation and further elaboration of NAAEC with the establishment of two separate advisory committees. As part of the CEC, a Joint Public Advisory Committee is established to provide advice to the Council, to provide technical, scientific, or other information to the independent and perma-nent Secretariat, and to perform other functions as directed by the Council. Each party to the agreement may also convene a National Advisory Committee, which could include representatives from nongovernment organizations.

Another avenue open to a nongovernmental organization or an individual is the possibility of making a submission to the Secretariat claiming that a party is failing to effectively enforce its environmental law. The submission could be accepted if the Secretariat finds that it will be aimed at promoting enforcement rather than at harassing industry (Article

14). This could make it possible for a Mexican to complain about the inadequate enforcement of environmental standards in Canada in an industry where the goods produced do not compete with Mexican exports and never leave Canada to be exported to Mexico (Johnson 1993). If the Secretariat is granted permission by the Council, it will prepare a factual record, including relevant technical, scientific, or other information, which, along with the documentary evidence from the submission, could be made public (Article 15). This could also prompt a country to initiate procedures for a formal dispute settlement.

The CEC's power to enforce is limited to the dispute settlement process discussed above. However, the real power of the CEC may simply be in its ability to publicize environmental misuse and government failure. One advocate of the NAAEC, a former Visiting Fellow at the World Resources Institute, stated:

> It would be up to member governments and the public to insist that the rather general provisions in the environmental agreement lead to new commitments on higher environmental standards on a realistic timetable, to insist that cleanup and technical assistance programs are fully funded, to insist that public participation is meaningful, to insist that monitoring and reporting on environmental compliance is regular and vigilant, and to insist that NAFTA's environmental provisions become a model for wider hemispheric and global trade and environmental collaboration (Hammonds 1993).

### A Survey of Public Interest in the Environmental Provisions

We thought we could learn more about how the environmental provisions of NAFTA might ultimately be applied to agricultural issues by meeting and talking with environmental and farm organizations with a strong Washington presence. We began by formulating a set of specific questions, but ultimately found the questions were more useful for providing structure to our discussion than for giving us answers. Thus, what follows is an integrated overview of our discussions rather than a tabulation of interview results.

We told each person interviewed that we intended to present the materials at an academic forum, and hoped that our findings would influence the direction of trade and environment research undertaken by agricultural economists. We found each person receptive to the notion that economic research could be directed toward their specific concerns, though often skeptical of the perspective of economics. Particularly welcomed was a closer scrutiny of the agriculture, trade, and environment nexus in North

America, since it seems to have received so little explicit attention so far. Thus, one of our main conclusions was that we, as a group, have considerable potential to influence how the three-way interface among agriculture, trade, and the environment is treated and understood in the policy arena.

### Environmental Groups: Where Are They Coming From?

"Trade and environment is the first battleground in defining sustainable development."

— Bill Snape (1994)
Attorney for Defenders of Wildlife

Environmental groups had an unprecedented role in shaping the outcome of the NAFTA. They shared a range of concerns, but differed in their emphases, strategies, and final positions taken. Some ultimately supported NAFTA and others stuck by their opposition.[4] Our conversations with some representatives of environmental organizations and our readings of articles and testimony offered by others led us to this simple conclusion: some saw the environmental provisions as "a glass half full," others saw them as "a glass half empty." We think, though, that all would say that their battle to force trade agreements to address a range of environmental issues has really just begun. There is no doubt that these groups will assure that every future agreement aimed at further economic integration in the Western Hemisphere will contain environmental components.

In our meetings, we learned that environmental groups see the NAFTA (like other multilateral agreements to come) to be more about a deeper integration of economies and societies than merely trade liberalization. Each group described itself as being engaged in defining new ground rules for sustainable development in this context of deeper economic integration. Several of those interviewed reminded us that economists do not know if freer trade, in the presence of environmental externalities, is globally welfare-improving or not. As economists, we may quibble with the measures promoted by environmental groups, or feel uncomfortable with their increasing comfort in trade forums, but it seems to us that these organizations may have successfully grasped the "moral authority" in the trade arena in the eyes of the public and many policy makers.

### What Do Environmental Groups Want, Specifically?

Table 6.1 highlights key concerns of environmental groups with whom we met directly. All environmental organizations wanted the NAFTA text to address a range of issues, including:

- monitoring of environmental quality resulting from trade liberalization;
- protection for national environmental laws;
- harmonization of sanitary and phytosanitary and other product standards;
- environmental problems along the U.S.-Mexican border;
- location of dirty industry, or "pollution havens";
- the legal relationship between NAFTA and IEAs; and
- the use of trade measures to enforce "environmentally-friendly" production and processing methods, or PPMs.

As described in the earlier sections of this chapter, the NAFTA and NAAEC jointly address these issues to some extent, but with varying directness and rigor. (Note that U.S.-Mexico border issues are addressed in side agreements not covered by this chapter, such as the Border Environmental Cooperation Commission.)

Pollution havens, SPS and SR measures, and IEA-NAFTA precedence issues are addressed directly in the NAFTA text—more or less satisfactorily in the opinion of NAFTA supporters, and less than adequately in the opinion of NAFTA opponents. NAFTA proponents emphasize the tremendous institutional innovation that NAAEC represents; others, like Defenders of Wildlife, say the side agreement's objectives of cooperation and enforcement of existing environmental laws were cast far too narrowly for their satisfaction.

Individuals participating in our meetings focused on several issues of importance to their respective environmental groups:

- The National Wildlife Federation (NWF) (a NAFTA supporter) emphasized that the agreement explicitly rules out reductions in SPS standards, even in the interest of harmonization. NAFTA opponents pointed out that the agreement fails to explicitly set minimum standards, although it could have done so using at least the highest current standard among the parties.
- NWF representatives pointed out that the agreement commits countries to avoiding the creation of pollution havens and creates platforms for "bringing public pressure to bear on governments." Opponents, like Greenpeace, argued that the pollution-haven provision rests on an unenforceable "gentlemen's" agreement.
- Supporters stressed the protection offered to the terms of IEAs; opponents said this protection is more "lip service" than substance.

**TABLE 6.1 Profiles of Environmental Groups**

| | |
|---|---|
| *Greenpeace USA*<br><br>*Members: 435,000*<br><br>*Staff:* 31<br><br>*NAFTA Stance:* Opposed | *Main Concerns:* NAFTA would undermine national policies to promote alternative energy and protect natural resources; that subsidies to encourage conservation, particularly of energy, would be subject to legal challenge by trading partners.<br><br>*Ag Issues:* Loss of family farm, dislocation of Mexican peasants.<br><br>*Use of CEC:* To address border concerns like maquiladaras, waste dumps, and power plant emissions. |
| *Defenders of Wildlife*<br><br>*Members: 70,000*<br><br>*NAFTA Stance:* Uncommitted (neither for nor against) | *Main Concerns:* Want legitimization of trade actions based on PPMs, a more open dispute settlement process, and protection of wildlife along border.<br><br>*Ag Issues:* Impacts on structure of Mexican agriculture; very involved in challenging fisheries harvesting practices in U.S. and other countries. |
| *Sierra Club*<br><br>*Members: 350,000*<br><br>*Staff:* 185<br><br>*NAFTA Stance:* Opposed<br><br>*Other:* Helped shape Clinton position on NAFTA prior to his presidency; pushed for renegotiation, not just side agreement. | *Main Concerns:* Effect on sanctity of U.S. environmental laws; role of public input and debate in dispute settlement; trade adjustment costs, particularly in Mexico; funding for border cleanup.<br><br>*Ag Issues:* Dislocation of Mexican peasant farmers resulting in pressures on forests and marginal lands; worker and environmental protection in Mexican agribusiness, particularly if labor surpluses develop due to large-scale migration from traditional agricultural regions.<br><br>*Use of CEC:* Will look for problems in "vulnerable" sectors like agriculture, mining, maquiladaras, tourism; will challenge CEC to address and solve these problems. |
| *National Wildlife Federation*<br><br>*Members:* 4.5 million<br><br>Staff: *500*<br><br>*NAFTA Stance:* Pro<br><br>*Other:* Proposed early form of CEC to the U.S. Trade Representative (USTR); only environmental group to support fast tract for NAFTA. | *Main Concerns:* Effects of increased trade and investment on pollution; possible downgrading of SPS and SR provisions (satisfied with NAFTA treatment, though concerned with interpretation); enforcement of national environmental laws. Tried to focus the debate on environmental issues specifically linked to trade.<br><br>*Ag Issues:* Is trade bad for small farms sector? What is the solution to rural adjustment problems in Mexico?<br><br>*Use of CEC:* Wants to pursue Council's role in promoting common indicators, life cycle analyses, ecologically sensitive national accounts, etc. Will expect Secretariat to investigate enforcement complaints. |

Neither NAFTA nor NAAEC address PPMs, yet this is perhaps the biggest trade and environment "battle" ahead. All the environmental groups agree that this is an omission, though they differ in their assessments of how PPM issues ought to be pursued. Some groups, such as the Sierra Club and Defenders of Wildlife, who want explicit license for nations to actively and unilaterally use trade measures (like "green countervails" or sanctions) to enforce the use of "environmentally friendly" PPMs by trade partners, were more willing than others to make this a basis for their political support of NAFTA (Snape 1994).[5] Others, such as the National Wildlife Federation, did not pursue PPMs in the context of NAFTA, but still seek a set of international rules to guide the limited use of trade measures related to PPMs within the context of multilateral agreement. NWF, in our interview, expressed verbal concern for how close this issue takes us to the edge of the "slippery slope" into protectionism. Even NWF, however, publicly states that the United States has a right to limit market access based on the way goods are produced and processed. Its president has testified that the U.S. "cannot set one standard on our producers here at home, and expect them to be able to compete fairly with foreign producers who do not protect the environment" (Hair 1993).

Environmental groups were split on the issue of the need to protect national environmental and conservation laws, particularly those that do not specifically contain trade provisions, from challenge by trade partners. NAFTA opponents, particularly Greenpeace, point to cases of legal challenge to Canadian, U.S., and state laws to suggest their fears are not groundless. NAFTA proponents, on the other hand, have made detailed arguments protesting this fear. NWF, for example, argued that the environmental provisions in NAFTA and NAAEC would not undermine U.S. domestic laws and regulations: for a challenge to be brought against U.S. law, it would have to be brought by Mexico or Canada, would have to be trade-related, and would, in any event, be more easily defended under NAFTA than GATT (see 1993 Congressional testimony of Jay D. Hair, NWF President, and Stewart Hudson, NWF Legislative Representative). In its testimony, NWF recounts why it is not concerned with NAFTA's impact on section 1538 of the Endangered Species Act (ESA), which generally prohibits exports and imports of endangered species. NWF claims the ESA should be free from challenge because it is consistent with NAFTA provisions pertaining to (1) nondiscrimination, that is, it applies to both U.S. and foreign traders; and (2) the mandatory trade restrictions of international agreements, in particular, the Convention on International Trade in Endangered Species of Wild Fauna and Flora (CITES), which is expressly protected by NAFTA.

Other U.S. laws, such as the Lacey Act, restrict trade in wildlife and protect certain species. For example, sea turtle legislation (Public Law 101-162, Title VI, section 609) generally inhibits the importation of "shrimp or products from shrimp which have been harvested with commercial fishing technology which may affect adversely ... species of sea turtles...." NWF asks, "Is it likely that Mexico will bring about a complaint to challenge this U.S. law?" It thinks a challenge is less likely with NAAEC than without. (In fact, in April 1993, the Department of State certified that Mexico has been making significant efforts to use turtle excluder devices.)

The Environmental Defense Fund, an organization of 50,000 members, including lawyers, scientists, and economists, with a pro-NAFTA stance, summarizes the limits (though not necessarily the failings, in its view) of the environmental provisions and side agreement (Gilbreath and Emerson 1993):

- The scope of the environmental dispute system is not nearly as broad as that for trade disputes, and remedies are not as easily obtained.
- Provisions for citizen cooperation and participation are modest.
- The outcome of the SPS provisions will depend on the interpretations of phrases such as "based on science" and "necessary to protect."
- The route to challenging a country's commitment to seek investment through weak environmental laws is long and tortuous.
- No provisions are made for the use of "green countervails."

The Sierra Club, the largest and best-known of the NAFTA opponents, spelled out in our interview what more it had wanted from the agreement, including: (1) stronger safeguards for national sovereignty; (2) the right to "enforce PPMs;" (3) total openness in dispute settlement; (4) the insurance of upward harmonization; and (5) stronger mechanisms *at the industry level* to ensure compliance with national laws. These same demands were echoed by other environmental groups who were less than satisfied with the final results.

### Farm Groups and the Environmental Provisions

Farm groups, while keenly interested in NAFTA, remained relatively uninvolved in shaping NAFTA's environmental provisions. Each of the three groups with whom we spoke—the Farm Bureau (pro-NAFTA), the Grange (NAFTA neutral), and the National Farmers Union (anti-NAFTA)—described their organization as "somewhat familiar" with the environmental provisions and "interested, but not directly involved" in their formulation. Despite their differing political stances on NAFTA, their key concerns regarding environmental aspects were in large part shared.

Farm groups were concerned, principally, with the treatment of SPS and SR measures, and the effects of an environmental agreement on trade and industry competitiveness. Enforcement issues were also ranked as major concerns by the Farm Bureau and the National Farmers Union. Their major worry regarding treatment of SPS and SR measures was the potential for a weakening of U.S. laws or standards, thereby aligning farm groups with environmental groups in this regard. Farm group membership worried, for example, that Mexico would be able to ship unsafe milk or meat to the United States.

The groups differed in their assessments of the effectiveness or adequacy with which the agreements addressed their major concerns. The Farm Bureau and the Grange are more or less satisfied with NAFTA's treatment of SPS, while the National Farmers Union expresses considerable skepticism regarding implementation of the provisions and the realities of border inspection. Both the Farm Bureau and the Grange believe NAFTA's provisions on SPS and SR are likely to help facilitate increased bilateral trade through improved transparency and equivalency. They stress the importance of a sound scientific basis for SPS measures, and recognize that factor endowments, product mixes, and production practices differ, so that applications of product standards may need to differ as well. The National Farmers Union is aligned with anti-NAFTA environmental groups in wanting to see product standards brought at least to the highest common denominator.

Farm groups had less knowledge of NAAEC than of NAFTA, but expressed doubts regarding the side agreement's need and likely effectiveness. The Grange is skeptical about NAAEC provisions and institutions, suggesting they create "uncertainty," will generate "nuisance complaints," and are more likely to consider "aesthetic" or "emotional" environmental issues than health and safety issues. Nonetheless, the Grange has adopted a wait-and-see attitude. The Farm Bureau doubts the need for the side agreement, feeling that NAFTA itself covered environmental issues adequately, and queries whether supplemental agreements are giving too much influence to environmental (and labor) groups. The groups with whom we spoke did not see themselves actively bringing issues to the CEC. The Farm Bureau expected it would take a more "reactive" role to issues raised, while the National Farmers Union said it was more likely to use "the trade route." All (including some environmental groups) expressed concern with the amount of resources necessary to bring issues and complaints to the CEC.

More mainstream farm groups might have been more involved in debate surrounding the environmental side agreement had it appeared that anti-NAFTA environmental forces were more fully garnering their goals. The

Farm Bureau, for example, would have sharply protested provisions allowing the use of trade measures to influence PPMs or to adjust for differences in standards. In an April 1994 letter to U.S. Trade Representative Mickey Kantor, Farm Bureau president Dean Kleckner writes:

> If trade is used to correct for differences among countries in labor and environmental standards, why not for differences in tax rates, internal social programs or even national resource advantages? Many countries would be quick to take advantage of the precedent we would be setting to justify trade barriers of their own, which could lead to a new worldwide wave of protectionism.

## The Nexus of Trade, Agriculture, and the Environment

We thought that the policy nexus between trade, agriculture, and the environment might be shaped by the interactions of farm and environmental groups. To a very limited extent, this was true. The intersection of the two sets of groups tended to center around two issues: (1) protection through SPS measures; and (2) the impacts of freer trade on small farms and sustainable agriculture.

Anti-NAFTA farm and environmental groups appear to have cooperated in stressing dangers to consumers when SPS provisions are weak or poorly enforced. In some eyes, this cooperation made for "strange bedfellows." The NWF, for example, expressed discomfort with the links between environmental groups and U.S. commodity interests, like fruits and vegetables and sugar. The NWF readily points to some U.S. border protection, like the ban on Mexican avocados because of the harmless seed weevil, as being politically motivated rather than scientifically based.

Alliance between food industry interests and environmental groups extends to PPM issues, too. Defenders of Wildlife, for example, has joined with the U.S. crab industry in filing a petition to halt imports of Chilean crab. Defenders of Wildlife is participating in the suit to argue that the Chilean fishing industry "is intentionally slaughtering numerous types of marine mammals for crab bait" (see 1993 testimony by Rodger Schlickeisen before House Committee on Merchant Marine and Fisheries). This is a case that may help define the environmental dimensions of the future trade negotiations between the United States and Chile.

The most interesting alliance we learned about during our meetings is that between anti-NAFTA environmental groups and anti-NAFTA farm groups representing "family farms." This coalition argues that freer trade benefits transnational corporate interests to the detriment of family farms, sustainable agriculture, and healthy rural communities. The relationships among trade, family farms, and sustainable agriculture have been little elaborated in the written testimony or statements of environmental groups. Groups with this stance told us that they had had few resources of their own to devote to an understanding of agricultural issues in the context of the trade-environment debate. However, the coalition has a strong spokesperson in Mark Ritchie, president of the Institute for Agriculture and Trade Policy in Minneapolis, who writes forcefully that world market forces and trade agreements have turned much of agriculture from "life giving to life threatening" (Ritchie 1993). While uncomfortable with the rigor and style of Ritchie's arguments, we felt equally frustrated that our profession has not communicated more effectively a solid understanding of the links between trade, the "industrialization" of agriculture, the environment, and a healthy food supply.

When we discussed agriculture issues with environmental groups and, likewise, environmental issues related to agriculture with farm groups, we found there was agreement on the following points:

- The PPM debate is likely to be very important for agriculture. Interviewees talked about concerns with pesticide regulation and how emphasis is likely to shift from residues issues to use in production. We found it highly believable that some groups would favor the use of trade measures to limit imports of products produced with pesticides banned or even simply not registered in the United States.
- Interviewees agreed that as economic integration moves further south (that is, between the NAFTA countries and South American nations), agricultural issues might receive closer scrutiny. In other words, U.S.-Mexico border issues may be replaced by broader concerns with land use, including deforestation, wildlife protection, and genetic diversity—issues that will interface more directly with production agriculture.

## Defining a Research Agenda

The individuals participating in our discussions had a number of valuable suggestions for a research agenda for agricultural economists. Specific suggestions included:

- more studies focusing on the environmental impacts of production shifts following liberalization in agriculture,
- development of natural resource accounting models applied to agricultural sector adjustment, and
- examination of the impacts of the displacement of traditional Mexican farmers on the environment and other social costs.

Environmental groups openly recognize that they have not adequately addressed the trade-environment-agriculture nexus, although some suggested they plan to do so in the future. This, perhaps, opens a window of opportunity for agricultural economists. One individual we interviewed suggested that the top priority for our research should, in fact, be to define the focal point of that nexus. Particularly in the context of NAFTA extensions to South America, we need to be thinking about how production shifts, generated by more open hemispheric markets, might incite concerns regarding loss of forests and wetlands, pesticide use, and other environmental amenities and disamenities which are associated with agriculture. More generally, our profession should be prepared to lay out and communicate the relationships among international trade in farm and food products, farm structure and producer welfare, sustainable agriculture, and consumer health, safety, and welfare.

SPS and SR issues are going to persist in challenging the development and implementation of trade agreements, even though they seem relatively well-traveled ground in relation to other environment and trade issues such as PPMs. There is work for economists to do in this area. Criteria—based on solid economic rationale—should be applied to assess if an SPS or SR measure augments or reduces societal well-being. This will depend on the public good dimension of the regulation relative to its role as a protectionist device. Empirical examples need to be pursued. Dave Orden and Donna Roberts, for example, have begun identifying some of the determinants of trade policies in selected SPS and SR cases. What has been the importance of economic factors, scientific evidence, and public opinion in past SPS and SR cases? Are policy decisions being made in a consistent and systematic manner?

Two other areas of trade-environment policy call for attention from agricultural economists. First, agricultural economists should take on the issue of trade measures used to enforce PPMs in agriculture. A convincing case must be made for valid differences in production and process methods depending on underlying economic and environmental factors. When encouraging adoption of more environmentally benign practices makes good economic and environmental sense, then the case for multilateral incentives less potentially damaging to international markets and relations than trade measures must be made (Marchant and Ballenger 1994). Second, agricultural economists can contribute to the design of "green" policies for agriculture that would not invite legal challenges under NAFTA or GATT. In particular, what are the characteristics of environmental programs for agriculture that redress rather than introduce market distortions?

## Conclusions

The title of our chapter asks if environmental side agreements will take center stage. We think they may because they create "living" institutions that have the potential to reshape the policy environment. Such institutions could be welfare improving if they lay the groundwork for a North American (or, ultimately, hemispheric) environmental policy that builds on the free flow of facts regarding environmental conditions, compliance and costs, sound methodologies for assessing environmental and economic impacts, and a truly democratic process in defining the policy agenda. On the other hand, if the institutions and processes are dominated by narrowly defined special interests, whether they be from the environmental community or industry, then NAFTA's influence on environmental policy is unlikely to be in the interest of broader societal well-being.

If the understanding of the agriculture, trade, and environment interface is incomplete in the environmental and farm group communities, then it is surely poor among the general public. This poor base makes it relatively easy for a narrowly defined interest to affect public perceptions and attitudes. As agricultural economists, we have an opportunity—perhaps an obligation—to "leave the wings" and to not let this happen.

## Notes

1. We analyze a hypothetical trade-environment agreement, in which South American countries agree to adopt U.S.-equivalent protections of agricultural workers from pesticide exposure in exchange for liberalized access to the U.S. market, in "Trade Agreements and Incentives for Environmental Quality: A Western Hemisphere Example." *Agribusiness*, Vol. 2, no. 1(1994):1-8.

2. Additional transboundary issues not discussed in this chapter are covered by the border agreements.

3. A closely related example involves a tax, rather than an SR measure, imposed by the Canadian province of Ontario. The tax is on aluminum cans and is designed to defray costs of recycling and disposal. Most U.S. beer is packaged using aluminum cans and is, therefore, subject to the tax. Canadian beer is generally packaged in glass bottles, which carry no recycling tax, raising the issue of discriminatory treatment possibly in conflict with NAFTA terms.

4. Organizations supporting NAFTA included the National Wildlife Federation, World Wildlife Fund, Conservation International, National Resource Defense Council, Environmental Defense Fund, and National Audobon Society; those opposed included Public Citizen, Sierra Club, Friends of the Earth, Greenpeace, Pesticide Action Network, and American Society for Prevention of Cruelty to Animals. Defenders of Wildlife neither supported nor opposed NAFTA.

5. Defenders of Wildlife president, Rodger Schlickeisen, in a recent letter to the *Washington Post* (June 25, 1994), writes, "No one is seriously proposing an immediate agreement allowing trade prohibition based on any and all production and process methods," but points out that if the World Trade Organization will not address environmentally harmful PPMs, "then the only way to force approval of 'green' production and process methods will continue to be through unilateral actions authorized by Congress."

## References

Abler, D. And D. Pick. "NAFTA, Agriculture, and the Environment in Mexico." *American Journal of Agricultural Economics*, Vol. 75, No. 3(August 1993):794-98.

Anderson, M. "The NAFTA and Environmental Quality: Issues for Mexican Agriculture." Ed. John Sullivan. *Environmental Policies: Implication for Trade*, USDA Economic Research Service Foreign Agricultural Economics Report 252, June 1994.

Blackhurst, R., and A. Subramanian. "Promoting Multilateral Cooperation on the Environment." In *The Greening of World Trade Issues*, K. Anderson and R. Blackhurst, eds. Ann Arbor, MI: University of Michigan Press, 1992.

Burfisher, M., S. Robinson, and K. Thierfelder. "Agricultural and Food Policies in a United States-Mexico Free Trade Area." *North American Journal of Economics and Finance* 3, No. 2(1992):117–39.

Gilbreath, J., and P. Emerson. "NAFTA: Negotiating a North American Environmental Policy." Paper presented at the International Symposium on Trade and the Environment, 10–12 November 1993, University of Minnesota.

Grennes, T., and B. Krissoff. "Agricultural Trade in a North American Free Trade Agreement." *The World Economy*, August 1993.

Hammonds, D.H. "NAFTA: Improving the Changes for Environmental Cooperation on Trade and Environment." Paper presented at the International Symposium on Trade and the Environment, 10–12 November 1993, University of Minnesota.

Hair, J.D. (President, National Wildlife Federation). Testimony on NAFTA and environmental concerns, before the U.S. House of Representatives Committee on Merchant Marine and Fisheries, 10 November 1993.

Hudson, S. (Legislative Representative, National Wildlife Federation). Testimony on NAFTA and environmental concerns, before the U.S. House of Representatives Committee on Merchant Marine and Fisheries, 10 November 1993.

Hudson, S. "The Environmental Impact of Trade Liberalization: Charting a Course Towards Sustainable Development." Paper presented at the International Symposium on Trade and the Environment, 10–12 November 1993, University of Minnesota.

Hudson, S., and R. Prudencio. "The North American Commission on the Environment and Other Supplemental Environmental Agreements: Part Two of the NAFTA Package." Staff Paper, National Wildlife Federation, Washington, DC, 4 February 1993.

Johnson, M. "NAFTA Green Opportunities." Draft Abstract, Ambassador's Lecture, Washington, DC, 15 November 1993.

Marchant, M., and N. Ballenger. "The Trade and Environment Debate: Relevant for Southern Agriculture?" *Journal of Agricultural and Applied Economics*,Vol. 26, no. 1(July 1994):108-28. Also issued as Staff Paper No. 337, Department of Agricultural Economics, University of Kentucky, April 1994.

Newman, M. "Pesticide Regulations and the NAFTA Negotiations." In *NAFTA: Effects on Agriculture*. An American Farm Bureau Foundation Project, 1991.

Ritchie, M. "Agricultural Trade Liberalization: Implications for Sustainable Agriculture." In *The Case Against Free Trade*. San Francisco: Earth Island Press, 1993.

Roberts, D. And D. Orden. "Determinants to Technical Barriers to Trade: The Case of U.S. Phytosanitary Restrictions on Mexican Avocadoes, 1972-1995." Unpublished manuscript, 1995.

Schlickeisen, R. (President, Defenders of Wildlife). "NAFTA and the Opportunity to Advance Sustainable Trading Practices." Testimony before the U.S. House of Representatives Committee on Merchant Marine and Fisheries, 10 November 1993.

Snape, W.J., III. "Searching for GATT's Environmental Miranda: Are `Process Standards' Getting Due Process?" Draft manuscript prepared for *Cornell International Law Review*, February 1994.

Taylor, J. "NAFTA's Green Accords: Sound and Fury Signifying Little." In *Policy Analysis*. Publication No. 198, CATO Institute, 17 November 1993.

Trueheart, C. "Fuming Over Cigarette Packs." *The Washington Post*, 17 May 1994, p. A7.

U.S. Department of Agriculture. "Agriculture in a North American Free Trade Agreement." Publication No. FAER 246, Economic Research Service, Washington, DC, September 1992.

U.S. Government Printing Office. *The NAFTA: Report on Environmental Issues*, November 1993.

# PART THREE

# Discovering the Critical Linkages: Trade, Renewable Resources and International Environmental Goods

# 7

# International Dimensions of Environmental Policy

## G.M. Heal

## Introduction

*International Dimensions of Environmental Policy*

Environmental policy has become unambiguously international in recent decades, to the point of being a significant source of contention between nations. As evidence of this, note that international conventions abound—the Montreal Protocol, the Framework Convention on Climate Change, and many others. In this chapter, an analysis is presented of some key analytical aspects of international environmental problems and of the policies which will be needed to correct them. The premise is that the issues which are intellectually deep and important in policy terms are not in fact to be found where the debate is currently at its most intense, but are to be found in certain emerging connections between equity and efficiency in the management of international environmental public goods. These issues are theoretically challenging, and are also practically important. A goal of this presentation is that the debate can be refocused on these issues.

There are three primary dimensions to the debate on international environmental matters:

- The relationship between trade policy and environmental policy. This covers matters such as "the greening of GATT," "environmental protection," hidden "green" tariffs, the relationship between NAFTA and the environment, etc. In the debates associated with these issues, environmentalists typically allege that GATT is

environmentally insensitive, while those who sponsor free trade argue that environmental concerns are sometimes merely a disguise for protectionism.
- The relationship between patterns of international trade (not trade policy), systems of property rights, and patterns of environmental use across countries.
- The management of public goods truly global in scope and scale, examples of which are the atmosphere, the stock of genetic diversity, and the ozone layer.

The first of these three issues has to date been the main focus of debate. I see this as a mistake: the debate about environmental policy and protectionism is reminiscent of debates in the 1970s about automobile safety standards and protectionism, and in general about protectionism and safety standards for consumer goods. At that time, it was seriously argued that consumer safety standards were a form of "hidden protectionism." We have learned since then that these concerns were exaggerated. The need for such standards has been accepted, and there has been some convergence of safety standards across countries which has minimized the problem. The disparities which remain generally are recognized as legitimate differences in the ways countries express concern for the physical well-being of their citizens, and also as having little impact in blunting the force of international competition. Although this is difficult to prove today, ten years from now we probably will see the current debates about "environmental protectionism" in much the same light.

That is not to deny the existence of interesting connections between trade patterns and patterns of environmental use. It is in fact noteworthy that traditional development strategies and the traditional division of labor within the international economy have emphasized natural resources and cash crops as sources of export revenue for poorer countries, and these are, of course, environmentally intensive. Consequently, many poorer countries, particularly in Latin America and Africa, have adopted environmentally-intensive development strategies. However, this is a different issue than the debate between trade policy and environmental protectionism referred to above. Because the relationship between patterns of international trade, property rights, and environmental use across countries (the second of the three debate issues itemized above), is the subject of the chapter by Chichilnisky, and of her additional papers (Chichilnisky 1993, 1994c), it is not addressed in depth here.

A very deep and important issue, as yet almost unrecognized, is the third of those listed above: the management of international environmental public goods. That issue is the thrust of this chapter.

## International Environmental Public Goods

There are several environmental problems which are global in their scope, and these have been reviewed by Chichilnisky and Heal (1993). A selection of major environmental concerns is itemized below:

- climate change associated with the emission of carbon dioxide,
- release of CFCs and the depletion of the ozone layer,
- loss of biodiversity due to pollution and to habitat change, and
- acid rain and the international transport of $SO_2$.

These have in common the fact that at the heart of each of these phenomena is a global public good. In the first two cases and the last case—climate change, ozone depletion, and acid rain—this public good is a characteristic in the earth's atmosphere. Biodiversity, as a source of knowledge and of intrinsic value, is also a public good (see Heal, 1994a). The remainder of this chapter will focus on just one of these problems—the possibility of climate change induced by human activities and the consequent need for $CO_2$ abatement policies. This topic provides all of the key economic characteristics common to most important global environmental problems, and illustrates well the connections between distribution and efficiency that arise in the management of global public goods.

The remainder of this section identifies the analytically distinctive features of these global environmental public goods, and examines the policies available for managing them efficiently, with emphasis on the use of tradable emission permits.[1] These permits have some interesting and very distinctive features in the connection that emerges between efficient patterns of management and the distribution of wealth. In subsequent sections, only international policy currently adopted—and jointly implemented—will be reviewed in the light of this analytical framework.

### Carbon Dioxide Issues

Once emitted into the atmosphere, carbon dioxide mixes rapidly and thoroughly on a global scale. Its atmospheric concentration is therefore a global public good. However, the $CO_2$ in the atmosphere is privately produced, as a by-product of the consumption and production activities of millions of firms and households. It is produced as a by-product of their heating, cooling, transportation, and production decisions. The atmospheric $CO_2$ concentration is therefore a privately-produced global public good. In the following section, recent research on the efficient provision of such goods is reviewed. In particular, this presentation draws heavily on three papers: an initial paper by Chichilnisky (1994a), a generalization by Chichilnisky and Heal (1994c), and a further extension by Chichilnisky, Heal, and Starrett (1993). A formal framework for analyzing the efficacy of policies for managing such public goods is presented in the next two subsections.

## A Model of Efficient Carbon Dioxide Abatement

Consider a world of $I$ countries, $I \geq 2$, indexed by $i = 1, ..., I$. Their well-being depends on consumption of private goods and on the state of the planet's atmosphere, so each has a utility function $u_i$, whose arguments are a vector of private goods $c_i \in R^n$ (with the typical element $c_{i,l}$) and also the quality of the atmosphere, $a$, which is a public good.

The quality of the atmosphere, $a$, is measured by the reciprocal or the negative of $CO_2$ concentration. The concentration of $CO_2$ is "produced" by emissions of carbon, which are positively associated with the production of private goods. This production is represented by $y_i$, a vector giving the production levels of the private goods in country $i$. We measure atmospheric quality in terms of reductions from an initial level, i.e., in terms of the abatement of $CO_2$ emissions by each country. Let $a_i$ be the abatement of country $i$, so that the total abatement, also used to indicate overall atmospheric quality, is $a = \Sigma_{i=1}^{I} a_i$. The abatement of carbon emission in country $i$ depends negatively on its production via an abatement function $\Phi$:

$$a_i = \Phi_i(y_i), \quad \text{and} \quad \frac{\partial \Phi_i}{\partial y_{i,l}} < 0 \; \forall \; i. \tag{1}$$

The marginal cost for country $i$ of abating carbon dixoide emissions in terms of the amount of good $l$ foregone is given by $MC_{i,l}(a_i^*) = 1/\Phi_{i,l}$, the reciprocal of the derivative of emission by country $i$ with respect to its output of the $l$th good.

Feasible allocations satisfy the above condition, and either the condition that for each country production equals consumption (2), or the condition that the total consumption of each private good worldwide is equalized (3):

$$c_i = y_i \; \forall \; i, \tag{2}$$

$$\sum_{i=1}^{I} c_i = \sum_{i=1}^{I} y_i. \tag{3}$$

The first of these conditions (2) requires that each country be self-sufficient and consume only what it produces. The second condition (3) allows *unrestricted lump-sum redistributions* across countries.

A Pareto-efficient allocation is one which solves the problem of maximizing the utility of a designated country *i*, subject to all other countries reaching prescribed utility levels (also subject, of course, to one of the feasibility conditions). There are two sets of conditions which may be necessary for Pareto efficiency:

$$\frac{\partial u_i}{\partial c_{i,l}} = \lambda_k \frac{\partial u_k}{\partial c_{i,l}} \quad \forall\ k \neq i,\ \forall\ l, \tag{4}$$

(equal marginal valuations)

where $\lambda_k$ is a Lagrange multiplier on the constraint that country $k$ reach a specified welfare level, and:

$$\frac{\partial \Phi_i}{\partial y_{i,l}} = \frac{-\dfrac{\partial u_i}{\partial c_{i,l}}}{\sum_k \lambda_k \dfrac{\partial u_k}{\partial a}}. \tag{5}$$

(Lindahl-Bowen-Samuelson)

The first of these conditions (4) states that the marginal social valuations of a consumption good should be the same in all countries. This condition is necessary only if we use the more general feasibility condition (3) permitting transfers between countries. The second condition (5), which must be satisfied with either definition of feasibility, is a modification of the traditional condition for efficient allocation of public goods (as in, for example, Atkinson and Stiglitz 1980), which requires equality of the marginal rate of transformation between a private good and the public good to the sum of the marginal rates of substitution between the private and public goods over all countries.

The following result was established by Chichilnisky (1994a) and by Chichilnisky and Heal (1994c):

PROPOSITION 1. *At a Pareto-efficient allocation in each country i, the marginal cost of abatement in terms of the private good 1 is inversely proportional to the marginal valuation of that private good, which is* $\lambda \partial u_i / \partial c_{i,l}$. *Marginal costs will be equal across countries if and only if marginal valuations of the private goods are equal.*

Thus, if it is possible to redistribute goods between countries so as to equalize their marginal valuations, marginal costs should be equalized for efficiency. If each country is required to consume what it produces, or trade internationally subject to a balance-of-trade constraint, then this will not be true. Efficiency in this case will not require the equalization of marginal costs. There is considerable policy significance to this result; i.e., it has been widely argued that the burden of $CO_2$ abatement should be borne by developing countries, because supposedly the marginal costs of abatement are self-evidently less there than elsewhere. Granting this supposition for the moment, we note that this argument rests on the presumption that for an efficient pattern of abatement worldwide, marginal abatement costs should be equalized. One should, therefore (on this view of matters), start abating where the costs on the margin are lowest and work upward from there. Proposition 1 calls this argument into question; indeed, it indicates that it is wrong. We need to start abatement not where the marginal abatement cost is lowest, but where the social opportunity cost of abatement on the margin [which is $(\partial\Phi_i/\partial y_{i,l})\lambda_i(\partial u_i/\partial c_{i,l})$] is lowest. This social opportunity cost is the product of the standard marginal cost of abatement in terms of consumption (which is $\partial\Phi_i/\partial y_{i,l}$) and the oppor-tunity costs of consumption in terms of utility [which is $\lambda_i(\partial u_i/\partial c_{i,l})$]. Marginal costs in the conventional sense may or may not be lower in developing countries. It is most doubtful, however, that the opportunity cost of consumption in terms of utility is lower there.

### Tradable Permits

The foregoing has characterized efficient allocations in the absence of any specific institutional framework. One particular framework which has received considerable attention recently is that of tradable emission permits, as used, for example, in the USA for the regulation of emissions of $SO_2$. This framework next is applied to the emission of carbon dioxide in the context of the simple model of the last section. Each country now has an endowment of permits to emit $E_i$ units of $CO_2$, where these endowments sum to the desired emission target, i.e., $\Sigma_i E_i = E^*$, where $E^*$ is the desired level of total emissions. Countries can trade these as price takers in a market in which there is a single price $P_e$ for emission permits. If the number of units of $CO_2$ emitted exceeds the number of permits a country has, the country must buy the difference in the permit market; otherwise, it can sell permits it holds in excess of its emissions and use the proceeds to buy private goods at prices $P_l$. Each country therefore seeks to maximize its utility subject to the budget constraint:[2]

$$c_i P = y_i P - P_e \{E_i + a_i\}, \tag{6}$$

where $P \in R^n$ is a vector of prices of private goods, and $P_e$ is the price of emission permits. It is assumed that in solving this problem, countries take the total level of emissions to be fixed at $E^{*}$.[3]

This budget constraint (6) can be rewritten as:

$$(c_i - y_i)P = -P_e\{E_i + a_i\}. \tag{7}$$

Here the left-hand side is country $i$'s *balance of trade*. This shows that a surplus of consumption over production (net imports) can be funded by the revenue generated by sales of permits in international markets. Controlling the initial endowments of emission rights, net of actual emissions, acts as a substitute for lump-sum international transfers by allowing countries to avoid the need to balance budgets internationally.

In the case of a fixed total level of emissions $E^{*}$, each country, in maximizing its utility subject to its budget constraint, chooses consumption levels and abatement levels to satisfy the following two sets of conditions:

$$\frac{\dfrac{\partial u_i}{\partial c_{i,l}}}{\dfrac{\partial u_i}{\partial c_{i,j}}} = \frac{P_l}{P_j} \tag{8}$$

(MRS = price ratio)

and

$$\frac{\partial \Phi_i}{\partial y_{i,l}} = -\frac{P_l}{P_e}. \tag{9}$$

(Price = marginal costs)

Both are intuitively obvious. The first just requires that for consumption goods, the marginal rates of substitution between private goods must equal the price ratios between these goods; the second requires that for each consumption good, its marginal cost in terms of abatement must equal its price relative to the price of an emission permit.

## Is the Market Efficient?

Does the trading of emission permits and private goods in competitive markets lead to an efficient outcome? Surprisingly to some economists, the answer is "no." This can be seen by a comparison of the conditions satisfied by utility maximization in competitive markets, (8) and (9), with the conditions needed for an efficient allocation of resources to abatement, namely (4) and (5). This comparison follows:

$$\frac{\partial u_i}{\partial c_{i,l}} = \lambda_k \frac{\partial u_k}{\partial c_{i,l}} \quad \text{vs.} \quad \frac{\dfrac{\partial u_i}{\partial c_{i,l}}}{\dfrac{\partial u_i}{\partial c_{i,j}}} = \frac{P_l}{P_j} \tag{10}$$

$$\text{(Pareto efficiency)} \qquad\qquad \text{(market)}$$

and

$$\frac{\partial \Phi_i}{\partial y_{i,l}} = \frac{-\dfrac{\partial u_i}{\partial c_{i,l}}}{\displaystyle\sum_k \lambda_k \frac{\partial u_k}{\partial a}} \; \forall \, l, \quad \text{vs.} \quad \frac{\partial \Phi_i}{\partial y_{i,l}} = -\frac{P_l}{P_e}. \tag{11}$$

$$\text{(Pareto efficiency)} \qquad\qquad \text{(market)}$$

We can see immediately that the equality needed in (11) holds only if the terms $\partial u_i/\partial c_{i,l}$ and $\lambda_k(\partial u_k/\partial c_{k,l})$ are independent of $i$ and $k$, i.e., the marginal social valuation of a consumption good is the same in all countries. Pareto efficiency implies this, but market equilibrium does not [see (10)].

It follows that competitive trading of emission permits and utility maximization subject to the budget constraints do *not* lead to the conditions needed for efficiency. There is an additional requirement represented by $\partial u_i/\partial c_{i,l} = \lambda_k(\partial u_k/\partial c_{k,l}) \; \forall \, l, \; \forall \, k \ne l$. This condition will not automatically be satisfied by price-taking, utility-maximizing behavior. It would be satisfied, however, if there were policy instruments available to redistribute resources without restriction across countries—for example, lump-sum redistributions. In the absence of such redistributive instruments, what is required to ensure that this extra condition is met and efficiency attained in the permit market?

The extra condition requires that the marginal social valuation for each good must be equal for every country. This is a condition on the distribution of wealth. It can be attained by a careful choice of the distribution of emission permits, which are part of each country's wealth. As shown in (7), careful choice of the distribution of emission permits is equivalent to lump-sum redistribution of wealth. Consequently, Chichilnisky, Heal, and Starrett (1993) were able to prove the following result:

PROPOSITION 2. *Let $E^*$ be a given total of emissions, distributed among countries as endowments of emission permits $E_i$ with $\Sigma_i E_i = E^*$. Countries trade emission permits subject to the budget constraints (7) so as to maximize utility, taking as given the total level of emissions. Then the resulting market equilibrium is efficient, at most, only for a finite number of ways of dividing the total $E^*$ into country allocations.*

## Why Distribution Matters

The results in Propositions 1 and 2 are robust. They hold not only for first-best or Pareto efficiency, as discussed above, but also for efficiency subject to an arbitrary abatement constraint (Heal 1993). In this case, it is still true that only certain specific distributions of emission rights are compatible with efficiency, defined now as maximization of the sum of utilities subject to feasibility constraints and also to a politically-imposed constraint on the level of emissions.

The intuitive explanation for this is as follows:

1. Trading emission permits naturally leads to the equalization of marginal abatement costs across countries. By obvious arguments, each country equates marginal cost of abatement to the price of an emission permit, which is the same for all countries.
2. Equalization of marginal costs is efficient only if marginal social valuations of consumption are equalized. Hence, permit trading is efficient only if marginal social valuations of consumption are equalized. This can be achieved only by the redistribution of wealth.
3. The allocation of emission permits affects a redistribution of wealth. The efficient allocations of permits are those which equate marginal valuations of consumption.

There is another way of explaining why only some distributions of quotas are efficient. Consider a two-country world economy with two goods—abatement and a private good. Figure 7.1 depicts the utility possibility frontier for this economy. Then each point on the utility frontier is characterized by a consumption level for the private good and an abatement level for each country, which together imply a total level of abatement. Write these as $\{c_1, c_2, a_1, a_2, a\}$, where $a = a_1 + a_2$ is total abatement. This is because each frontier point is a complete general equilibrium of the two-country economy. Now suppose that country 1 has a strong preference for clean air and country 2 has a low preference. Then points on the frontier that favor country 1, i.e., have high utility levels for country 1, will have more total abatement than those that favor country 2. As we go along the frontier from $\{\max u_1, 0\}$ to $\{0, \max u_2\}$,

FIGURE 7.1. The Utility Possibility Frontier for a Two-Country World Economy with Two Goods: Abatement and a Private Good.

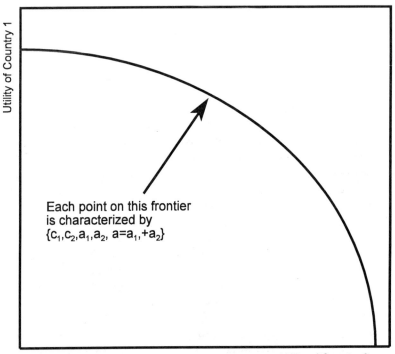

Utility of Country 2

the total level of abatement will decline monotonically. So, if we pick a specific efficient allocation of resources, this is characterized by $\{\hat{c}_1, \hat{c}_2, \hat{a}_1, \hat{a}_2, \hat{a} = \hat{a}_1 + \hat{a}_2\}$. It follows that if we pick as the level of total abatement the level $\hat{a}$, then for efficiency we must pick the corresponding individual country levels $\{\hat{a}_1, \hat{a}_2\}$.

A third way of demonstrating this point is to note that we have to satisfy more conditions than at a competitive equilibrium with private goods. The extra condition is that everyone must consume the same amount of the public good. Achieving more targets typically requires more instruments; the extra instruments are the distribution of quotas. A useful comparison is with a Lindahl equilibrium, the normal market equilibrium concept for public goods, where the extra instruments are provided by country-specific prices. Recall that at a Lindahl equilibrium,[4] the prices for public goods will typically be different for different consumers, so that with Lindahl markets, different countries would pay different prices for emission permits. In this case, permit trading would not equalize marginal abatement costs across countries.

The fact that only a few distributions of emission permits are efficient has surprised different groups for different reasons:

- To "Coasians," it is surprising because creating property rights should be sufficient on its own to cure the inefficiency resulting from externalities. The distribution of these property rights should not matter according to the conventional wisdom in this area.
- To welfare economists, it is surprising because markets should be efficient with public goods only if we have Lindahl prices, i.e., different prices for a public good for each consumer of that good. In the present context, control of the distribution of property rights replaces Lindahl prices and missing markets.

## Joint Implementation and Permit Trading

Clause 4 of the Rio Convention on Climate Change, established by the 1992 Earth Summit in Rio, introduced the concept of joint implementation. This consists of joint ventures between developed countries and certain less developed countries to decrease the sum total of their emissions of greenhouse gases; these measures aim at reducing carbon emissions within the territories of the developing countries.

A formal analysis of joint implementation is based on a distinction made in the Rio Convention between two categories of countries. These are the so-called Annex 1 countries (industrial countries) and Annex 2 countries (developing countries). The Rio convention assigns carbon emission targets to the former (Annex 1) countries; these targets are to reduce emission levels to 1990 values by the end of the century. However, no targets are assigned to the Annex 2 (developing) countries.

Joint implementation is a form of emissions trading. It gives industrial (Annex 1) countries the ability to "buy" emission rights from Annex 2 countries. The situation of Annex 1 countries can be modeled as in the previous section. For this group as a whole, total emissions are specified, and each has an emission target of its 1990 emission levels. Annex 2 countries have to be represented as a separate group of countries with no targets: they have the right to emit at whatever level is optimal for them to select. So, formally, their emission rights would be given by their utility-maximizing emission levels. The Annex 2 countries then may sell these rights to Annex 1 countries by cutting back their own emissions below these levels. As an example, suppose that Mexico's equilibrium emission level is $E^*$ with no emission constraint. Mexico can restrict emission to $E^* - \delta$ and sell emission rights of $\delta$ to an Annex 1 country at whatever is the going quota price.

The experience of joint implementation to date has been in relatively small projects involving five countries in total. One is an agreement involving Norway and Mexico, funded primarily by the Global Environment Facility (GEF) of the World Bank. Mexico initiated an effort to replace small electric appliances, such as light bulbs, in a manner which diminishes energy use and carbon emissions. A second project involves the Netherlands in cooperation with Poland and India. Here, Poland aims at replacing its use of coal energy by natural gas, thereby decreasing its carbon emissions. Such projects raise complex issues in assessing the true incremental contribution of the project to abatement in the developing country—the so-called "additionality" of the abatement. These projects also raise, and leave ambiguous, the question of whether emission targets are implicitly being set for and accepted by the participating developing country. This is a politically sensitive issue, as many developing countries take the view that because industrial countries are responsible historically and currently for the greater part of $CO_2$ emissions, the burden of adjustment should be placed on them, and that only industrial countries should be subject to emission targets.

In both of these examples, the nature of the cooperation is a bargain between an industrialized country and one or two less developed countries, by which the former, in cooperation with the GEF, "purchases" rights to continue its current emission practices through ensuring decreased emissions from the developing countries. The experience to date suggests several policy issues, which have been the subject of discussion in the U.N. Framework Convention for Climate Change.

### *The Potential of Joint Implementation*

The first and most obvious issue in evaluating joint implementation is its effectiveness if taken to its natural conclusion, i.e., the purchase by industrialized countries of rights to continue present emission practices by ensuring decreased emissions from developing countries. Developing countries emit, at most, 30 percent of the world carbon emissions. If the aim is to decrease world emissions, for example by 60 percent, as is often proposed, then even a complete cessation of carbon emissions by all developing countries would not make this goal feasible. Abatement of the type contemplated at present requires the active decrease of carbon emissions by industrial countries, who are the main emitters. Joint implementation cannot be a substitute.

An argument in favor of joint implementation is that it can lead to improvements in the positions of all the countries engaged in the bargain. This argument is supported on the evidence that the bargain is freely agreed upon among the countries involved. If countries do not stand to gain, why would they enter the deal? These arguments are correct within a restricted institutional framework, but they fail to provide a thorough analysis of the situation. What is chosen depends on the alternatives available. A bargain can indeed be better than no bargain at all, but it could be worse than other alternative bargains. With more information about the alternatives available, a country can typically improve its trading position. Indeed, the most frequently voiced concern about joint implementation is that a few countries could "steal the march" on others by taking advantage of a thin market with little information. All of this is simply a restatement of a well known fact: efficient trading requires that information is well-distributed among all the traders. It also requires competitive trading, which is in turn a function of the number of traders. Two traders typically do not make a competitive market. These two principles—market information and market depth—are widely applied in most well-organized markets across the world, and are necessary for market efficiency. This leads us naturally to consider a multilateral extension of joint implementation, i.e., an institution in which trading is conducted with well-distributed informational flows, and where market depth can be achieved through the simultaneous participation of all countries.

### A Migration Path to Multilateral Trading

From the previous remarks, another argument emerges in favor of joint implementation. The joint ventures or "bilateral trading" practices which characterize joint implementation can be viewed as the first step in the development of a well-organized, multilateral market. It is often the case that bilateral trading precedes, and leads to, multilateral trading. Examples are provided by the Chicago commodity markets and by Lloyds of London's insurance market, both of which started with bilateral trading among a few parties. The challenge is therefore to build a well-defined institutional structure of which joint-implementation ventures represent a first development step. This requires the simultaneous construction of a multilateral organization with the clear understanding that today's joint ventures are to provide data and knowledge about how the multilateral organization will work. The eventual aim is to develop an organization in which countries can achieve an efficient allocation of their resources, through decentralized trading within well-organized and efficient mechanisms. Within such a framework, all of the results set out above on the relationship between distribution and efficiency will apply; only particular ways of distributing emission rights will be compatible with Pareto efficiency.

## Conclusions

The last two decades have seen the emergence of several environmental problems truly global in their scope. These have several distinctive aspects. One is the uncertainty which is associated with them [see Chichilnisky and Heal (1993) for a review of this dimension of global environmental issues]. Another distinctive feature is that the problem is associated with, or carried by, a global public good. These problems include: climate change associated with the emission of $CO_2$, the release of CFCs and the depletion of the ozone layer, the loss of biodiversity due to pollution and to habitat change, and acid rain and the international transport of $SO_2$.

At the heart of each of these phenomena is a global public good, which is privately produced in spite of being a public good. In three of the four cases—climate change, ozone depletion, and acid rain—this public good is a characteristic in the earth's atmosphere. Biodiversity, as a source of knowledge and of intrinsic value, is also a public good (see Heal 1994a). The efficient provision of global, privately-produced public goods poses interesting challenges, both for economic theory and for policy choice and implementation. The main distinctive feature which has emerged in the case of the atmosphere as a global, privately-produced public good is the interconnection between equity or distribution and efficiency. This runs quite contrary to the orthogonality of equity and efficiency formalized for competitive markets with private goods in the first and second theorems of welfare economics. It introduces an interesting element into the evaluation of alternative distributions; that is, rather than being purely a matter of ethical judgments about justice and fairness, this now involves a more objective set of criteria relating to efficiency as well.

Although these issues are developed and illustrated in the concrete context of using tradable quota markets as a way of controlling the global emission of carbon dioxide, they of course apply much more generally. The same points will hold in the context of any privately-produced public good, and will therefore apply in the context of all of the global environmental issues mentioned above. The first stages of analyzing the applications to other global environmental goods are detailed in Heal (1994a) and in Chichilnisky (1994b).

Joint implementation, a part of the approach currently being explored to international regulation of $CO_2$ emission, can be seen as a precursor to the trading of emission permits, though probably an inadequate precursor justified only if there is a clear migration path toward a more multilateral and organized market. Such a market will be for privately-produced global public goods, and as such will display all of the characteristics of the permit markets considered above.

## Notes

1. For an introductory discussion of tradable permits, see Dales (1972). Their application to global warming is reviewed from a policy perspective by Tietenberg and Victor (1994) and also by Chichilnisky and Heal (1994b).

2. In understanding the right-hand side of this budget constraint, remember that abatement $a_i$ is equal to the difference between the country's "natural" level of emissions $e_i^N$ (the level it will produce if it sets abatement at zero) and its actual emissions $e_i : e_i^N - e_i = a_i$. So the difference between actual emissions $e_i$ and target emissions $E_i$ is $e_i - E_i = e_i^N - a_i - E_i$. For simplicity, the terms in $e_i^N$ have been dropped.

3. An alternative assumption is used in Heal and Lin (1994), who admit the possibility of strategic behavior by countries.

4. For details, see Atkinson and Stiglitz (1980).

## References

Atkinson, A.B. and J.E. Stiglitz. *Lectures on public economics*. McGraw Hill, 1980.

Burniaux, J-M., J.P. Martin, G. Nicoletti and J.O. Martins, "GREEN: a multi-sector, multi-region general equilibrium model for quantifying the costs of curbing $CO_2$ emissions", OECD Resource Allocation Division, economics Department Working Paper No. 116, 1992.

Chichilnisky, G. "The Abatement of Carbon Emissions in Industrial and Developing Countries: Commentary" Invited presentation, OECD Conference The Economics of Climate Change, June 14-16 ,1993, forthcoming in OECD: *The Economics of Climate Change* (ed. T. Jones), 1994.

Chichilnisky, G. "North-South Trade and the Dynamics of Renewable Resources" *Structural Change and Economic Dynamics*, Cambridge University Press, December 1993.

Chichilnisky, G. "North-South trade and the global environment", *American Economic Review*, September 1994.

Chichilnisky, G. "Property rights and the dynamics of North-South trade". This volume.

Chichilnisky, G. "Biodiversity and values" in L. Guruswamy and J. McNeeley (eds) *Biological Diversity: Exploring the Complexities*, Cambridge University Press, forthcoming.

Chichilnisky, G. and G.M. Heal. "Who should abate carbon emissions? An international perspective." *Economics Letters*, 44(1994):443-49.

Chichilnisky, G. and G.M. Heal. "Global environmental risks", *Journal of Economic Perspectives*, Fall, 1993.

Chichilnisky, G. and G.M. Heal. "Tradeable emission permits: principles and practice", a report to the OECD Working Party Number 1, 1994.

Chichilnisky, G. and G.M. Heal. "Efficient abatement and marginal costs," Working Paper, Columbia Business School, 1993, forthcoming in *Proceedings of the Second Nordic Conference on Environmental Economics*, ed. B. Kristrom, Kluwer Academic Publishers, The Netherlands, 1995.

Chichilnisky, G., G.M. Heal and D.A. Starrett. "International emissions markets: equity and efficiency". Working paper, Stanford Institute for Theoretical Economics, American Economic Association Papers and Proceeding, May 1996, forthcoming.

Dales, J.H. *Pollution, Property and Prices.* University of Toronto Press, 1972.

Heal, G.M. "Markets and biodiversity", in L. Guruswamy and J. McNeeley (eds) *Biological Diversity: Exploring the Complexities,* Cambridge University Press, forthcoming.

Heal, G.M. "Political targets and efficient abatement", Working Paper, Columbia Business School, *Proceedings of the Second Nordic Conference on Environmental Economics,* ed B. Kristrom, Kluwer Academic Publishers, the Netherlands, 1995.

Heal, G.M. and Y. Lin. "Equilibrium and efficiency in permit markets". Working paper, Columbia Business School, 1994.

Tietenberg, T. and D.G. Victor. "Tradeable permits for controlling global warming: implementation issues." Paper presented at the American Economic Association meeting, Boston, January 1994.

9 7 - 110

MDC's
LDC's
019
013
Q20
F14
F11

D23

# 8

# Property Rights and the Dynamics of North-South Trade

*Graciela Chichilnisky*

## Introduction

*Property Rights, Trade, and Resource Dynamics*

This chapter focuses on how the lack of property rights in North-South trade of primary resources can distort trade and threaten the sustainability of development. This issue is examined within a two-region world economy where one region, the North, represents the industrial countries, and the other, the South, the developing countries. The lack of property rights characterizes a class of environmental problems arising from the use of renewable resources as inputs in the production of traded goods. Typical examples are rain forests used for timber, or destroyed to give way to the production of cash crops such as coffee, sugar, and palm oil. In many developing countries, these resources are extracted from unregulated common property sources; and that ownership is shared with future generations. Focus is placed on renewable resources because it can be argued that sustainable development is all about the proper management of the world's renewable resources. The atmosphere can be considered a renewable or self-regenerating resource, as are bodies of water, forests, fisheries, and biodiversity in general. To a great extent, the global environment is described by the dynamics of the productive use of the earth's renewable resources.

There are two significant departures from traditional trade theory. The first is that one input in production is an environmental resource. This resource is self-renewable and in principle exhaustible, such as a forest or a fishery. Its *population dynamics* are represented by a differential equation which describes the demographic progress of the species, its stock through time. This is a major departure because it adds an underlying dynamic—an ecological dynamic—to the functioning of the market. Thus, this analysis blends elements of general equilibrium theory and dynamic analysis. The second major departure from traditional theory is that the regions are characterized by their property rights regimes based on the source from which resources are extracted. In the North, property rights are well defined, while in the South, the environmental resource is unregulated common property.

A seamless merging of a general equilibrium model of trade with a dynamic system describing population dynamics is a major contribution of this study. Their merging is achieved by a simple formalization: the two systems meet at one point; they use the resource as an input to the production of traded goods. This, in turn, affects all economic variables, including all prices of inputs and produced goods, in a typical general equilibrium manner.

This simple formalization carries unexpected explanatory power. It allows us to solve the entire two-country model and to analyze its properties in a simple, explicit fashion. Using this explicit solution, a rigorous comparative dynamics exercise is carried out to analyze the impact of different systems of property rights in the two regions on their prices, production levels, international trade, and welfare.

It is shown that differences in property rights are sufficient to explain differing trade patterns between two otherwise identical regions, even if these regions have the same endowments, preferences, and technologies. Private and public gains from trade, and private and public comparative advantages are shown to differ. The weaker the property rights, the larger the difference. The current pattern of specialization in resource-intensive goods by the South is shown to be inefficient for both the South and the North.

The succeeding sections of this chapter provide the following. Lemma 1 studies population dynamics, and the connection between property rights and the long-run supply curve of the renewable resource. The next step is to analyze market behavior. The general equilibrium model of North-South trade is defined, and solved in one explicit resolving equation provided in the Appendix. Theorem 1 then is used to establish the patterns of trade implied by the difference in property rights between the two regions. Corollary 1 establishes that the overuse of resources is not due to lower prices in the South. The Appendix formalizes the model of North-South trade with variable property rights for an environmental input.

## Resource Dynamics

### *The Dynamics of Renewable Resources*

The strategy for studying the dynamics of the renewable environmental resource $E$ under different property rights regimes is as follows. Emphasis is first placed on the dynamics of the resources without, and then with, economic use. From this steady-state behavior, the supply curve of resources is derived as a function of market prices. Then, it is shown how the long-run supply curve of the resource varies with the property rights regimes.

A standard manner in which renewable resources—such as forests and fisheries—are modeled is to assume a "population growth curve" that describes the demographic progress of the species. If $z_t$ is the stock or population size at time $t$, then changes in $z$ over time are denoted by:

$$\dot{z}_t = H(z_t), \tag{1}$$

where the function $H$ has the form like an inverse U, i.e., it is increasing in $z$ (population size) first, and then decreasing as overcrowding occurs. A well-known case is when $H(z)$ is quadratic in $z$, i.e.,

$$\dot{z} = H(z) = \beta z - \gamma z^2, \text{ with } \beta, \gamma > 0. \tag{2}$$

Integrating both sides of (2) yields the classic logistic curve:

$$z_t = \beta z_0 / [\gamma z_0 + (\beta - \gamma z_0)\exp(-\beta t)]. \tag{3}$$

Equation (3) represents the population growth without economic intervention and within a stable ecological environment.

Now assume that the resource is *harvested*, or extracted for use as an input to production. Let $E_t \geq 0$ be the total harvest at time $t$. The new growth equation (ecology with economic intervention) is:

$$\dot{z} = H(z_t) - E_t. \tag{4}$$

$E$ depends on the stock of $z$ and input $x$:

$$E = F(z, x) \tag{5}$$

Let $q$ be the opportunity cost of the input $x$, where $x$, for example, is labor or capital, and let $p_E$ be the market value of the resource; $q$ and $p_E$ are constant over time. The profit from the production of $E$ is:

$$\pi_t = p_E F(z_t, x_t) - q x_t. \tag{6}$$

The optimal behavior under a private property regime implies that:

$$F' = \partial F(x)/\partial x = q/p_E. \tag{7}$$

The problem then is reduced to analyzing a single first-order differential equation.

To examine the stability of the steady-state solution, the adjustment mechanism for the input $x$ is the quantity of the input applied to harvesting the resource, which increases with profits, i.e.,

$$\dot{x}_t = \mu\pi_t, \text{ where } \mu > 0. \tag{8}$$

The solution path of the adjustment process defined by (8) depends on its initial value; the natural initial value is the long-run population size in its natural environment, i.e., the long run-stock without economic encroachment. In this event, the population size tends in the long run to the steady state $z^s$, where $z^s$ is a function of $p_E$ and $q$:

$$z^s = z^s(p_E/q). \tag{9}$$

The corresponding harvest or extraction is

$$E^s = E^s(p_E/q). \tag{10}$$

### Resource Supplies in the Long Run

The solution $z^s(p_E/q)$ in (9) describes the behavior of the renewable resource stock under private property regimes. Note that $E^s = z^s(p_E/q)$ is an increasing function of the relative market value of the resource, $p_E$. For each $q$, let $E^s = E^s(p_E)$ denote the supply curve of the resource $E$ in a stationary state as an increasing function of $p_E$. $E^s(p_E)$ represents the social supply of the resource $E$ as it is derived from (7), i.e., maximizing profits and internalizing fully the impact of each unit's extraction on the productivity of the following units. The next step is to study the variation of the stationary stock of $E$, or, equivalently, of the steady-state solution $z^s$, with respect to different property rights regimes.

### Comparative Dynamics of the Stock of Resources with Respect to Property Rights

For each property rights regime, the production function in (5) is redefined to reflect the extent to which the harvester takes into consideration the externalities that its harvesting produces on the other harvesters within that regime. For example, in the private property regime, the harvester fully internalizes the impact of its catch on the productivity of the next unit of input by taking into account the marginal productivity of the catch (7). With unregulated common property resources, this may not be the case, leading in a limiting case to the so-called "tragedy of the commons," as discussed in Lemma 1 below. In order to compare the supply curves in each case, the private marginal cost curves associated with the production of a *common property resource* (E) are derived explicitly.

Let there be $N$ "harvesters" of a common property resource, indexed as $I = 1, ..., N$. Let $x_i$ be the input of harvester $I$ to harvest the common property resource $E$. Let $x = \Sigma\ x_i$. It is assumed that the inputs of all harvesters are identical and interchangeable, so that for each stock $z$, the total harvest can be expressed as a function $E = F(x)$ of the total input. It is also assumed that all harvesters are symmetric, so that for a stock $z$, each harvester obtains as its output a fraction of the total output equal to the fraction that it supplies of the total input, formally $E_i = F(x)(x_i/x)$. For a stock $z$, each harvester chooses its input level $x_i$ to maximize the value of its share of outputs net of costs, $p_E E_i(x_i) - qx_i$, taking as given the output levels of others, $E_j$, for $j \neq I$. Here, $p_E$ is the market-induced price of the resource, which is an exogenous parameter for the competitive harvester, and $q$ is the "opportunity cost" of the input $x_i$. Finally, $F(x)$ is assumed to be strictly concave, so that for each stock $z$, the production of the environmental good $E$ is characterized by diminishing returns, arising perhaps from the application of increasing amounts of variable input $x$, to a fixed body of land or water.

LEMMA 1. *Under the assumptions listed above, the long-run private supply curve for the common property resource lies below the social supply curve.*

*Proof.* Consider a given level of the stock $z$, and let $F(z, x) = F(x)$. Then the marginal product of the input $x$ is $F'(x)$, and the average product is $F(x)/x$. By strict concavity, $F(x)/x = F'(x)$. Let the private marginal product of the input be $Pmp$ and the social marginal product be $Smp$. With identical harvesters, if harvester $I$ uses inputs $x_i$, his/her yield is, by assumption, $y_i = x_i F(x)/x$, i.e., average yield per unit of input times amount of input. Thus, harvester $I$'s production function for $E$ is given by $y_i = x_i F(x)/x$. Hence,

$$Pmp_i = F(x)/x + x_i\{[xF'(x) - F(x)]/x^2\} = F(x)/x + x_i/x[F'(x) - F(x)/x].$$

Note that as the number of harvesters becomes large, $x_i/x$ goes to zero, and the private marginal product becomes the average product. In this limiting case, we recover the well-known result that harvesters equate input prices to average return rather than to marginal product, the basis of the "tragedy of the commons." Since $Smp_i = F'(x)$,

$$\begin{aligned} Smp_i - Pmp_i &= F'(x) - F(x)/x - (x_i/x)[F'(x) - F(x)/x] \\ &= [F'(x) - F(x)/x](1 - x_i/x) < 0. \end{aligned} \tag{11}$$

Therefore, the social marginal product of the input is lower than the private one. Since $F$ is concave in $x$, for each given $z$ and $p_E$, the steady-state quantity harvested under a common property regime is larger than the corresponding amount under private property. Thus, the long-run steady state of the stock is smaller in the case of common property resources than the same steady state with private property. In a limiting case, the extraction with common property regimes is sufficiently high so that no steady state with a positive stock exists.

The dynamics of the renewable resource show how the stock depends on property rights. The supply of resources is clearly dependent on their relative market price, $p_E/q$, and increasing with the price $p$ /$q$.

The next step is to explain prices through market behavior. To simplify matters, the input used in the extraction of $E$ will be capital $K$ in the following, and hence $q = r$, the rental rate of capital. The two systems, resource dynamics and market equilibrium, determine simultaneously prices and resource use. This is formalized using a model of North-South trade.

## A General Equilibrium Model of North-South Trade

The model is a two-good, two-input, two-country model similar to the classic Heckscher-Ohlin model. Its equations and its solution are given in the Appendix. In terms of its underlying analytical structure, however, there is a major difference with the classic model. Here, one input is a renewable environmental resource with its own ecological dynamics. In the Heckscher-Ohlin model, inputs are exogenously fixed throughout. In particular, the supplies of inputs, such as environmental resources $E$, are price dependent here, in contrast with the Heckscher-Ohlin theory where they are fixed. This difference is crucial, because it permits treatment of the relationship between the market and the ecological dynamics.

The steady-state behavior of the supply of the resource, $E^s = E^s(p_E)$, is generally an increasing function so that its inverse is $p_E = p_E(E)$. This equation is used to compute the solution of the model. Its variation with property rights, which was established in Lemma 1 above, is crucial for determining the patterns of trade and welfare in the world economy under different property rights regimes. The slope of the supply equation for resources, equation (A.3) in the Appendix, varies with property rights—namely the parameter $\alpha$. Thus, property rights are linked with the supply of resources to the economy in a crucial way.

The general equilibrium for this North-South model is formalized as follows. Assume that the two regions are identical in most respects except property rights. The endowment of capital input, $\overline{K}$, is fixed in each region. Part of capital is used to extract $E$, and the remaining capital endowments, together with the extracted $E$, are used as inputs in the production of two goods, A and B, where B is assumed to be more intensive in the use of the environmental resources, and A is capital intensive. The production functions of A and B, where $A = f(K_A, E_A)$ and $B = g(K_B, E_B)$, are concave and constant returns to scale. The utility function, $U(A, B)$, is strictly concave, homothetic, and identical across regions. $E^s = E^s(p_E)$ was derived in the previous section from the ecological dynamics of the renewable resource interacting with the optimal economic extraction rate. To simplify the computation of the solution, $E^s$ is assumed to have a simple form, i.e., $E^s = \alpha P_E / P_B + E^o$, where $\alpha > 0$ depends on the property rights regimes for E. A large $\alpha$ represents ill-defined property rights, such as the case of common property resources.

Utility $U(A, B)$ is maximized subject to a budget constraint at given price vector $(p_E, r, P_A, p_B)$. Under appropriate (strict) concavity assumptions, this yields an *aggregate demand* vector for commodities, denoted $(D_A, D_B)$ in each region.

Given price vector, the quantity of the input E supplied according to the supply functions $p_E = p_E(E)$, and the remaining K used for the production of goods, the supply of goods and the demand for inputs can be derived from input market-clearing conditions.

The *excess demand* for each region is $\Phi(p_B, r, p_E) = D(p_B, r, p_E) - S(p_B, r, p_E)$. At equilibrium, the excess demand in the world is zero. Thus, the world equilibrium price vector $(P_A^*, P_B^*, r^{*N}, P_E^{*N}, r^{*S}, P_E^{*S})$ is solved by zero excess demand condition, where superscripts indicate regions.

The difference in the property rights determines trade. As mentioned, *two* types of supply curves for the environmental common property resource are considered. One is the *private supply curve*, derived from the private marginal cost of extracting the resource, the other, the *social supply curve*, is derived from the social marginal costs of extraction, which takes account of the negative externalities that one user has on others (see Lemma 1). One supply curve for the North is considered, its social supply curve, and two for the South, both the social and the private supply curves. Using the two different curves in the South (private and social) leads to different concepts of comparative advantages and of gains from trade.

A new concept of comparative advantage must now be defined: Region S is said to have a comparative advantage in the production of good B, which is intensive in the use of the input E, when for each price $p_E$ the supply of E relative to that of K in region S is larger than the corresponding relative supply in region N at the same time. It is necessary to differentiate between private and public comparative advantages as follows. *Private comparative advantage* in region S is defined by using the private supply curve for E in the South; *public comparative advantage* is defined by using the social supply curve for E.

Different supply curves will also give rise to different production possibility sets; these are used in the following analysis to define gains from trade. Consider at each price vector the quantity of $E$ supplied according to the private supply curve $E = E^\pi(P_E)$, and the corresponding quantity of $K = K(r)$. With these two quantities of $E$ and $K$, it is possible to compute all of the combinations of outputs $A$ and $B$ which are feasible using the production functions $f$ and $g$. This set is denoted $PP^\pi(P)$. Taking the union for all $p$, the private production possibility set $PPS^\pi = U_p PP^\pi(P)$, which is assumed to be convex, is obtained. Performing the same procedure, but using the social supply curve $E = E^\sigma(P_E)$, yields the public production possibility set $PPS^\sigma = U_p PP^\sigma(P)$, which is also convex.

Gains from trade are defined as usual. They are given by the increase in utility $U(A, B)$ associated with a move from an equilibrium allocation in autarchy (each country in isolation) to a world equilibrium. *Public gains from trade* are computed by comparing welfare in autarchy and at a world equilibrium, with respect to the model with public production possibility sets. *Private gains from trade* are defined in the same fashion, but using the private production sets.

Since private and public supply curves are similar in the North, the North's public and private production possibility sets are also similar. Thus, private and public gains from trade are the same in the North. This is not so in the South. The weaker the property rights in the South, the larger will be the divergence between the public and private supply curves, and between the private and public production possibility sets. Therefore, the weaker the property rights in the South, the larger will be the divergence between its private and its public gains from trade.

## North-South Trade and the Dynamics of Renewable Resources

The next step is to integrate all of this information into a coherent whole. The following result analyzes the properties of the market equilibria of the North-South model, and uses Lemma 1's results on the long-run behavior of resources with different property rights regimes.

In order to emphasize the role of property rights, we can assume that both countries are entirely symmetric except for property rights. Therefore, both have the same endowment of capital, which is used either as an input to the extraction of resources $E$ with the identical technology, or as an input, together with $E$, for the production of two internationally tradable goods. The technologies of the production are identical, and the utility $U(A, B)$ is identical across countries as well.

According to the Heckscher-Ohlin model, these countries have no motive for trade: autarky should prevail. Indeed, if private property regimes would hold in both countries, these two regions will not trade. The autarkic solution is a Pareto-efficient world equilibrium.

Now consider the differences in property rights across the regions. Even though both countries extract $E$ using $K$ and the same technology, as shown in Lemma 1, for any given market price, the quantity extracted in a steady state will be higher in the South, which has ill-defined property rights. This introduces an illusory difference between the countries, with the South appearing to have more abundant resource supplies than the North. Hence, the two countries trade.

It is possible to compute the level of trade and prices by considering another world economy identical to this—without considering property rights, but taking into account that the South (for whatever reason) has a different supply function for $E$ than the North. Indeed, the South has a more price-responsive or "flatter" supply curve for $E$ than does the North, as established in Lemma 1. An interesting and useful property of the North-South model which was developed in Chichilnisky (1993) is the existence of a single equation, called the "resolving equation," which depends on all the exogenous parameters of the model and from which the equilibrium values of the terms of trade $P_B^*$ can be computed. Once this value $P_B^*$ is known, all other endogenous variables of the model can be computed from it. This resolving equation, which has been used previously to carry out detailed comparative static exercises explicitly and rigorously in the North-South model, allows us to carry out comparative dynamics as well, since one of the parameters relates to the long-run dynamic behavior of stock in the resource as a function of the property rights.

THEOREM 1. Assume that the North and the South have the same technologies, preferences, and natural endowment of environmental inputs. If the South has ill-defined property rights for the environmental input, then at a world equilibrium, the South will export environmentally-intensive goods. The South will exhibit private gains from trade, but in a steady state it extracts more environmental resources, and it produces and exports more environmentally-intensive goods ($B$) than is Pareto efficient.

*Proof.* Recall that the two regions are identical, but because of the differences in property rights, the South's supply of $E$ is given by the private supply curve $E^\pi(P_E)$ while the North's is its social supply $E^\sigma(P_E)$. Consider at world equilibrium prices, $p_A^*$ and $p_B^*$; the corresponding factor prices, $p_E^*$ and $r^*$, are the same in both regions because the two regions have the same technologies. From Lemma 1 above, the South supplies more environmental resources than does the North at the same prices; hence, the South produces a larger amount of the traded good $B$ than does the North. Intuitively, this is a consequence of the fact that $B$ is intensive in the input $E$, which is more "abundant" in the South. Since this theorem assumes that the two regions have the same homothetic utilities, and the two regions face the same relative prices for goods $A$ and $B$, the North and the South demand goods $A$ and $B$ in the same proportions. Since, in equilibrium, the supply of $B$ in the South is proportionately larger when the international markets clear, the South must export $B$ and the North must import $B$; that is, the South is an exporter of environmentally-intensive goods.

Since the two countries are identical except for property rights, when the two have well-defined property rights, they do not trade (autarky). By the first welfare theorem, the private property competitive equilibrium is Pareto efficient. Moving from autarky to trade increases the equilibrium price of $B$, and hence $E$ increases in the South, which implies that the South produces more than Pareto efficiency requires. □

Note that the environmental overuse described in Theorem 1 is induced by a competitive market response to the lack of property rights in the South.

COROLLARY 1. *If exports of the environmentally-intensive good B by the South lead to the equalization of the price of environmental resources used as inputs in the two regions, the South will still use more environmental resources than the North (and more than is Pareto optimal) unless property rights for the common property resources are improved in the South. If property rights are not improved in the South, then the exports of environmentally-intensive goods and their domestic production would have to be curtailed in order to achieve patterns of consumption which duplicate the social optimum.*

This follows directly from Theorem 1 and Lemma 1. The significance of this corollary is to emphasize that the overuse of environmental resources by the South is not necessarily caused by prices being lower in the South than in the North, as it is often thought. Equalizing prices through the international market will not resolve the problem of overuse of environmental resources.

## Conclusions

It has been shown that different property rights regimes for environmental resources can account for the pattern of trade between the North and the South. The South exports environmentally-intensive goods, even if it is not well endowed with them. Improving the property rights will lead to higher prices for the environmental inputs, lower extraction and exports by the South, and lower consumption by the North. All in all, property rights improvements in the South could check the main economic source of overuse: prices which are below social costs.

Similar examples hold for land resources. Recently, the government of Ecuador allocated a piece of the Amazon (the size of the state of Connecticut) to its Indian population, a clear property rights policy.

Under the conditions of our theorem, this policy should lead to a better use of the forests' resources and to a more balanced pattern of trade between Ecuador and the U.S. Jose Maria Cabascango, the representative of the Indigenous Nationalities of Ecuador (which comprises about two million people), has expressed their resistance to the overuse of the Amazon for oil exploitation, or for growing cash crops for the international market.

Property rights may change slowly, however, because they require expensive legal infrastructure and enforcement. Poor countries may find themselves unable to accommodate such policies quickly. But the improvement of property rights for indigenous populations in developing countries, which comprise most of the world's population, certainly should be considered a major policy goal. This represents a small but apparently growing trend in Brazil, Bolivia, Colombia, Ecuador, the French Guyana, and Venezuela. Support from international organizations in establishing legal frameworks and enforcing the rights of indigenous populations should be more desirable. Conversely, any policy designed to remove the rights of locals and increase the land available for cash crops oriented solely to the export market should be suspect. Indeed, recent studies show that 90 percent of the tropical deforestation occurs with the purpose of transforming forests for agricultural use, much of it for cash crops for the international market (Amelung 1991; Barbier, Burger, and Markandya 1991; Binkley and Vincent 1990; Hyde and Newman 1991). The World Bank's emphasis on exports of agricultural cash crops as a foundation for development is, in this light, contradicting the North's stated desire to preserve global environmental assets. Such policy contradictions should be resolved immediately, since they lead to an enormous and dangerous waste of resources.

It seems worth noting that environmental overuse in the South does not occur solely because the locals overconsume their resources, but because they export these resources to a rich international market at prices which are below social costs. This is why the global environmental issue is inextricably connected with North-South trade. The South overproduces, but primarily because the North overconsumes. The international market transmits and enlarges the externalities of the global commons. No policy which ignores this connection can work.

## Appendix

### The Equilibrium Solution of the North-South Model

Factor endowments in the two regions are variable, depending on factor prices. Taking the South as an example: The fixed endowment of capital $\overline{K}$ is used in the extraction of $E^s$ and in goods production. Hence,

$K^E < \overline{K}$, and the supply of capital for the production of goods $A$ and $B$ is $K^s = \overline{K} - K^E$. By a fixed-proportions technology in each sector, efficient production plans satisfy $B^s = E^B/a_1 = K^B/c_1$, and $A^s = E^A/a_2 = K^A/c_2$, where the superscript $s$ denotes supply. Recall that $E^A + E^B = E^s$ varies with prices, and so does $K^A + K^B = K^s = \overline{K} - K^E$.

Assume that $B$ is more resource intensive when compared to $A$, so that $D = (a_1c_2 - a_2c_1) > 0$. Equations (A.1) and (A.2) define an equilibrium:

$$P_A = a_1 p_E + c_1 r, \tag{A.1}$$

and

$$P_B = a_2 p_E + c_r, \tag{A.2}$$

where $P_A$ and $P_B$ are the prices of $A$ and $B$, respectively, $p_E$ is the price of the resource, and $r$ is the rental on capital. As shown in the text, the environmental resource $E$ supplied in equilibrium $E^s$ is an increasing function of $P_E$ for any given $q = r$. To simplify the computation of solutions, let

$$E^s = \alpha p_E/p_B + E^o, \tag{A.3}$$

where $\alpha > 0$ depends on the property rights regimes for $E$. A large $\alpha$ represents ill-defined property rights, such as the case of common property resources. The parameter $\alpha$ can vary as a continuum, indicating a variety of "shades" of property rights between the two extreme cases. Because of Lemma 1, the less the externalities which one harvester produces for others are internalized, the larger will be the slope of $E^s$, $\alpha$. Similarly,

$$K^s = \overline{K} - K^E, \text{ so that } K^s = \beta r + \overline{K}, \text{ for some } \beta > 0, \tag{A.4}$$

indicating that when the opportunity cost of capital $r$ is higher, less capital is used in extracting $E$, and $K^E$ is lower (as shown in Lemma 1); therefore, more capital $K^s$ is available for the production of goods $A$ and $B$. For a given property rights regime, factor supplies vary with factor prices, so that *the overall production possibility frontier exhibits substitution in the total use of capital and environmental resources.* In equilibrium, all markets clear. Since the economies are identical except for property rights, there are nine exogenous parameters: $a_1$, $a_2$, $c_1$, $c_2$, $\beta$, $\overline{K}$, $E^o$, and $\alpha(N)$ and $\alpha(S)$. After adding a price-normalization condition, a total of twenty-six independent equations is obtained. There are twenty-eight endogenous variables, fourteen for each region: $p_A$, $p_B$, $p_E$, $r$, $E^s$, $E^d$, $K^s$, $K^d$, $A^s$, $A^d$, $B^s$, $B^d$, $X_B^d$, so the system is underdetermined so far up to two variables, which reflects the fact that demand has not yet been specified.

We consider a demand specification which allows us to obtain the simple analytic forms:

$$U(A, B) = B + k, \text{ if } A \geq A^{d*}, k > 0, \text{ and}$$
$$U(A, B) = B + \gamma A \text{ otherwise, } \gamma = -k/A^{d*} < 0.$$

Then for $p_B > 1/\gamma$, agents demand $A^{d*}$, thereby choosing $k$ and $\gamma$ in $U$ appropriately.

Thus, we have a system of twenty-eight equations on twenty-eight variables, depending on nine exogenous parameters. The economies of the two regions are identical except for the parameters $\alpha(N)$ and $\alpha(S)$, which depend on the property rights for the common property resource in each region.

## References

Amelung, T. "Tropical Deforestation as an International Economic Problem." Paper presented at the Egon-Sohmen Foundation conference on "Economic Evolution and Environmental Concerns," Linz, Austria, 30-31 August 1991.

Barbier, E.B., J.C. Burger, and A. Markandya. "The Economics of Tropical Deforestation." *AMBIO* 20,2(1991):55–58.

Barbier, E.B., J.C. Burgess, B.A. Aylward, and J.T. Bishop. "Timber Trade, Trade Policies, and Environmental Degradation." Publication No. LEEC DP 92-01, London Environmental Economic Center, 1992.

Binkley, C.S., and J.R. Vincent. "Forest-Based Industrialization: A Dynamic Perspective." World Bank Forest Policy Issues Paper, The World Bank, Washington, DC, 1990.

Chichilnisky, G. "A General Equilibrium Theory of North-South Trade." In *Essays in Honor of Kenneth Arrow, Vol. 2: Equilibrium Analysis*, W.P. Heller, R.M. Starr, and D.A. Starrett, eds., pp. 3–56. Cambridge: Cambridge University Press, 1986.

Chichilnisky, G. "North-South Trade and the Global Environment." *The American Economic Review* 84,4(September 1994):851–74.

Chichilnisky, G. "North-South Trade and Renewable Resources." In *Structural Change and Economic Dynamics*. Oxford: Oxford University Press, 1993.

Chichilnisky, G. "On the Mathematical Foundations of Political Economy." *Contributions to Political Economy* 9(1990):25–41.

Chichilnisky, G. "Terms of Trade and Domestic Distribution: Export-Led Growth with Abundant Labor Supply." *Journal of Development Economics* 8(1981):163–92.

Chichilnisky, G. "Trading Blocks with Endogenous Technology and Increasing Returns." Working Paper, Columbia University, September 1994.

Chichilnisky, G. "Traditional Comparative Advantages vs. External Economies of Scale: NAFTA and the GATT." Invited presentation to the United Nations-ECLAC conference on "Trade Liberalization in the Americas," Washington, DC, June 1992. (To appear in the conference proceedings and in *Journal of International Comparative Economics*.)

Hyde, W.F., and D.H. Newman. "Forest Economics in Brief—With Summary Observations for Policy Analysis." Draft Report, Agricultural and Rural Development, The World Bank, Washington, DC, 1991.

# 9

# Environment, Welfare and Gains from Trade: A North-South Model in General Equilibrium

*Xinshen Diao and Terry L. Roe*

## Introduction

Environmental effects on welfare and gains from North-South trade are modeled by adapting the traditional Heckscher-Ohlin framework to account for pollution generated from production and affecting health and utility. As incomes grow, a greater proportion of income is spent on health including expenditures to mitigate environmental effects. Expenditures on health range from a high of 12 percent of gross national product in the U.S. to an average of about 4 percent in developing countries (World Bank 1993). Based on data from 25 countries, Gertler and van der Gaag (1990) estimate that health care expenditures rise by about 1.32 percent for every one percent increase in a country's gross national product. Consequently, health has become an important impetus for environmental protection in wealthy countries, as trade disputes between U.S. and Mexico over phytosanitary standards (Robert and Orden 1995), and the EC's ban on beef imports from the U.S. and other developing countries containing growth hormones (Runge and Nolan 1990) suggest. Agricultural pollutants that enter the food chain have received considerable attention in the U.S. (Caswell 1991). U.S. epidemiological evidence suggests that 2-3 percent of all cancers associated with environmental pollution occur from exposure to pesticide residues on food stuffs. Emissions of particulates are suspected of causing 20,000 to 30,000 premature deaths each year in the U.S. (Chivian 1993). High levels of morbidity and shortened life expectancies in developing countries have direct environmental linkages. The World Bank

(1992) presents persuasive evidence that unsafe water, inadequate sanitation, and suspended particulate matter are particularly deleterious to health in these countries.

As rich countries tend to be more willing than poor conuntries to pursue policies that alleviate negative environmental impacts, they have expressed concern about the possible effects of different policies on trade and comparative advantage. The conflicts and potential for conflicts between trade and environmental policies, especially the effects of environmental protection on trade patterns and gains from trade, have also become a North-South issue. Most of the trade based-models tend to predict that more stringent abatement policies negatively affect countries' comparative advantage, thus inducing pollution-intensive industries to migrate to the South where environmental standards are more lax. Pethig (1976) and Siebert (1979) were among the first to examine pollution's effect on productivity in a trade context. After accounting for the externality, comparative advantage in the pollution-intensive industry is found to lie with the country whose shadow price for pollution is low relative to the other country. From their continuous good model, Copeland and Taylor (1994) reach a similar conclusion—the higher-income country tends to choose stronger environmental protection, and to specialize in relatively clean goods. Other research focusing on resource productivity effects include studies by McGuire (1982) and Merrifield (1989). The former used a Heckscher-Ohlin framework to obtain more general results than the previous studies. The latter considered international capital mobility, and the likelihood of specialization and the closing of polluting industries among countries in the presence of externalities. Chichilnisky (1994) studies the effect of property rights on comparative advantage in the presence of a potentially exhaustible resource and obtains a similar result; she found that regions in which property rights for the environmental resource are poorly defined tend to export resource-intensive goods.

The typical approach to model a pollution externality is to treat it as proportional to output (e.g., Siebert 1979; and Kohn 1991), or as an input into the production process (e.g., Pethig 1976; McGuire 1982; Merrifield 1989; Copeland and Taylor 1994). However, inputs used in the production process typically yield a pollution by-product, which is not necessarily proportional to output, nor is pollution typically an input per se. Moreover, some forms of pollution affect health or utility through consumption of market goods. The health effects through consumption have direct trade implications if the pollution is *embodied* in the good. Further, pollution as a by-product of inputs used in production will have different effects if the pollution remains within the country compared to the case where it is transnational in nature.

The approach developed here treats pollutants as a by-product of the inputs employed in the production process. To emphasize the North-South health-pollution-trade linkages, identical but nonhomothetic preferences are assumed so that the richer North consumes higher levels of health than the South. Three types of pollution—local-*disembodied*, global-*disembodied* and *embodied* pollution—are modeled in a single analytical framework. The Walrasian equilibrium, Pareto optimal, and the regulator's problem are considered for each type of pollution. For the embodied case, we find the first best policy instrument is not only a tax on the polluting input, but also a subsidy on the nonpolluting input if the input is intensively used. We analyze the effects of pollution-abating instruments on trade and welfare for both the small and large country assumptions, and find that a pollution control policy does not necessarily have an adverse effect on the country's comparative advantage. That is, a policy to control pollution does not necessarily reduce exports from the polluting sector. Hence, a country's comparative advantage in trade is still determined by factor proportion theory (the Heckscher-Ohlin theorem). Further, the direct effect of Pigouvian taxes on welfare can be undone when the terms of trade between North and South are permitted to adjust, suggesting the need for compensatory payments.

The remainder of the chapter is organized into four major sections followed by a brief conclusion. The basic model and the Walrasian equilibrium are laid out in the first section. The Pareto optimal solutions to each of the local, global, and embodied cases are analyzed in the next section. The third section focuses on the regulator's problem and a number of propositions for these three cases. In the final section we develop numerical examples to further clarify the conceptual model and its implications. The numerical examples also serve to illustrate the nature of a number of analytical predictions that are indeterminate, and the Nash game that emerges for the regulator's problem. The chapter lays the groundwork for the possible next step of constructing a North-South applied general equilibrium model calibrated to world data.

## The Model

There are two open economies: the North and the South, in which two tradable goods are produced. Each of the two production sectors contains a large number of identical firms which employ labor ($L$) and capital ($K$) to produce these two tradable goods ($X$ and $Y$). The technologies are constant returns to scale and identical across countries. The sector $X$ is capital intensive, while $Y$ is labor intensive, i.e., the input capital/labor ratio is higher in $X$. The inputs are mobile between sectors in each country, but immobile across countries. The North is assumed to be wealthier than the South by being endowed with more capital but an equal amount of labor. The key departures from the Heckscher-Ohlin model are the following two assumptions: (1) Pollution is a by-product of input $K$ employed in the production of $X$, and (2) the two countries have identical but nonhomothetic preferences over goods $X$, $Y$, and health.

The first assumption is based on the observation that most pollutants are produced by inputs, and the same input used in different industrial processes can release different amounts of pollutants. The health effects of pollution are produced either through the environmental degradation (which we call *disembodied* effects) or through the consumption of a good within which contaminants are embodied (which we call *embodied* effects). The second assumption captures the phenomenon that demand for health increases in greater proportion to an increase in income.

The production, pollution, health, and utility functions are specified below:

### Production Technologies

$$X^i = F(L_x^i, K_x^i),$$
$$Y^i = G(L_y^i, K_y^i),$$

where $L_j^i$, $K_j^i$ denote inputs allocated to the production of the $j$th commodity ($j = X, Y$) in the $i$th country, where $I = n$ (North), $s$ (South). Since firms are identical in each sector, the sectoral production functions can be obtained by aggregation. $F(\cdot)$ and $G(\cdot)$ are strictly increasing, concave, continuously differentiable and homogeneous of degree one in arguments.

### Pollution

When good $X$ is produced, pollution is generated. The effect of pollution on the environment can take one of two forms, embodied or disembodied. Embodied pollution affects utility through the *consumption* of $X$. Examples are organic and inorganic impurities in food tissues, such as bacteria and bacteriological toxins, pesticides, herbicides, and heavy metal deposits. Disembodied pollution is not attached or bound to the individual good demanded. Disembodied pollution can be local (country-specific) or global (worldwide), such as air pollution caused by suspended particulate matter, ozone depletion, toxic gases from manufacturing plants, and diseases caused by airborne bacteria resulting from plant or municipal wastes. Each of these types of pollution are analyzed separately.

Disembodied pollution ($PO^i$) in the $i$th country is assumed to be generated as a by-product from the employment of input ($K_x$) in the production of $X$:

$$PO^i = f(K_x^i),$$

where $f(\cdot)$ is identical across countries, differentiable and strictly increasing in $K_x^i$. Local-disembodied pollution only affects the quality of the environment locally. The index of quality is expressed as a departure from some uniform environmental standard $(E^*)$:

$$E^i = E^* - PO^i.$$

Likewise, global-disembodied pollution affects the environment globally, i.e.,

$$E = E^* - (PO^n + PO^s). \tag{1}$$

Embodied pollution is expressed as the concentration $(po^i \equiv PO^i/X^i)$ in, e.g., parts per million per unit of X. Since $F(\cdot)$ is homogeneous of degree one, the concentration of pollutants $(po^i)$ is scale neutral, which implies homogeneity of degree zero in $(L_x, K_x)$. Hence, the pollution concentration function can be expressed as:

$$po^i = g\left(\frac{K_x^i}{L_x^i}\right).$$

Similarly, the function $g(\cdot)$ is assumed to be identical across countries and strictly increasing in $K_x^i/L_x^i$, i.e., increasing in $K_x^i$ and decreasing in $L_x^i$. Consequently, the level of embodied pollution is determined by the relative input levels, not their absolute levels. At the same level of output X, if input capital/labor ratio increases (decreases), the level of embodied pollution is higher (lower). Since pollution $(po^i)$ is *embodied* in a good, the environmental problem is equivalent to the purity problem of the polluted good. Let the purity index of an unpolluted good be unity, then the existing purity index of a polluted good can be defined as:

$$E_i = 1 - po^i, \quad \text{such that } 0 \le po^i < 1.$$

$E_i$ denotes the purity of X consumed in the $i$th country, and $po^i$ denotes the pollutant embodied in X which is produced by the $i$th country. Since pollution is embodied in a tradable good, only for the X-exporting country is the purity of X consumed equal to the purity of X produced, while for the X-importing country, the purity of the X it consumed is a weighted average of the purity produced in both countries.

$$E_j = (1 - po^j)\gamma + (1 - po^i)(1 - \gamma).$$

The weight $(\gamma)$ is determined by the proportion of X produced domestically in the total demand, i.e., $\gamma = X_j^j/X_j$, where the superscripts denote where produced, and the subscripts denote where consumed. Thus, $X_j^j$ represents the amount of X produced and consumed in the importing country, and $X_j$ represents the total consumption of X in this country.

## Utility

Several considerations affect the specification of utility. Following the Heckscher-Ohlin model, the specification should permit identical preferences among agents in the North and South, and avoid the problem of aggregation. For the purpose of this paper, it should be consistent with the observation that the North consumes higher levels of health relative to other normal goods than the South. These considerations are most easily handled by specifying a quasi-homothetic form of utility [e.g. Gorman polar form (Gorman 1953), or a Stone-Geary form]. Arguments of the utility function are goods $X$, $Y$, and health ($H$):

$$U_i = U(X_i, Y_i, H_i). \tag{2.a}$$

Health is produced by goods and environmental quality:

$$H_i = H(X_i, Y_i, \tilde{E}_i), \tag{2.b}$$

where $\tilde{E}_I = \{E^i, E, E_i\}$ depending on the case being analyzed. This function is assumed to be identical across countries, differentiable, strictly increasing in $(X_i, Y_i, \tilde{E}_i)$ and concave in $(X_i, Y_i)$. Hence, environmental degradation affects health and utility negatively.

In the two disembodied cases, pollution affects health and utility through environmental degradation as exemplified in the case of cancers from ozone depletion. Obviously, it is an externality to consumers. However for the embodied case, pollution affects health through the consumption of $X$. When consumers choose $X$ and $Y$ to maximize their utility, the consumed level of embodied pollution is determined. But consumers still cannot choose $E_i$ (the purity per unit of $X$), as the level of the embodied pollution is determined in the production process. Hence, the purity is still an externality to consumers. The embodied property of this type of pollution implies that the term $E_iX_I$ enters utility function jointly. Hence, we redefine a composite utility function for the embodied case as follows:

$$U_i = U(E_iX_i, Y_i),$$

where $U(\cdot)$ is strictly increasing.

### The Competitive Equilibrium with Pollution

A competitive equilibrium for this model is a set of prices $(P_x, P_y, w, r)$, a commodity bundle $(X^i, Y^i, X_i, Y_i)_{l=n,s}$, and a set of input allocations $(L_x^i, L_y^i, K_x^i, K_y^i)_{l=n,s}$, with a pair of environmental qualities $(\tilde{E}_s, \tilde{E}_n)$, such that: (1) all agents treat prices parametrically; (2) producers maximize their profits; (3) consumers maximize their utilities subjecting to their budget constraints, treating environmental qualities $\tilde{E}_I$ as a parameter; (4) in each country, the demand for the inputs are equal to their endowments, i.e., $L_x^I + L_y^I = \bar{L}^I$, $K_x^I + K_y^I = \bar{K}^I$, $I = n, s$; (5) in the world, the demand for each good is equal to the supply of this good, i.e., $X_s + X_n = X^s + X^n$, $Y_s + Y_n = Y^s + Y^n$. Thus, the Walrasian equilibrium implies that the level of pollution, $PO^I$ ($po^i$), and hence the environmental quality, $\bar{E}_I$ ($I = n, s$) is determined by the equilibrium levels of $L_x^I$ and $K_x^I$.

Given that the North is endowed with more $K$ than the South, and the production of $X$ is capital intensive, at the equilibrium, the North produces more $X$ than the South, while the South produces more $Y$ than the North, i.e., $X^n > X^s$ and $Y^n < Y^s$.

For a nonhomothetic utility function, if we further assume that health is relatively more responsive to $Y$ (a healthy good) than $X$, then, the share of income spent on the nonpolluted good in the North is larger than in the South. Thus, together with $X^n > X^s$ and $Y^n < Y^s$, the trading patterns are determined, that is, the North (South) exports (imports) $X$ and imports (exports) $Y$.

As $\bar{E}_I$ is determined by the level of inputs employed in the production of $X$, in the case of local-disembodied pollution, producers in the North produce more pollution, i.e., $PO^n > PO^s$ ($X^n > X^s$ implies that $K_x^n > K_x^s$). Hence the environment is more degraded in the North than in the South, i.e., $E^n < E^s$. For the global-disembodied pollution, $PO^n > PO^s$ holds; however, from equation (1), both countries face the same level of environmental degradation ($E$). By the factor price equalization theorem (Woodland 1982), the wage and capital rental rate are equalized across countries, and hence the input ratios in the production of $X$ and $Y$ are equalized as well. Since embodied-pollution is homogenous of degree zero in $K_x/L_x$, the purity of $X$ produced and consumed are the same in both countries, i.e., $po^n = po^s$, and $E_n = E_s$.

## Pareto Optimality with Three Types of Pollution

Since the externality affects consumer's utility, the competitive equilibrium is not Pareto optimal. By comparing the necessary conditions for Pareto optimality with those for a competitive equilibrium, we are able to identify first best policy instruments and correctly specify the regulator's problem for each of the three cases, local-disembodied, global-disembodied, and embodied. For a two-country model, Pareto optimal conditions for each country cannot be derived separately as the two economies are interdependent. By maximizing one country's social welfare function subject to its endowments, and a constraint which requires that the level of the other country's welfare be at least equal to the level derived in the competitive equilibrium, a Pareto optimal solution for the world is obtained.

## Optimal Analysis for the Case of Local-Disembodied Pollution

The optimal problem for the local-disembodied case is stated mathematically as:

$$Max_{(X_i, Y_i, L_j^i, K_j^i, PO^i)} \; U(X_n, Y_n, H(X_n, Y_n, E^* - PO^n))$$

$$s.t.: \; U(X_s, Y_s, H(X_s, Y_s, E^* - PO^s)) = U_s^*,$$

$$X_s + X_n = F(L_x^s, K_x^s) + F(L_x^n, K_x^n),$$

$$Y_s + Y_n = G(L_y^s, K_y^s) + G(L_y^n, K_y^n),$$

$$PO^i = f(K_x^i),$$

$$L_x^i + L_y^i = \overline{L}^i,$$

$$K_x^i + K_y^i = \overline{K}^i, j = x, y; i = s, n.$$

Assuming an interior solution, the rearranged first order conditions characterizing a constrained optimum to this problem are:

$$\frac{U_{X_i} + U_{H_i} H_{X_i}}{U_{Y_i} + U_{H_i} H_{Y_i}} - \frac{G_{L_y^i}}{F_{L_x^i}} = 0 \, , \tag{3.a}$$

$$\frac{U_{X_i} + U_{H_i} H_{X_i}}{U_{Y_i} + U_{H_i} H_{Y_i}} - \frac{G_{K_y^i}}{F_{K_x^i}} = \frac{-\lambda_e^i f_{K_x^i}}{F_{K_x^i}(U_{Y_i} + U_{H_i} H_{Y_i})} \, , \tag{3.b}$$

**with notation**

$$F_{L_x} \equiv \frac{\partial F}{\partial L_x}, \; F_{K_x} \equiv \frac{\partial F}{\partial K_x}, \; G_{L_y} \equiv \frac{\partial G}{\partial L_y}, \; G_{K_y} \equiv \frac{\partial G}{\partial K_y}, \; f_{K_x} \equiv \frac{\partial f}{\partial K_x}, \; U_{X_i} \equiv \frac{\partial U}{\partial X_i},$$

$$U_{Y_i} \equiv \frac{\partial U}{\partial Y_i}, \; H_{X_i} \equiv \frac{\partial H}{\partial X_i}, \; H_{Y_i} \equiv \frac{\partial H}{\partial Y_i}, \; \lambda_e \text{ is the shadow price for pollution and}$$

$$\lambda_e = - U_H H_E < 0.$$

In the Walrasian equilibrium, the right-hand side of (3.b) is zero. The term $U_H H_E$ takes into account the effects of environment on health and of health on utility. It is positive by construction of equations (2.a) and (2.b). These results, of course, indicate that a Walrasian equilibrium (in which $\lambda_e$ is not considered) is not Pareto optimal.

The relationship between marginal products of inputs and their shadow prices, and the shadow price of pollution in the polluting sector $X$ is:

$$\frac{F_{L_x^i}}{F_{K_x^i}} = \frac{\lambda_l^i}{\lambda_k^i - \lambda_e^i f_{K_x^i}} \tag{3.c}$$

In contrast, the corresponding result for the clean sector $Y$ is:

$$\frac{G_{L_y^i}}{G_{K_y^i}} = \frac{\lambda_l^i}{\lambda_k^i}$$

where $\lambda_l$ is the shadow price of labor, and $\lambda_k$ is the shadow price of capital. $\lambda_l/(\lambda_k - \lambda_e f_{Kx}) < \lambda_l/\lambda_k$, as $\lambda_e < 0$ and $f_{Kx} > 0$. Since the function $F(\cdot)$ is concave, the policy implication of (3.c) is that a Pareto optimal outcome is characterized by producers of $X$ facing a price of input $K_x$ augmented by the social cost of the effect of pollution on utility, thus increasing the ratio of $L_x/K_x$ relative to the Walrasian equilibrium. As pollution depends only on the use of $K_x$, less pollution is generated, and hence a higher environmental quality ($E^i$) is obtained. The term $\lambda_e f_{Kx}$ can also be used to formulate an optimal tax on the input $K_x$, as a policy instrument for the regulator in the third section of this chapter.

## Optimal Analysis for the Case of Global-Disembodied Pollution

For the global-disembodied case, the optimal problem is expressed as:

$$Max_{(X_i, Y_i, L_j^i, K_j^i, PO^i)}\ U(X_n, Y_n, H(X_n, Y_n, E^* - PO^n - PO^s))$$

$$s.t.:\ U(X_s, Y_s, H(X_s, Y_s, E^* - PO^n - PO^s)) = U_s^*,$$

$$\cdots,\ PO^n + PO^s = f(K_x^n) + f(K_x^s),\ \cdots,$$

plus other constraints listed in the preceding subsection. The difference between the local and global cases for the optimal problem is that environmental quality is globally affected by the pollution produced by the two countries, and hence requires a single constraint equation for it. The rearranged first order conditions are the same as in the local-disembodied case. However, the shadow price of pollution becomes

$$\lambda_e = -U_{H_n} H_{nE} - \lambda_u^s U_{H_s} H_{sE} < 0, \tag{4}$$

where $\lambda_u^s$ is the shadow price associated with the South's utility constraint. $\lambda_e$ now is the same for both countries and depends upon the marginal environmental effect on both countries' health and utility. The form of technical rate of factor substitution in sector $X$ is the same. But as the shadow price of pollution, $\lambda_e$ now takes into account the negative impacts on both countries, the ratio $L_x/K_x$ relative to the preceding subsection increases more.

### Optimal Analysis for the Case of Embodied Pollution

The special feature of the embodied pollution is its negative impact on health associated with the ingestion of $X$. The effect of pollution on health is included in the argument, $E_i X_i$. For the trade pattern noted in the first section, the maximization problem in the embodied pollution case is written as:

$$Max_{(X_i, Y_i, L_j^i, K_j^i, po^i)} \ U(1 - po^n)X_n^n, \ Y_n)$$

$$s.t.: \ U((1 - po^s)X_s^s + (1 - po^n)X_s^n, \ Y_s) = U_s^*,$$

$$X_n^n + X_s^n = F(L_x^n, K_x^n),$$

$$X_s^s = F(L_x^s, K_x^s),$$

$$Y_n + Y_s = G(L_y^n, K_y^n) + G(L_y^s, K_y^s),$$

$$po^i = g\left(\frac{K_x^i}{L_x^i}\right), \ j = x, y; \ i = n, s, \cdots,$$

plus the endowment constraints. The rearranged first-order conditions differ from the disembodied cases. Taking the North as an example, they are:

$$\frac{U_{X_n}(1 - po^n)}{U_{Y_n}} - \frac{G_{L_y^n}}{F_{L_x^n}} = \frac{-\lambda_e^n g_{L_x^n}}{F_{L_x^n} U_{Y_n}},$$

$$\frac{U_{X_n}(1 - po^n)}{U_{Y_n}} - \frac{G_{K_y^n}}{F_{K_x^n}} = \frac{-\lambda_e^n g_{K_x^n}}{F_{K_x^n} U_{Y_n}}$$

The shadow price of the embodied pollution in the North and South are:

$$\lambda_e^n = - U_{E_n X_n} X_n^n - \lambda_u^s U_{E_s X_s} X_s^n < 0,$$

$$\lambda_e^s = - U_{E_s X_s} X_s^s < 0.$$

(5.a)

where $U_{E_i X_i} = \partial U / \partial (E_i X_i)$. The second term of $\lambda_e^n$ accounts for the marginal effect of embodied pollution on utility in the South associated with exports from the North that are consumed in the South, $X_s^n$. The shadow price of the embodied pollution in the South is associated only with contaminants from its own production, $X_s^s$. These results, of course, indicate that a competitive equilibrium is not Pareto optimal.

The relationships between factors and shadow prices are given by:

$$\frac{F_{L_x^n}}{F_{K_x^n}} = \frac{\lambda_l^n - \lambda_e^n g_{L_x^n}}{\lambda_k^n - \lambda_e^n g_{K_x^n}}.$$

(5.b)

From this result, note that not only is the denominator increased by the shadow price of embodied pollution, but the numerator is decreased by it, since the marginal physical products of pollution concentration are $g_{Lx} < 0$ and $g_{Kx} > 0$, and $\lambda_e^n < 0$. The policy implication of equation (5.b) is to induce producers in sector X to use more labor and less capital relative to the Walrasian equilibrium. To achieve this objective, taxing $K_x$ alone is not sufficient to internalize this externality. If the cost of labor is reduced by a policy, producers in sector X are motivated to substitute labor for capital. That is the reason we evaluate numerically a subsidy policy in the third section.

The differences among the necessary first-order conditions for the types of externalities considered here yield the key result that optimal environmental policy cannot be the same for the different types of pollution. For local-disembodied pollution, the shadow price of environmental quality in each country depends only on the country's own marginal utility (3.b). As the North has a higher level of GNP and a lower level of environmental quality, the shadow price for pollution is higher, i.e., $-\lambda_e^n > -\lambda_e^s$. The shadow price for global-disembodied pollution (4) is equal across countries since $\lambda_e$ depends on the summation of the two countries' marginal utility of environmental degradation. For embodied-pollution, the shadow price in the exporting country (the North) depends on the two countries' marginal utility, while in the South the shadow price depends only on its own (5.a). The other mentioned departure is a subsidy for each unit of labor $L_x$, employed in the production of X.

## The Regulator's Problem: Internalizing the Externality

### The Case of Local-Disembodied Pollution

The regulator's problem for each country is to increase social welfare by internalizing the externality for that country. As pollution is the function of capital input employed in the production of X, from the preceding section, the analysis implies that internalization can be accomplished by an optimal tax on $K_x$, and its form and level are suggested by (3.c). As the shadow price is dependent only on each country's marginal utility, if one ignores the possible effect of a tax on the world equilibrium price, each country's regulator can determine the tax policy unilaterally. We first analyze the effects of a tax on $K_x$ for the small country case where world market prices are given. The effects of the input tax in this case are referred to as the direct effects.

Given the assumptions and structure developed in the first section of this chapter, the following proposition is presented.

PROPOSITION 1. *Holding world price constant, a positive ad valorem tax on $K_x$ in either country affects: wage positively, capital rental rate negatively, the tax included cost of capital in the polluting industry negatively; (ii) the supply of Y positively and X negatively; (iii) the demand for $K_x$ negatively, and hence $PO^i$ negatively; (iv) GNP (including the lump sum tax transfer) negatively.*

The proof is available from the authors upon request.

Since the relationship between the demand for goods and pollution is not clear, the *direct* effect on consumers' demand (holding world prices constant) of a $K_x$ tax is indeterminate without adding more structure to the model.

PROPOSITION 2. *For the small country local-disembodied case, an optimal tax on $K_x^i$ raises the ith country's utility independently of the other country's choice of a tax on $K_x^{i*}$.*

The proof is available from the authors upon request.

Changes in the supply or demand will cause the world equilibrium prices to change. Change in one world price, e.g., $P_x$ as one country (e.g., the North) imposes tax can be derived by differentiating the world market equilibrium condition:

$$Q_{x_n}(P_x, P_y, E^n, t^n) + Q_{x_s}(P_x, P_y, E^s, t^s) = 0 ,$$

with respect to $t^n$, and treating $P_y$ as numeraire, where $Q_{xi}(\cdot)$ is the ith country's excess demand for X. Allowing the change in $E^i$ to only depend on $t^i$, yields:

$$\frac{\partial P_x}{\partial t^n} = -\frac{\dfrac{\partial Q_{X_n}}{\partial E^n}\dfrac{\partial E^n}{\partial t^n} + \dfrac{\partial Q_{X_n}}{\partial t^n}}{\dfrac{\partial Q_{X_n}}{\partial P_x} + \dfrac{\partial Q_{X_i}}{\partial P_x}}.$$

Recall that $Q_{Xi} = X_i - X^i$, $X_i$ and $X^i$ denote demand and supply, respectively. Hence, $\partial Q_{Xn}/\partial E^n = \partial X_n/\partial E^n$, and $\partial Q_{Xn}/\partial t^n = \partial X_n/\partial t^n - \partial X^n/\partial t^n$. Since the denominator is negative by the stability conditions (Samuelson 1947), $\partial P_x/\partial t^n$ has the sign of the numerator. It is not surprising that, without functional form assumptions for utility, $\partial X_n/\partial E^n$ cannot be signed. However, as $E^n$ is an externality term, it is reasonable to assume that the value of $\partial X_i/\partial E^i$ would be small. Further, if the market demand is independent of $E^i$, then $\partial X_i/\partial E^i = 0$. Hence, the sign of $\partial P_x/\partial t^n$ is determined by the sign of $\partial Q_{xn}/\partial t^n$. If $\partial Q_{xn}/\partial t^n > (<) 0$, then $P_x$ rises (falls). Proposition 1 (ii) tells us that the tax effect on the supply of $X$ is negative, and positive for $Y$. Further, the demand for both goods falls when GNP falls [Proposition 1 (iv)]. By Walras' law, the excess demand of $X$ would rise, i.e., $\partial Q_{xn}/\partial t^n > 0$, which implies that $P_x$ rises in this case.

When prices are permitted to adjust, the welfare of the two countries is affected differently. Changes in utility from pollution abatement and price adjustment can be obtained by totally differentiating the indirect utility function:

$$dV_i = \frac{\partial V}{\partial GNP_i}(X^i - X_i)dP_x + \frac{\partial V}{\partial GNP_i}dGNP\big|_P + \frac{\partial V}{\partial E^i}(dE^i\big|_t + dE^i\big|_P).$$

Recall that $X^i - X_i$ is positive (negative) for the North (South).

PROPOSITION 3. *Given that an increase in $P_x$ has a "small" effect on $E^i$, i.e., $dE^i/_t$ is small, the North (an X-exporting country) is made better off by an optimal tax, and the South (an X-importing country) is made worse off if the South's import volume is larger. The South is better off only when the trade volume of $X$ is small and the positive change in the utility from the abatement effect is large.*

The direct effects of the tax are $(\partial V/\partial GNP_i)dGNP\big|_P + (\partial V/\partial E^i)dE^i\big|_P$, which are positive for an optimal tax rate by Proposition 2. The sign of $(\partial V/\partial E^i)dE^i\big|_t$ is negative if $P_x$ rises. Hence, if this term is small, $dV_n$ is positive for the North. However, the term $(X^i - X_i)dP_x$ is negative for the South (X-importing country). Thus, $dV_s < 0$, if its excess demand for $X$ is large and dominates the positive effect of the policy on its utility. Only when the trade volume of $X$ is small, and the positive abatement effects on the South's utility is large, can the South be made better off when $P_x$ rises.

In contrast to the analyses in the preceding section, if no transfer payments are made among countries, then a country (the South in this case) can be made worse off when the imposition of pollution taxes cause the terms of trade to change in favor of the other country. The South could be made no worse off if a portion of the environmental tax revenues received in the North are transferred to the South. For this reason, the optimal level of $t^i$ is at least a second best policy. The level and the direction of transfers are derived in the numerical analysis.

The implications of these results (and those in the other two cases considered below) suggest that in the absence of international transfers, a country is unlikely to impose environmental taxes if the losses in welfare from changes in the terms of trade dominate welfare gains from environmental enhancement. Countries that experience gains from environmental taxes that improve their terms of trade may be encouraged to overtax the polluting factors if the incremental losses from overtaxing are smaller than the gains from changes in the terms of trade. These results also contradict the notion that a country's comparative advantage will be compromised by the adoption of a pollution control policy in the sector for which it holds a comparative advantage.

### The Case of Global-Disembodied Pollution

Proposition 1 and 3 derived in the preceding subsection still hold, while Proposition 2 has had to be revised, for in the case of global-disembodied pollution, intervention in one country affects the other country's welfare directly.

We can use a one-shot Nash game to characterize the interdependence of regulator's choices on the other country. A strategy for each country's regulator is to abate pollution using the tax suggested by results reported in the second section. Given world price, the indirect utility for each country is:

$$V_i = V_i(GNP_i(t^i), E(t^n, t^s)) = V_i^*(t^n, t^s).$$

PROPOSITION 4: *For the small country case, if pollution is global, then the Nash equilibrium, if one exists, will not necessarily lead to a Pareto Superior outcome without cooperation between regulators of the two countries.*

Given world price $P_x$, changes in both countries' social welfare with non-cooperation between regulators can be represented in a Nash table (Table 9.1). If after taxing, the absolute value of a negative change in the $i$th country's utility associated with the reduction in its GNP is greater than the positive change in utility caused by the improvement of environmental quality, i.e.,

If
$$\left| \frac{\partial V_i}{\partial GNP_i} \frac{\partial GNP_i}{\partial t^i} \right| \geq \frac{\partial V_i}{\partial E} \frac{\partial E}{\partial t^i} \tag{6}$$

**TABLE 9.1 Nash Table**

| South | North | |
|---|---|---|
| | No pollution abatement | With pollution abatement |
| No pollution abatement | $(t^n = 0, t^s = 0) \rightarrow$ <br><br> $dV_n = 0, dV_s = 0$ | $(t^n > 0, t^s = 0) \rightarrow$ <br><br> $dV_n = \dfrac{\partial V_n}{\partial GNP}\dfrac{\partial GNP_n}{\partial t^n}dt^n$ <br><br> $+ \dfrac{\partial V_n}{\partial E}\dfrac{\partial E}{\partial t^n}dt^n$ <br><br> $dV_s = \dfrac{\partial V_s}{\partial E}\dfrac{\partial E}{\partial t^n}dt^n$ |
| With pollution abatement | $(t^n = 0, t^s > 0) \rightarrow$ <br><br> $dV_n = \dfrac{\partial V_n}{\partial E}\dfrac{\partial E}{\partial t^s}dt^s$ <br><br> $dV_s = \dfrac{\partial V_s}{\partial GNP}\dfrac{\partial GNP_s}{\partial t^s}dt^s$ <br><br> $+ \dfrac{\partial V_s}{\partial E}\dfrac{\partial E}{\partial t^s}dt^s$ | $(t^n > 0, t^s > 0) \rightarrow$ <br><br> $dV_n = \dfrac{\partial V_n}{\partial GNP}\dfrac{\partial GNP_n}{\partial t^n}dt^n$ <br><br> $+ \dfrac{\partial V_n}{\partial E}(\dfrac{\partial E}{\partial t^s}dt^s + \dfrac{\partial E}{\partial t^n}dt^n)$ <br><br> $dV_s = \dfrac{\partial V_s}{\partial GNP}\dfrac{\partial GNP_s}{\partial t^s}dt^s$ <br><br> $+ \dfrac{\partial V_s}{\partial E}(\dfrac{\partial E}{\partial t^s}dt^s + \dfrac{\partial E}{\partial t^n}dt^n)$ |

for the $i$th country, then, $t^i = 0$ is a rational choice for the $i$th country's regulator. If (6) holds for both countries, then, $t^n = 0$, $t^s = 0$ are chosen. Thus, the Nash equilibrium is the status quo. Only if (6) does not hold for both countries, would $t^n > 0$ and $t^s > 0$ be chosen, and the Nash solution is Pareto optimal.

Similar to the local-disembodied case, when world market prices are allowed to change, the North (South) experiences an improvement (deterioration) in its terms of trade, thus increasing $dV_n$ and decreasing $dV_s$ for any strategy except the status quo. This increases incentive for the North to choose $t^n > 0$ and for the South to choose $t^s = 0$. An example in the fourth section shows that it might be a Nash equilibrium in the large country case.

## The Case of Embodied Pollution

There are two distinguishing properties of the embodied case. First, equation (5.b) implies that the regulator needs to tax $K_x$ *and* to subsidize $L_x$, where the subsidy rate, $s^i = \lambda_e^i g_{Lxi}/w$ and the tax rate, $t^i = -\lambda_e^i g_{Kxi}/r$. Second, for the X-exporting country (North), its shadow price of pollution, $\lambda_e^n$, depends on both countries' marginal utilities of environmental quality, since the pollutants are contained in the tradable good X (5.a). Based on these properties, Proposition 1 has to be supplemented by Proposition 5.

PROPOSITION 5: *For a small country, an ad valorem subsidy s on $L_x$ affects w, r, $X^i$ and $Y^i$ in the opposite directions to the effects of a tax on $K_x$, with an exception of the effect on GNP, which is negative for both.*

The proof is similar to the proof of Proposition 1. It can also be shown that because the effects of s are opposite to those of t, their joint effects on $L_x$ and $K_x$ are indeterminate.

PROPOSITION 6: *Given that X is capital intensive, taxing $K_x$ only (i.e., if t > 0 and s = 0), causes the concentration of pollution (po) to rise.*

The tax effect on the input ratio $K_x/L_x$ can be derived from Proposition 1, part (i), changes in wage, and the real cost of capital used in production of X. Since $K_x/L_x$ depends negatively on the wage/capital cost ratio in sector X, as wage rises and per unit cost of capital falls, more capital and less labor are used in sector X, i.e., $\partial(K_x/L_x)/\partial t > 0$. The pollution concentration is a function of the capital/labor ratio, i.e., $\partial po/\partial(K_x/L_x) > 0$. Hence, $\partial po/\partial t > 0$, which completes the proof of Proposition 6. Proposition 6 implies that to reduce the embodied pollution and improve social welfare, not only a tax needs to be placed on the polluting input, but also a subsidy placed on the nonpolluting input.

Another implication of embodied pollution is that, for the small country case, unilateral action by the South has no effect on the North, since the South does not export X, while unilateral action by the North benefits the South through the import of a healthier X. In the large country case, the world price re-equilibrates following a country's imposition of an abatement policy. Proposition 1 and 5 imply that if any country (or both) tax $K_x$ only, then the total supply of X falls and Y rises, and $P_x$ might rise. Further, if any country (or both) subsidize $L_x$ only, then the total supply of X rises and Y falls, and $P_x$ might fall. However, the joint effects of a tax on $K_x$ and a subsidy to $L_x$ are indeterminate. The numerical example in the next section is used to show the nature of this relationship.

## An Example Economy

In order to further clarify the conceptual model and its implication, the numerical examples are developed in this section. The functional forms used are consistent with the structure presented in the first section. The parameters chosen for each function are available from the authors upon request.

Eight equilibria are calculated for each of the *disembodied* and *embodied* cases. For brevity, we largely focus on those results that are noted as being indeterminate in the analytical analyses.

## The Local-Disembodied Pollution Case

Table 9A.1 reports the results of the local-disembodied case for the North. Since the results for South are similar, they are skipped for brevity. Column 1 (PE) shows that the Pareto optimal solution results in an increase in the production and consumption of $Y$ and $H$, and a fall in $X$. Pollution ($PO$) falls and utility ($U_n$) rises in the North with the binding constraint requiring that the South be made no worse off. The results in Column 2 (RSB) support the predictions of Propositions 1 and 2. When both countries tax and world prices adjust (Column 3), the price $P_x$ rises. Thus, welfare rises in the North, but falls in the South, where the terms of trade effects dominate the welfare increasing effects of the pollution tax (Proposition 3). We study the transfer needed to make the South no worse off in a later subsection.

The contrast between unilateral action with world prices fixed [Column 4 (RSN) and 5 (RSS)] and unilateral action with world prices equilibrated [Column 6 (RWN) and 7(RWS)] provides insights into terms of trade effects. Since pollution is local, when only the North taxes at fixed world prices, the solution is identical to the results reported in Column 2 (RSB), where both countries tax at fixed world prices, and likewise for the South. This outcome substantiates the analytical results that, for a small country, unilateral and bilateral actions are equivalent. (We will see that this is not true for the embodied pollution case later.) When prices adjust, the welfare of the South always falls regardless of whether it imposes a pollution tax. Further, when only the South taxes and prices adjust, even though the pollution rises in the North, the North's welfare still increases as the result of changes in the terms of trade.

## The Global-Disembodied Pollution Case

Results for this case are reported in Table 9A.2 for the North. As pollution is global, the effects of unilateral action differ from the local case (Column 4 and 5). For the small country (world prices are fixed), unilaterally taxing $K_x$ in one country benefits the other country from the reduction in pollution. Further, as mentioned in the analytical model, welfare improvement of the no-action country exceeds the taxing country. Consequently, taking no action permits a country to free ride on the other's pollution control policy. When world prices adjust, this result is dramatically changed. Changes in the terms of trade make the South worse off regardless of which country acts unilaterally. Table 9A.3 shows that the Nash solution is for the North to tax and the South not to tax. To obtain a Pareto optimal outcome (where both countries tax), a transfer from North to South is required. However, it can be shown that such a transfer reduces the welfare gain of the North to a level that is below the gain it would experience in the Nash equilibrium.

### The Embodied Pollution Case

Results for this case are reported in Table 9A.4. In contrast to the disembodied cases, when both countries take action (i.e., they tax $K_x$ and subsidize $L_x$), the supply of $X$ increases and $Y$ falls in both countries for the small country case (Column 2). This result implies that as the optimal subsidy rate is higher than the tax rate, the labor subsidy effect on supply of $X$ dominates the negative effects of the $K_x$ tax. Thus, when world prices adjust, the price of $P_x$ falls (Column 3). Utility increases in both countries, but increases more in the South, which implies that the environmental effect dominates the terms of trade effect.

For the embodied case, we also examine the effects where both countries impose the previously determined optimal tax on $K_x$ only. The results are reported in Table 9A.4, Columns 4 and 5. We observe that for the small country, if only the pollution input $K_x$ is taxed, the pollution concentration per unit of $X$ rises since the input ratio $K_x/L_x$ rises (Column 4). The ratio rises because $X$ is capital intensive and a tax causes the rental rate of capital to fall more than the effect of the ad valorem tax. Hence, welfare falls (Proposition 6). This is an important counter-intuitive result. It suggests that, in the *embodied* case, and for a small country, taxing the polluting input only (no labor subsidy) may cause the tax inclusive price of this input to fall, thus increasing the concentration of pollution per unit of $X$, and decreasing utility! For the large country, only taxing $K_x$ causes $P_x$ to rise (Column 5) and pollution concentration to fall. The terms of trade effect makes the North better off and the South worse off in this situation.

### Trade Effects

As mentioned, the total effects of input taxes on trade are analytically indeterminate as well. Simulation results of these effects are reported in Table 9A.5. Exclusive of output price changes (i.e., the small country case) optimal taxes cause the North's exports of $X$ to fall and the South's exports of $Y$ to rise in both disembodied cases, while the exports of $X$ rise and $Y$ fall for the North and South, respectively, in the embodied case. After output prices are permitted to re-equilibrate, the North's exports of $X$ rise for the global-disembodied and embodied cases, but fall for the local-disembodied case. The South's exports of $Y$ rise in all three cases. Thus, when world prices re-equilibrate, a country's comparative advantage is not reduced for the cases of global-disembodied and embodied types of pollution. Only for the case of local-disembodied pollution is the North's comparative advantage in X decreased.

### Transfer Effects

If the welfare effects caused by the change in the terms of trade dominate the effects caused by environmental policy, so that one country is made worse off, then compensatory payments from the gainer to the loser might be considered. We simulate such scenarios for the disembodied cases, where the North transfers tax revenue to the South at a level that leaves the South no worse off than before the imposition of taxes. These results are reported in Table 9A.6.

Based on the optimal tax rates, the North's total tax revenues are 0.5 percent and 0.99 percent of GNP for the local and global disembodied, respectively. The amounts of revenue that have to be transferred to the South so that the South is made no worse off are 10.25 percent and 10.87 percent of the North's total tax revenues for the local and global cases, respectively. These amounts are only equivalent to 0.05 percent and 0.11 percent, respectively, of the North's GNP. The corresponding change in welfare levels are reported in Table 9A.7. Note that after the transfers, the Pareto optimal levels of welfare reported above are obtained. Hence, these results indicate that the optimal tax rates are second best policies for both countries.

### Conclusions

The effects of environment on trade and welfare are analyzed in a modified general equilibrium Heckscher-Ohlin framework where health appears as an argument in a quasi-homothetic utility function. This form of the function is used to capture the notion that the North is willing to spend more to alleviate environmental effects on health than the South. Environmental effects on health and welfare depend on three types of pollution which we characterize as local-disembodied, global-disembodied and embodied. Pollution is produced by an input as a by-product of production.

The results show that an optimal tax can, in principle, improve each country's welfare if the country is small in the world market. However, for a large country or region, changes in the terms of trade may cause one country to be made better off at the expense of the other. Then, a Pareto improvement can only be reached by an optimal tax with compensation, which suggests that some form of compensatory payment may be required to encourage the other country to pursue abatement policies.

We explore the strategic interdependence that arises in the case of global-disembodied pollution. Characterizing the interdependence as a one-shot Nash game, we find that a Nash equilibrium is not necessarily Pareto optimal. Under cooperative behavior, both countries can improve their welfare by jointly imposing a pollution control tax with a necessarily compensatory transfer.

For the case of embodied pollution, the optimal tax for the exporting country not only depends on its own marginal welfare loss of pollution, but also on the losses the country's exports caused on consumers in the importing country. Further, if only the polluting input is taxed, then its after tax rental rate falls if this input is intensively used. Hence the effectiveness of this instrument to lower the embodied pollutants is limited and can even be negative. Instead, a tax on the polluting input in combination with a subsidy to the non-polluting input can reduce pollution and improve the country's welfare if the country is small in the world market.

Regardless of whether pollution is local or global, disembodied or embodied, an abatement policy adopted by both countries or by one country unilaterally will not necessarily lower a country's comparative advantage in both small and large country cases, i.e., reduce its exports of the polluting good.

## Appendix: Simulation Results for the Example Economy

TABLE 9A.1 Simulation Results in the North for Local-Disembodied Pollution

|  | PE (1) | RSB (2) | RWB (3) | RSN (4) | RSS (5) | RWN (6) | RWS (7) |
|---|---|---|---|---|---|---|---|
| $X^n$ | 0.9974 | 0.9880 | 0.9974 | 0.9880 | 1.0 | 0.9932 | 1.0042 |
| $Y^n$ | 1.0023 | 1.0105 | 1.0023 | 1.0105 | 1.0 | 1.0059 | 0.9963 |
| $X_n$ | 0.9969 | 0.99998 | 0.9974 | 0.99998 | 1.0 | 0.9986 | 0.9988 |
| $Y_n$ | 1.0019 | 0.99997 | 1.0024 | 0.99997 | 1.0 | 1.0013 | 1.0011 |
| $H_n$ | 1.0005 | 1.00014 | 1.0011 | 1.00014 | 1.0 | 1.0007 | 1.0004 |
| $U_n$ | 1.00004 | 1.00008 | 1.0006 | 1.00008 | 1.0 | 1.0004 | 1.0002 |
| $PO^n$ | 0.9967 | 0.9908 | 0.9967 | 0.9908 | 1.0 | 0.9941 | 1.0026 |
| $K_x/L_x$ | 0.9956 | 1.0072 | 0.9956 | 1.0072 | 1.0 | 1.0008 | 0.9948 |
| $t^n$ |  | 0.0144 | 0.0143 | 0.0144 | 0.0 | 0.0144 | 0.0000 |
| $r/w$ |  | 0.9787 | 0.9902 | 0.9787 | 1.0 | 0.9851 | 1.0052 |
| $r^*/w$ |  | 0.9929 | 1.0044 | 0.9929 | 1.0 | 0.9992 | 1.0052 |
| $P_x/P_y$ |  | 1.0000 | 1.0058 | 1.0000 | 1.0 | 1.0032 | 1.0026 |
| $GNP_n$ |  | 0.99997 | 1.0027 | 0.99997 | 1.0 | 1.0015 | 1.0012 |

*Definitions:* PE = Pareto optimal solution; RSB = both countries tax, world prices fixed; RWB = both countries tax, world prices adjust; RSN = unilateral action where only the North taxes, world prices fixed; RSS = unilateral action where only the South taxes, world prices fixed; RWN = unilateral action where only the North taxes, world prices adjust; RWS = unilateral action where only the South taxes, world prices adjust; $r^* = r(1 + t^n)$. All solutions are reported comparing with a Walrasian equilibrium as a numeraire.

**TABLE 9A.2 Simulation Results in the North for Global-Disembodied Pollution**

| | PE (1) | RSB (2) | RWB (3) | RSN (4) | RSS (5) | RWN (6) | RWS (7) |
|---|---|---|---|---|---|---|---|
| $X^n$ | 0.9966 | 0.9755 | 0.9975 | 0.9755 | 1.0 | 0.9863 | 1.0111 |
| $Y^n$ | 1.0043 | 1.0213 | 1.0022 | 1.0213 | 1.0 | 1.0120 | 0.9902 |
| $X_n$ | 0.9931 | 0.9999 | 0.9941 | 0.9999 | 1.0 | 0.9971 | 0.9969 |
| $Y_n$ | 1.0043 | 0.9999 | 1.0055 | 0.9999 | 1.0 | 1.0026 | 1.0029 |
| $H_n$ | 1.0014 | 1.0008 | 1.0026 | 1.0003 | 1.0005 | 1.0012 | 1.0014 |
| $U_n$ | 1.0002 | 1.0004 | 1.0015 | 1.0001 | 1.0003 | 1.0006 | 1.0008 |
| $PO^n$ | 0.9943 | 0.9811 | 0.9950 | 0.9811 | 1.0 | 0.9880 | 1.0068 |
| $K_x/L_x$ | 0.9937 | 1.0146 | 0.9880 | 1.0146 | 1.0 | 1.0015 | 0.9862 |
| $t^n$ | | 0.0318 | 0.0311 | 0.0318 | 0.0 | 0.0314 | 0.0 |
| $r/w$ | | 0.9574 | 0.9838 | 0.9574 | 1.0 | 0.9702 | 1.0140 |
| $r^*/w$ | | 0.9856 | 1.0122 | 0.9856 | 1.0 | 0.9985 | 1.0140 |
| $P_x/P_y$ | | 1.0000 | 1.0132 | 1.0000 | 1.0 | 1.0065 | 1.0070 |
| $GNP_n$ | | 0.9999 | 1.0062 | 0.9999 | 1.0 | 1.0029 | 1.0033 |

*Definitions:* PE = Pareto optimal solution; RSB = both countries tax, world prices fixed; RWB = both countries tax, world prices adjust; RSN = unilateral action where only the North taxes, world prices fixed; RSS = unilateral action where only the South taxes, world prices fixed; RWN = unilateral action where only the North taxes, world prices adjust; RWS = unilateral action where only the South taxes, world prices adjust; $r^* = r(1 + t^n)$.

**TABLE 9A.3  Nash Equilibrium, Large Country Case**

| North<br>South | No tax | Tax |
|---|---|---|
| No tax | $dV_n = 0;$<br>$dV_s = 0$ | $dV_n = 0.621;$<br>$dV_s = -0.701$ |
| Tax | $dV_n = 0.840;$<br>$dV_s = -0.897$ | $dV_n = 1.481;$<br>$dV_s = -1.536$ |

Note: $\{t_n > 0, t_s = 0\}$ is the Nash equilibrium.


**TABLE 9A.4  Simulation Results for the North with Embodied Pollution**

| | PE<br>(1) | RSB<br>(2) | RWB<br>(3) | RSK<br>(4) | RWK<br>(5) |
|---|---|---|---|---|---|
| $X^n$ | 1.0538 | 1.0723 | 1.0266 | 0.9417 | 0.9918 |
| $Y^n$ | 0.9363 | 0.9234 | 0.9706 | 1.0568 | 1.0079 |
| $X_n$ | 1.0284 | 0.9958 | 1.0082 | 0.9998 | 0.9862 |
| $Y_n$ | 0.9827 | 0.9991 | 0.9877 | 0.9981 | 1.0143 |
| $U_n$ | 1.0149 | 1.0080 | 1.0030 | 0.9967 | 1.0048 |
| $po^n$ | 0.7573 | 0.8184 | 0.8599 | 1.0376 | 0.9734 |
| $s^n$ | | 0.1493 | 0.1493 | 0.0 | 0.0 |
| $t^n$ | | 0.0767 | 0.0767 | 0.0767 | 0.0767 |
| $r/w$ | | 0.9705 | 0.9188 | 0.8951 | 0.9536 |
| $r^*/w^*$ | | 1.2283 | 1.1629 | 0.9637 | 1.0413 |
| $P_x/P_y$ | | 1.0000 | 0.9730 | 1.0000 | 1.0326 |
| $GNP_n$ | | 0.9978 | 0.9910 | 0.9993 | 1.0160 |

*Definitions*: PE = Pareto optimal solution; RSB = both countries tax, world prices fixed; RWB = both countries tax, world prices adjust; RSK = both countries tax $K_x$ only, world prices fixed; RWK = both countries tax $K_x$ only, world prices adjust; $r^* = r(1 + t^n)$; $w^* = w(1 - s^n)$.

TABLE 9A.5  Changes in Excess Supplies After Tax

| | Local-Disembodied | | Global-Disembodied | | Embodied | |
|---|---|---|---|---|---|---|
| | Small Country | Large Country | Small Country | Large Country | Small Country | Large Country |
| Excess supply of X (North) | −0.0615 | −0.0026 | −0.1255 | +0.0115 | +0.6428 | +0.1344 |
| Excess supply of Y (South) | +0.0503 | +0.0031 | +0.1357 | +0.0249 | −0.3190 | +0.0892 |

TABLE 9A.6  Tax Revenue, Transfer and Their Percentages of GNP

| | South | | North | |
|---|---|---|---|---|
| | Local-Disembodied | Global-Disembodied | Local-Disembodied | Global-Disembodied |
| Total tax revenue | 0.0255 | 0.0664 | 0.0646 | 0.1294 |
| (Tax revenue/GNP) % | 0.2340 | 0.6067 | 0.4958 | 0.9894 |
| Total transfer | | | 0.0066 | 0.0141 |
| (Transfer/Tax revenue)% | | | 10.2449 | 10.8651 |
| (Transfer/GNP)% | 0.0606 | 0.1285 | 0.0508 | 0.1075 |

**TABLE 9A.7  Comparisons of the Utility Levels Before and After Transfer**

|  | South | | North | |
| --- | --- | --- | --- | --- |
|  | Local-Disembodied | Global-Disembodied | Local-Disembodied | Global-Disembodied |
| No tax | 5.153 | 5.093 | 6.24399 | 6.205 |
| Tax without transfer | 5.149 | 5.085 | 6.248 | 6.214 |
| Tax with transfer | 5.153 | 5.093 | 6.24426 | 6.206 |
| Pareto optimal | 5.153 | 5.093 | 6.24426 | 6.206 |

# References

Caswell, J., ed. *Economics of Food Safety.* New York: Elsevier, 1991.

Chichilnisky, G. "Property Rights and the Dynamics of North-South Trade." *The American Economic Review* 84, No. 4 (September 1994): 851-74.

Chivian, E., ed. *Critical Conditions: Human Health and the Environment.* Cambridge: MIT Press, 1993.

Copeland, B.R., and M.S. Taylor. "North-South Trade and the Environment." *The Quarterly Journal of Economics* 109, No. 3(August 1994): 755 - 87.

Gertler, P., and J. van der Gaag. *The Willingness to Pay for Medical Care: Evidence from Two Developing Countries.* Baltimore: Johns Hopkins University Press, 1990.

Gorman, W.M. "Community Preference Fields." *Econometrica* 21(1953): 63 - 80.

Kassouf, A. "Estimation of Health Demand and Health Production Functions for Children in Brazil." Ph.D. dissertation, University of Minnesota, 1993.

Kohn, R.E. "Global Pollution: A Heckscher-Ohlin-Samuelson Model of Pigouvian Taxation." *Eastern Economic Journal* 27, No. 3(1991): 337-43.

Low, P., ed. *International Trade and the Environment,* Discussion Papers No. 159. Washington, DC: The World Bank, 1992.

McGuire, M. "Regulation, Factor Rewards, and International Trade." *Journal of Public Economics* 17(1982): 335-54.

Merrifield, J. "The Impact of Selected Abatement Strategies on Transnational Pollution, the Terms of Trade, and Factor Rewards: A General Equilibrium Approach." *Journal of Environmental Economics and Management* 15(1989): 59-84.

Pethig, R. "Pollution, Welfare and Environmental Policy in the Theory of Comparative Advantage." *Journal of Environmental Economics and Management* 2(1976): 160-79.

Robert, D., and D. Orden. "Determinants of Technical Barriers to Trade: The Case of U.S. Phytosanitary Restrictions on Mexican Avocados, 1972-1995." ERS (USDA) Working paper, 1995.

Runge, C.F., and R.M. Nolan. "Trade in Disservices: Environmental Regulation and Agricultural Trade." *Food Policy* 15, No. 1(1990): 3-7.

Samuelson, P.A. *Foundations of Economic Analysis.* Cambridge, MA: Harvard University Press, 1947.

Siebert, H. "Environmental Policy in the Two-country Case." *Zeitschrift Fur Nationalokonomie* 39, No. 3-4(1979): 259-74.

Woodland, A.D. *International Trade and Resource Allocation.* Amsterdam: North Holland, 1982.

World Bank. *World Development Report* 1992. New York: Oxford University Press, 1992.

_____ . *World Development Report 1993.* New York: Oxford University Press, 1993.

# 10

# Quantifying Trade and Environment Linkages Through Economywide Modeling

*John Whalley*

## Introduction

The trade and environment issue has acquired a high profile in the last two years, particularly following the GATT panel report on the tuna/dolphin dispute between Mexico and the United States, the subsequent discussion of trade and environment in the GATT[1], and the formation of a working group on trade and environment at the Marrakesh meeting. However, most people's sense of the quantitative significance of trade and environment linkages continues to be highly imprecise. It is unknown whether or not the issues being discussed in these forums relate to matters of limited consequence for overall economic performance from the global economy (which is a presumption for many narrowly-focused sectoral or product issues), or whether these are some of the most central issues affecting both the performance of the trading system and wider global environmental management over the next few decades.

An attempt has been made in this study to survey the limited quantitative literature in this field emerging from economywide modeling, drawing together preliminary findings from five recent studies which touch on the quantitative dimensions of linkage between trade and environment. These are, in the main, numerical general equilibrium exercises which involve calibration of models to various benchmark or base case data sets, followed by counterfactual analysis around base cases. What emerges is a picture of seemingly little consequence for global system performance of some of the proposed environmentally motivated trade actions, such as trade actions to offset advantages accruing to exporters from countries with relatively lax environmental standards, or the trade implications of sectorally focused trade actions, as in some of the species-related cases. On the other hand, some areas of environmentally motivated policy relatively neglected by the trade community, such as carbon taxes, seemingly have major (and under some scenarios, potentially dramatic) consequences for world trade, since large taxes affecting a major portion of aggregate global economic activity are involved.

A brief description of the content of these modeling exercises follows, and the initial results emerging from them. A tentative summary conclusion is then offered of what seems to be their major implications is then offered.

## Models Capturing Trade and Environment Linkages

Recent modeling works which have sought to capture trade and environment linkages, or have done so indirectly as a result of other modeling efforts, mainly reflect numerical general equilibrium modeling. These models have their origins in the tax and trade-based numerical general equilibrium models of the late 1970s, and early 1980s (see Shoven and Whalley 1984, 1992; DeMelo, Dervis, and Robinson 1982). In these models, production and demand structures are specified and represented usually by some type of convenient functional form (Cobb-Douglas, CES, LES). Parameter values are specified through a calibration procedure to a benchmark, or base case, equilibrium data set. In the past, such models have been used to analyze nonenvironmental policy interventions (such as tax, trade, and other areas), and it is only recently that models more explicitly oriented towards environmental concerns have evolved.

In these more recent models, the environmental component is usually specified through some explicit interaction between physical production processes and environmental characteristics, such as levels of emissions and pollutants. Thus, as changes take place in the underlying real behavior of the economy (such as, increased trade), impacts in terms of environmental characteristics can be directly captured by the model. Usually these models are used in so-called counterfactual form, that is, with calibration to a benchmark equilibrium and with some hypothetical change considered which then moves the economy to a counterfactual equilibrium.

One recent example of models capturing these interactions is a study by Beauséjour, Lenjosek, and Smart (1995). This is a model which was originally motivated by an attempt to analyze the environmental impacts of the Canada-U.S. trade agreement, but has since been used to analyze more general economy-environment interactions. Table 10.1 sets out the

**TABLE 10.1.** Economy-Environment Model Structure Used by Beauséjour, Lenjosek, and Smart

---

**Economic Component**

**General:**
- Single-period or static general equilibrium model; no capital accumulation through saving
- Three regions: Canada, the U.S., and the rest of the world
- Rest of the world not explicitly modeled

**Production Structure:**
- Seventeen industries producing 18 commodities using labor, capital, 7 sector-specific resource factors, and 18 intermediate inputs
- Labor and capital are homogeneous and mobile among industries
- Substitution possible among capital, labor, and resource inputs, and between domestic and foreign intermediate inputs

**Final Demand:**
- An aggregate of consumption and investment
- Function of income and relative prices
- One consumer in each region; excess demands for goods (and capital) accommodated by the rest of the world

**Government:**
- Provision of government services part of service industry
- Indirect taxes, tariffs, and subsidies included
- Net government revenue redistributed to consumers in a non-distortionary manner

**Foreign Trade Sector:**
- Capital is perfectly mobile among regions at the constant world rental rate
- Prices for certain resource commodities and all commodities produced in the rest of the world are exogenous
- All other domestic commodity prices adjust to equilibrate a region's merchandise trade balance with its service payments on imported capital

Environmental Component

**Scope:**
- Air pollution issues of greenhouse warming, acid deposition, and smog
- Five pollutants modeled: nitrogen oxides, methane, volatile organic compounds, sulphur oxides, and carbon dioxide

**Emissions of Air Pollutants:**
- arise from the combustion of fossil fuels (in both stationary and mobile sources) and from industrial processes
- Occur in fixed proportion to the levels of polluting intermediate use, polluting production, and polluting consumption

**Pollution Reduction:**
- Substitution among relatively "dirty" fuel inputs
- Decreased production in polluting industries
- Application of "abatement capital" to reduce emissions from the use of a given fuel or industrial process

**Economic Instruments for Controlling Air Pollutants:**
- Air pollution taxes:
- Various taxes on fossil fuels at uniform rates or at rates proportional to the emission of air pollutant (e.g., a carbon tax)
- Emission charges
- Quantitative emission standards—economywide and industry-specific
- Tradable permit systems among industries

---

*Source:* Beauséjour, Lenjosek, and Smart (1995).

broad structure of the model; a single-period or static general equilibrium model capturing three trading regions—Canada, the United States, and the rest of the world. For each region, a number of industries are specified, each using primary factor inputs as well as intermediate production, with substitution possible among the various inputs. The final demand specification in the model covers both consumption and investment, with consumption a function of both incomes and relative prices. Single consumers are specified in each region, so that no distributional impacts within the region are captured. The government taxes various activities as in traditional tax models, with the revenues redistributed to consumers in lump-sum form. In the foreign trade area, a combination of price taking and price making behavior is captured, reflecting trade in resources and other products. The environmental component of the model is an overlay on top of the economic component, with five different forms of pollutants specified—nitrogen oxide, methane, organic compounds, sulphur oxide, and carbon dioxide. Air pollutants arising from the use of fossil fuels are introduced into the model by assuming fixed coefficient emissions relative to each type of production. Changes in pollutant activity within the model take place both by substitution among fuels of differing emission intensity, as well as through changes in the industrial composition of the economy, between high and low-polluting industries. The model then can be used to analyze various kinds of environmentally-based policy interventions, including air pollution taxes and emission standards. Environmental impacts on trade are captured through the regional linkage component of the model.

A study in a similar vein is a recent model more explicitly focused on trade and environment linkages developed by Perroni and Wigle (1994). Table 10.2 presents the structure of this model in schematic form. Perroni and Wigle calibrate their model to a 1986 global data set covering three major regions, and a variety of pollutant activities. The regions are: (1) North America, (2) other developed countries, and (3) low and middle income countries. The economic component of the model is similar to that in Beauséjour, Lenjosek, and Smart. Emissions generated through productive processes interact with various specified natural and geographical processes, including absorption and transmission of particulants through the atmosphere and oceans. In the model this leads to a direct impact on global environmental standards, and hence environmental quality for consumers.

Unlike Beauséjour, Lenjosek, and Smart, Perroni and Wigle directly capture the welfare effects of changes to environmental standards in explicit utility evaluations in their model, embodied in the form of damage functions. The model covers six goods and sectors chosen, so as to allow a separation between industries with more emissions from those with less,

TABLE 10.2 Perroni and Wigle's Model Treatment of Economy-Environment Linkages

| FIRMS | | E | | E |
|---|---|---|---|---|
| | Production | M | Natural | N |
| | and | I | and | V |
| | Abatement | S | Geographical | I |
| | Processes | S | Processes | R |
| Market Process | | I | | O |
| | | O | | N |
| | | N | | M |
| | | S | | E |
| | | | | N |
| | | | | T |
| CONSUMERS | Valuation | | | |

*Source*: Perroni and Wigle (1994).

and also to allow separation of higher-technology from lower-technology industries. Having calibrated their model to a 1986 benchmark data set, they are then able to analyze the effects of increased trade on environmental characteristics by looking at the effects of alternative trade policy scenarios, including removal of all global trade barriers in their model.

A third recent model-based analysis is that by Low (1992), which, while in partial rather than full general equilibrium form, is nonetheless relevant to the trade and environment debate. Low uses a model-based calculation to analyze the effects of possible trade barriers being adopted in the United States to countervail perceived lax standards of key trading partners including Mexico, and analyzes their impacts on trade. This is done using an analysis of data on pollution abatement costs by type of expenditure and by sector for the United States, which are then used to infer what size trade barrier might be introduced under an assumption of zero such costs (or unmeasurable costs) being incurred by firms in Mexico. The effects of new trade barriers designed to offset cost advantages due to standards differentials are then analyzed using a partial equilibrium structure, which captures relevant demand-supply elasticities. Impacts on the level of trade, in the original base period data, can then be evaluated. This study by Low has attracted substantial attention because of the conclusion that the trade impacts of such policies in this case are small. These, in turn, are linked to the data on abatement costs. Abatement cost data are displayed in Table 10.3 and are relevant to the discussion here because they show the relatively small costs involved.[2]

TABLE 10.3  Data on Pollution Abatement Operating Costs by Type of Expenditure, 1988, Used by Low (in millions of U.S. dollars)

| SIC No. | Products/ Equipment | Total Gross Cost (1) | Total Industry Output (2) | Abatement Costs per Unit of Output (3) | Payments to Government | | | Costs by Form of Pollutant Abated | | | | |
|---|---|---|---|---|---|---|---|---|---|---|---|---|
| | | | | | Total | Public Sewage Services | Solid Collection Disposal | Total | Air | Water | Solid Waste Hazardous | Solid Waste Nonhazardous |
| 20 | Food/kindred prod. | 1,160 | 351,515 | 0.33 | 399 | 348 | 51 | 762 | 158 | 326 | 13 | 265 |
| 21 | Tobacco manuf. | 38 | 23,832 | 0.16 | 6 | 5 | 1 | 32 | 12 | 10 | 1 | 9 |
| 22 | Textile mill prod. | 177 | 64,768 | 0.27 | 62 | 50 | 12 | 115 | 31 | 49 | 7 | 29 |
| 24 | Lumber/wood prod. | 236 | 72,065 | 0.33 | 20 | 10 | 10 | 216 | 84 | 48 | 17 | 68 |
| 25 | Furniture/fixtures | 118 | 39,226 | 0.30 | 11 | 6 | 5 | 107 | 34 | 7 | 37 | 30 |
| 26 | Paper/allied prod. | 1,343 | 122,556 | 1.10 | 142 | 108 | 34 | 1,202 | 372 | 520 | 33 | 277 |
| 27 | Printing/publishing | 206 | 143,907 | 0.14 | 42 | 25 | 17 | 165 | 72 | 10 | 22 | 61 |
| 28 | Chemicals/allied prod. | 3,075 | 259,699 | 1.18 | 182 | 154 | 27 | 2,893 | 706 | 1,274 | 467 | 446 |
| 29 | Petroleum/coal prod. | 2,006 | 131,415 | 1.53 | 31 | 15 | 16 | 1,975 | 1,176 | 547 | 143 | 109 |
| 30 | Rubber/misc. plastics | 278 | 94,200 | 0.30 | 51 | 27 | 24 | 227 | 63 | 35 | 35 | 94 |
| 31 | Leather/leather prod. | 23 | 9,664 | 0.24 | 8 | 6 | 2 | 15 | 3 | 6 | 1 | 6 |
| 32 | Stone/clay/glass prod. | 439 | 63,059 | 0.70 | 28 | 17 | 11 | 411 | 248 | 51 | 26 | 87 |
| 33 | Primary metal industries | 1,809 | 149,080 | 1.21 | 63 | 48 | 16 | 1,746 | 966 | 469 | 136 | 175 |
| 34 | Fabricated metal prod. | 762 | 158,834 | 0.48 | 73 | 49 | 24 | 689 | 135 | 268 | 169 | 117 |
| 35 | Machinery, except elect. | 430 | 243,261 | 0.18 | 57 | 38 | 18 | 373 | 68 | 101 | 91 | 113 |
| 36 | Electric/electrical equip. | 659 | 186,951 | 0.35 | 86 | 63 | 24 | 573 | 92 | 190 | 163 | 128 |
| 37 | Transportation equip. | 975 | 354,048 | 0.28 | 83 | 60 | 22 | 892 | 216 | 239 | 268 | 169 |
| 38 | Instruments/related prod. | 198 | 114,528 | 0.17 | 23 | 18 | 5 | 175 | 22 | 62 | 49 | 42 |
| 39 | Misc. manuf. industries | 77 | 34,869 | 0.22 | 13 | 6 | 7 | 64 | 10 | 15 | 10 | 30 |
| | Total | 14,009 | 2,617,477 | 0.54 | 1,379 | 1,053 | 326 | 12,630 | 4,467 | 4,223 | 1,687 | 2,253 |

Sources: Low (1992); U.S. Department of Commerce, Bureau of the Census (1988).

A further and final model set is comprised of analyses by Whalley and Wigle (1991) and by Piggott, Whalley, and Wigle (1993) in two interrelated modeling studies. These two global models capture international trade effects of policies dealing with carbon emissions, which have been used to analyze the effects of major policy interventions intended to address global warming, such as a possible carbon tax set at levels designed to stabilize global carbon emissions at early 1990s levels (the so-called "Toronto call," after the statement of such an objective at a 1989 global scientific conference in Toronto). In the first of these papers, the possible international impacts of carbon tax options are directly evaluated. In the second, the extent of subregional or even unilateral country reduction in carbon emissions, which would optimally be unilaterally undertaken to deal with global warming, are analyzed using a model extension with an explicit parameterization of preferences.

Table 10.4 sets out the structure of the first model, which is not dissimilar from that in other models. There is a production and demand structure in each region, with CES production functions defined over primary factors and other inputs. The primary factors, in turn, are broken down into energy and non-energy inputs, which cover greenhouse and non-greenhouse, and carbon and non-carbon products. This leads to production of composite energy and, in turn, the eventual production of energy-intensive and non-energy-intensive products. International trade then takes place in energy-intensive and other goods, and carbon-based products. Table 10.5 details the regions and countries in these models, with model calibration in both taking place to a 1986 global data set around which alternative counterfactual analyses are performed.

## Model Results and Analyses

The models summarized in the previous section have been used for a variety of different analyses, and their results provide significant input for the debate on trade and environment interactions. Results are in some cases preliminary, and in other cases the trade component of results is a by-product of analyses primarily directed towards other issues. But given the relative absence of such quantification thus far, these results are important for current debate.

Beauséjour, Lenjosek, and Smart (forthcoming) use their static general equilibrium model of economy-environment interactions in Canada and the United States, largely to provide results on the effect of tax and regulatory options used to limit carbon emissions in both countries. Their main results are cross-country, looking at the relative effectiveness of carbon taxes and fossil fuel taxes, and analyzing the relative significance of each. Their model does, however, have the capability to analyze the

**TABLE 10.4 Production and Demand Structures in the Whalley/Wigle Global General Equilibrium Model Used to Evaluate Carbon Tax Options**

A. <u>Factors and Goods in Each Region</u>

<u>Endowments</u>
- Carbon-based energy resources (CR)
- Non-carbon-based energy resources (ER)
- Sector-specific factors in energy-intensive manufacturing (SF)

<u>Produced Goods</u>
- Carbon-based energy products (CP)
- Non-carbon-based energy products (EP)
- Composite energy (E)
- Energy-intensive goods (EI)
- Other goods (OG)

B. <u>Structure of Production in Each Region</u> (CES[a] Functions used at each stage)

<u>Stage 1: Production of Energy Products</u>

```
PF     CR     PF     ER

   CP              EP
```

<u>Stage 2: Production of Composite Energy</u>

```
CP     EP

   E
```

<u>Stage 3: Production of Energy-Intensive and Other Goods</u>

```
E  SF  PF          E      PF

   EI                 O
```

C. <u>Arguments in Final Demands</u>

EI, OG, E

D. <u>Commodities in Which International Trade Takes Place</u>

EI, OG, CP

---

[a]CES denotes "constant elasticity of substitution."

*Source*: Whalley and Wigle (1991).

**TABLE 10.5  Regions in the Whalley/Wigle Global Equilibrium Model Used to Evaluate International Incidence Effects of Carbon Taxes**

---

1. EUROPEAN COMMUNITY (of the 12)

2. NORTH AMERICA (U.S., Canada)

3. JAPAN

4. OTHER OECD

    Austria, Switzerland, Finland, Iceland, Norway, Sweden, Australia, New Zealand

5. OIL EXPORTER (OPEC countries, plus major non-OPEC exporters)

    Algeria, Libya, Nigeria, Tunisia, Mexico, Venezuela, Indonesia, Iran, Iraq, Kuwait, Saudi Arabia, United Arab Emirates

6. REST OF THE WORLD (developing countries and centrally-planned economies)

    This is a residual category containing all other countries, including USSR, Eastern Europe, China, Brazil, India, and other developing countries not in category 5.

---

*Source*: Whalley and Wigle (1991).

effects of these and other policy interventions on both production and trade. Earlier preliminary work from this effort suggested, for instance, that the effects of regional trade agreements, such as the Canada-U.S. trade agreement, on various kinds of emissions overall may be relatively small, concluding that of the five emissions they consider, some increase and some fall.

In Perroni and Wigle (forthcoming), the focus is somewhat different because the model is explicitly focused on environment-trade interactions. Their model results suggest that increased international trade generally has little impact on environmental quality. They also conclude that the magnitude of welfare effects of environmental policies are not significantly affected by simultaneous changes in trade policies when environmental policies are enacted. Also, the size and regional distribution of the gains in trade liberalization appear to be little affected by environmental policies. The tentative conclusion reached is that the extent of trade and environment interactions may perhaps be smaller than might have been suggested by the intensity of recent debate on this topic.  In Low (1992), the focus on trade and environment linkages is direct, and more explicitly on one particular economy-environmental interaction. The purpose is to assess what might happen to Mexican exports to the United States if the United States were to levy a special import tax designed to offset pollution abatement control costs incurred by U.S. domestic industries, under the assumption that such costs in Mexico are either zero or unmeasured. The approach is to identify pollution-intensive or "dirty" industries as those with the highest pollution abatement or control expenditures. These industries are then examined in terms of their contribution to Mexico's exports, and a simulation is used to assess the effects of a special import tax on these exports along the lines discussed.

Low emphasizes that such expenditures currently incurred by U.S. industries represent only a small component of total costs, with only 18 out of 123 industries paying more than 1 percent of the value of their output in pollution abatement costs. The highest such expenditure is one industry with 3 percent; the weighted average is approximately 0.5 percent. On this basis alone, the impact of a special import tax, while still dependent on assumed values of elasticities, would likely be small.

Using a simple elasticity-based approach and 1986 data, Low calculates that the imposition of such a tax would cause a reduction of less than 2 percent in Mexico's exports. This compares with an approximate real doubling of Mexican trade with the United States between 1985 and 1992, suggesting that such potential environmentally-based trade measures—over which there has been such agonizing—if actually implemented, would have only a small effect on direct trade flows because the cost components involved are small.

In contrast to these results, the work of Whalley and Wigle (1991), and Piggott, Whalley, and Wigle (1993) shows potentially large effects on international trade flows from major policy intervention such as a carbon tax. Their published papers report no direct numbers on trade impacts, since this was not their major focus, but in the presence of large carbon taxes which apply to a significant input component for manufacturing (and where the tax rates required range as high as 800 percent in order to generate reductions in labor emissions to stabilize globally at 1990 levels), the cost component feeding through to manufactures is large. The result is a potentially major impact on international trade in manufactures and changes in trade patterns. Global consumption of energy-intensive manufactures falls sharply, and with it global trade. Some scenarios suggest that a tax at high levels such as these could have more major consequences for trade in the global economy than any other developments in the global economy in the post-war years. Thus, for example, in the Whalley and Wigle (1991) study, there are major changes in net trade patterns between energy-intensive goods and other goods for major regions. Japan, for instance, changes from being a net exporter of energy-intensive manufactures to a net importer. Europe, including eastern Europe, changes from a net importer to a net exporter situation, and the EC also changes from a net exporter to a net importer position. In Piggott,

Whalley, and Wigle (1993) there are further incidental analyses of trade impacts from carbon taxes, and some of their unpublished results also suggest large trade impacts from a major global carbon tax.

Thus, the preliminary indications now beginning to emerge from model-based quantitative analyses seem to suggest that the direct trade and environment interactions that have been the subject of most debate and discussion in the GATT and other forums, including those associated with relatively lax standards, may have only limited consequences for overall global economic performance. While there are still only a few quantitative results for broader environmental actions, the logic would seem to be that the same would likely be true for the potential use of environmentally-based trade measures to deal with narrower sectoral or product issues such as tuna/dolphin.

On the other hand, the trade consequences of major environmental interventions not figuring prominently in the trade and environment debate, such as a possible global carbon tax, seemingly could be considerably more substantial. In an extreme case, they might even reverse the growth in world trade in manufactures that we have seen in the last four decades of GATT-based trade liberalization. No doubt this quantitative picture will be further refined in the years ahead, and because of the relatively recent emergence of these issues, it is only now that the primary quantitative work outlined here is beginning to be undertaken; but initial indications seem to offer the themes discussed above as potential inputs for the debate.

## Notes

1. See the GATT research volume on trade and environment edited by Anderson and Blackhurst (1992), as well as Low (1992) and Whalley (1991). See also the recent discussion of "Climate Change Policy and International Trade" in Barrett (1994).

2. Low's conclusion is consistent with that reached by Tobey (1990), who uses an econometric approach to test the significance of pollution effects in a Hechsher-Ohlin-Vanek model. Commodity's relative pollution intensities are defined in terms of pollution abatement costs incurred in production using similar U.S. data, with endowment data from Leamer (1984), and trade data from U.N. trade statistics. Tobey's conclusion is that stringent environmental regulations imposed on industries in the late 1960s and early 1970s by most industrial countries have not affected trade patterns to any measurable extent in the most heavily polluting industries. A more recent paper by Levinsohn (1994) concludes that differing environmental regulations across U.S. states have little effect on location decisions, in part because once again the cost shares involved are small.

## References

Anderson, K., and R. Blackhurst, eds. *The Greening of World Trade Issues.* Ann Arbor, MI: University of Michigan Press (and London: Harvester Wheatsheaf), 1992.

Barrett, S. "Climate Change Policy and International Trade." In *Climate Change: Policy Instruments and Their Implications.* Proceedings of the Tsukuba Workshop of the Intergovernmental Panel on Climate Change, Working Group III, Tsukuba, Japan, January 1994.

Beauséjour, L., G. Lenjosek, and M. Smart. "Economic Instruments for Controlling Emissions of Carbon Dioxide: A CGE Analysis of Economic and Environmental Impacts." *The World Economy* 18.3(May 1995).

DeMelo, J., K. Dervis, and S. Robinson. *General Equilibrium Analysis and Developing Countries.* Cambridge: Cambridge University Press, 1982.

Leamer, E.E. *Sources of International Comparative Advantage: Theory and Evidence.* Cambridge, MA: The MIT Press, 1984.

Levinsohn, A. "Environmental Regulations and Manufacturers' Location Choices: Systematic Evidence from the Census of Manufactures." Unpublished paper presented at the Trans-Atlantic Public Economics Conference on Market Failures and Public Policy, Turin, Italy, 19–21 May 1994.

Low, P. "Trade Measures and Environmental Quality: Implications for Mexico's Exports." In *International Trade and the Environment*, P. Low, ed. Washington, DC: The World Bank, 1992.

Perroni, C., and R. Wigle. "International Trade and Environmental Quality: How Important Are the Linkages?" *Canadian Journal of Economics* XXVII, No. 3(August 1994):551-67.

Piggott, J., J. Whalley, and R. Wigle. "How Large Are the Incentives to Join Sub-Global Carbon Reduction Initiatives?" *Journal of Policy Modeling* 15, nos. 5-6(October-December 1993):473-90.

Shoven, J., and J. Whalley. "Applied General-Equilibrium Models of Taxation and International Trade: An Introduction and Survey." *Journal of Economic Literature* XXII, No. 3(September 1984):1007–51.

_____ . *Applying General Equilibrium.* Cambridge: Cambridge University Press, 1992.

Tobey, J.A. "The Effects of Domestic Environmental Policies on Patterns of World Trade." *Kyklos* 43, No. 2(1990):191-209.

U.S. Department of Commerce, Bureau of the Census. *Manufacturers' Pollution Abatement Capital Expenditures and Operating Costs.* Washington, DC, 1988.

Whalley, J. "The Interface Between Trade and Environmental Policies." *Economic Journal* 101, No. 405(March 1991):180-89.

Whalley, J., and R. Wigle. "The International Incidence of Carbon Taxes." In *Economic Policy Responses to Global Warming*, R. Dornbusch and J.M. Poterba, eds. Cambridge, MA: The MIT Press, 1991.

# PART FOUR

# Measuring the Critical Linkages

# 11

## On Measuring the Environmental Impact of Agricultural Trade Liberalization

*Kym Anderson and Anna Strutt*

### Introduction

One of the great contributions of agricultural and trade policy analysts during the past decade has been to provide clear and convincing assessments of the economic consequences of farm trade liberalization. In particular, the quantification of the real income effects of multilateral trade reform helped to persuade agnostics and skeptics of the economic virtues of reducing domestic agricultural price supports, which in turn allowed the Uruguay Round eventually to come to a successful conclusion. During the Round one of the positive consequences of the effort to quantify the conventional economic effects of agricultural policy reform is that we now have a large array of partial and general equilibrium models of national, regional, and global markets for farm (and other) products.

Virtually none of those models, however, paid attention to the consequences of policy reform for the natural environment. Yet it was clear even before the ink was dry on the Uruguay Round agreements, signed in April 1994, that any future multilateral trade negotiations would be forced to consider environmental in addition to conventional economic effects of trade-related policy reform. This observation is driven by a conviction held by numerous environmental groups that trade liberalization is bad for the environment—notwithstanding the preambles to the GATT1947 and the WTO1995. Those feelings are strong not only at the global level, but also, and in some cases more so, at regional levels.

For example, despite the paucity of firm evidence on the environmental consequences of freeing up trade within North America, that conviction was expressed so strongly that leaders in Washington and Mexico City perceived that NAFTA would pass the U.S. Congress only if accompanied by a side agreement to protect the environment. Moreover, environmental groups see NAFTA as but the beginning of their battle to force trade agreements to address environmental issues, not least because they perceive (correctly) that such agreements are increasingly about much deeper integration than that resulting from the lowering of border restrictions on trade (Ballenger and Krissoff 1994).

It is therefore important, both for the sake of the environment and to reduce the risk of the next round of multilateral trade negotiations being frustrated by unsubstantiated claims about adverse environmental effects of trade reform, to begin now to improve our understanding of the linkages between trade-related policy reform and the environment, and in particular to quantify their significance. Quantification is necessary because the sign of some effects cannot be determined *a prior*, because for priority setting we need to know their *relative* importance, and for the pragmatic reason that it is easier to attract attention to an issue with numbers than without.

To date, few models have been developed to quantify the physical environmental effects of economic reforms such as trade liberalization (Dean 1992; Anderson and Blackhurst 1992), and even less effort has been expended in placing a monetary value on those physical effects through combining models of the economy and the natural environment (Powell 1993). The purpose of this chapter is to assess what would be involved in evaluating the environmental effects of agricultural trade liberalization. Throughout, attention is focused on (1) global environmental effects of Uruguay Round-type multilateral trade reforms, although most of the discussion also applies to regional, national, or sub-national environmental effects of regional and unilateral trade liberalization and indeed to other policy and market changes as well; and (2) agriculture, because it has received much less attention by analysts than industrial pollution and energy consumption.

The chapter begins by reviewing the main concerns of environmental groups as they relate to agriculture. It then looks briefly at what has been written already about the global environmental effects of decreasing agricultural support prices, before discussing ways to improve our quantitative knowledge of those effects and their economic significance. Many of the environmentalists' concerns about trade are misplaced from an economist's perspective, partly because it is typically aspects of production or consumption rather than trade *per se* that cause environmental problems, and so solutions lie with more efficient measures than trade policy instruments. Nonetheless, there is no doubt that like any other market or policy change, trade-related farm policy reforms will have both positive and negative consequences for the natural environment. How large are those effects likely to be in quantitative terms, what value does society place on them, and how might policy reforms be modified and/or supplemented to improve the level and distribution of society's net welfare (including the value society places on the goods and services provided by the natural environment)? These are questions modelers need to have in mind when designing new models or modifying existing ones. But before turning to some thoughts on how one might proceed, it is helpful to reflect on what it is that concerns environmentalists about trade policy reform.

## What Concerns Environmentalists About Trade Liberalization?

Only the more extreme environmentalists claim that international trade itself is a significant contributor to environmental degradation. They have in mind the pollution involved in the transport of goods between countries. There are more efficient ways than banning trade for dealing with such concerns, of course. As such concerns become serious, so parties will get together to negotiate international environmental agreements (e.g., the Basel convention on trade in hazardous substances and waste).

If trade *per se* is not the main cause of the problems perceived by environmentalists, the economic theory of distortions and welfare suggests that trade policy instruments are unlikely to be the first-best way to overcome those problems (Bhagwati 1971). Why, then, all the fuss about the environmental effects of trade liberalization? It stems in large part from the fact that reductions in distortions to international trade increase real incomes and stimulate a change in the mix and international location of production and consumption. Both of these effects worry some environmentalists in high-income countries, and that in turn concerns people in poorer countries, who fear they may face additional trade restrictions as a result.

With respect to higher incomes, some environmentalists assume the consequent increase in spending will place greater demands on the environment. That assumption, however, is questionable, because income growth brings with it at least three important changes in behavior patterns. One is that population growth tends to decline as incomes rise, which reduces one important source of pressure on both urban and rural environments of developing countries. Another is that education investment expands with income, and with it comes more skillful management of all resources, including the private use of the natural environment. And third, modernizing communities with rising incomes and improving education tend eventually to improve private property rights and put more stringent environmental policies in place (Radetzki 1992; Grossman 1994). Not only does the demand for pollution abatement policies appear to be quite income elastic (at least beyond a certain threshold), but also the cost of complying falls as trade liberalization expands the opportunities to acquire more environmentally benign production technologies and consumer products and inputs.

Environmentalists may be disappointed that governments adopt less-stringent environmental standards and charges than they would like, but the appropriate response in most circumstances is for them to advocate tougher domestic environmental standards in their own and other countries as incomes rise, rather than to argue against those income rises through trade liberalization. The main exceptional circumstance is when the environmental effects of greater spending spill over national boundaries. The spillovers could be physical, as with carbon emissions and large-scale deforestation (climate change, reduced biodiversity) and CFCs and halons (ozone depletion). Or the spillovers could be (for want of a better word) psychological, as with a concern for plant or animal rights globally. One possible solution when there are international spillovers is to seek international environmental agreements [e.g., the Montreal convention on CFC phase-out and the Convention on International Trade in Endangered Species (CITES)]. But such agreements typically are very difficult to reach, not least because of large differences across countries in incomes, and hence in the willingness of people to place a high value on the goods and services of the natural environment. In those circumstances, the wealthier and more concerned environmentalists will look for other ways to influence the environmental damage of other countries (as they perceive it), and the use of their own country's trade policy as a stick or carrot to influence behavior in other countries may be one of the few options they have (debt relief for nature swaps or other foreign aid being additional possibilities).

With respect to changes in the mix and international location of production that would accompany agricultural trade liberalization, environmentalists are concerned in at least two ways. They fear that in the highly protected countries of Western Europe, the rural countryside and villages will be less visually attractive and less populated as farmers respond to lower domestic food prices by "getting bigger or getting out." And they fear that the higher food prices in international markets, following reduced exports/increased imports by the highly protectionist economies, will raise land prices in tropical and Southern Hemisphere countries, which will stimulate greater deforestation (to expand the area of agricultural land) and heavier doses of agricultural chemicals (which not only degrade the local environment but also cause greater chemical residues in food that the reforming countries might import). These concerns are understandable, but they are based on only a small number of the direct and indirect environmental effects involved in the relocating of production that would be induced by trade reform. A diagram showing those effects is given in Figure 11.1. A crude beginning to understanding their relative importance can be obtained even with existing models of world food markets, as illustrated in the next section. But much more comprehensive modeling is possible and desirable, as discussed in the subsequent section.

### Effects of Farm Trade Liberalization on the Quantity and Location of Farm Production and Input Use

To illustrate how one might start to examine the effects on the global environment of reducing agricultural support policies, Anderson (1992a, b) drew on some estimates of the production effects of a multilateral reform as simulated by the Tyers and Anderson (1992) model of world food markets. Those estimates were from an extreme simulation: it assumed complete removal of all farmer support policies in all industrial countries and U.S. land set-asides in 1990, and full adjustment in that same year. Even with such a huge liberalization and instantaneous adjustment, the estimated impact on world food output in aggregate is negligible and the relocation of production is minor; i.e., grain and meat production would have been 5 or 6 percent lower in industrial countries and 3 to 8 percent higher in developing countries. The big declines would have been in Japan and Western Europe, but that would have been partly offset by increases in North America and Australasia. The latter rich regions would have accounted for more than a quarter of the increases, with developing countries providing the balance (Figures 11.2 and 11.3).

Figure 11.3 suggests that for the regions where production would fall, the reductions would be a fairly large proportion of output. But for the regions expanding production, the increases are a relatively small proportion of their current output, especially for grain. The difference is because the price decreases in the former regions are much larger than the price increases in the latter regions. This has important implications for environmental degradation and chemical residues in food, especially because the contracting regions are relatively densely populated, and so use farm chemicals and intensive livestock methods much more than the expanding regions. In the case of fertilizer and pesticides, for example, the highly protected countries use more than ten times as much per agricultural hectare as Australasia and most developing countries (Figure 11.4). Furthermore, land-scarce Western Europe and Japan crop twice as much of their total land area as does the rest of the world on average, so

FIGURE 11.1. Main Effects of Agricultural Production on the Natural Environment.

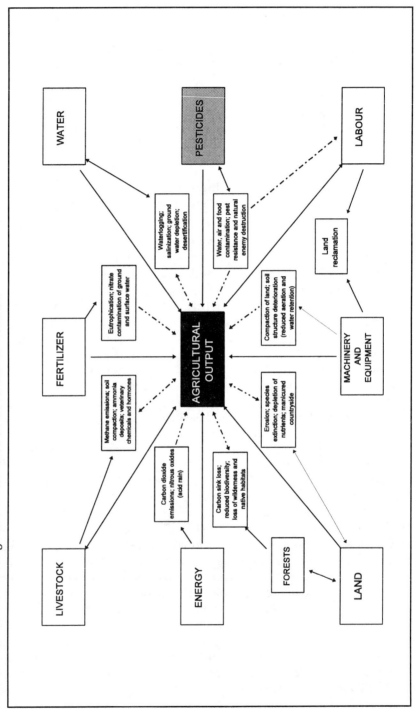

the extent of contamination of their soil, water, and air from the use of farm chemicals is even greater than Figure 11.4 suggests, relative to other countries. That is, the relocation of crop production from those densely populated protectionist countries to the rest of the world would cause a much larger reduction in degradation in the former compared with any increased degradation in the latter, where chemical use would expand from a low base and to still modest levels.

Figure 11.5 summarizes these effects by depicting the market for farm chemicals in the two regions, where for diagrammatic simplicity it is assumed *laissez faire* operates in input markets. Suppose $P$ is the infinitely elastic supply price for these inputs in both regions, so $Sp$ and $Sp'$ are the

**FIGURE 11.2. Shares of Various Countries in Global Changes in Food Production.**

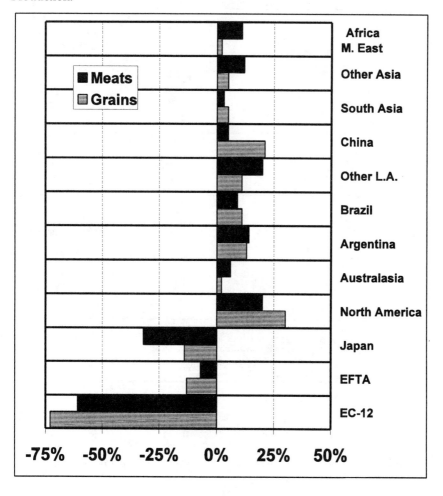

private supply curves; $Ss$ and $Ss'$ are the social marginal cost curves for using farm chemicals in the two regions (the divergence being larger in the more densely populated protectionist region); and $D$ and $D'$ are the input demand curves prior to output price subsidies/import barriers being reduced in the protectionist region. The reform reduces the demand for chemicals substantially in the reforming region, to $Dr$, while it expands the demand slightly in the rest of the world, thanks to higher international food prices, to either $Dr'$ or $Dr''$ (the difference in magnitudes of the shifts

**FIGURE 11.3.** Proportional Changes in Food Production of Various Countries Following Full Liberalization of Industrial Country Policies, 1990.

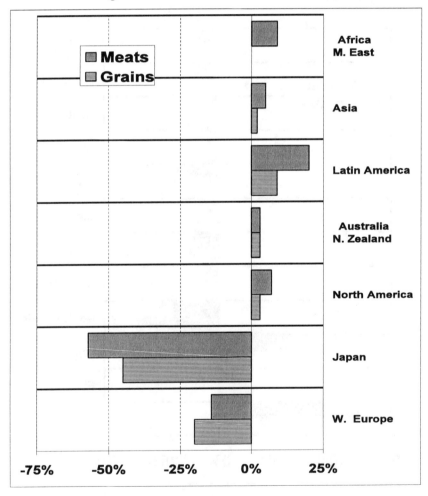

FIGURE 11.4. Relationship between Agricultural Producer Subsidy Equivalent (PSE) for 1979-89 and the Use of Chemicals and Pesticides per hectare of Arable and Pasture Land.

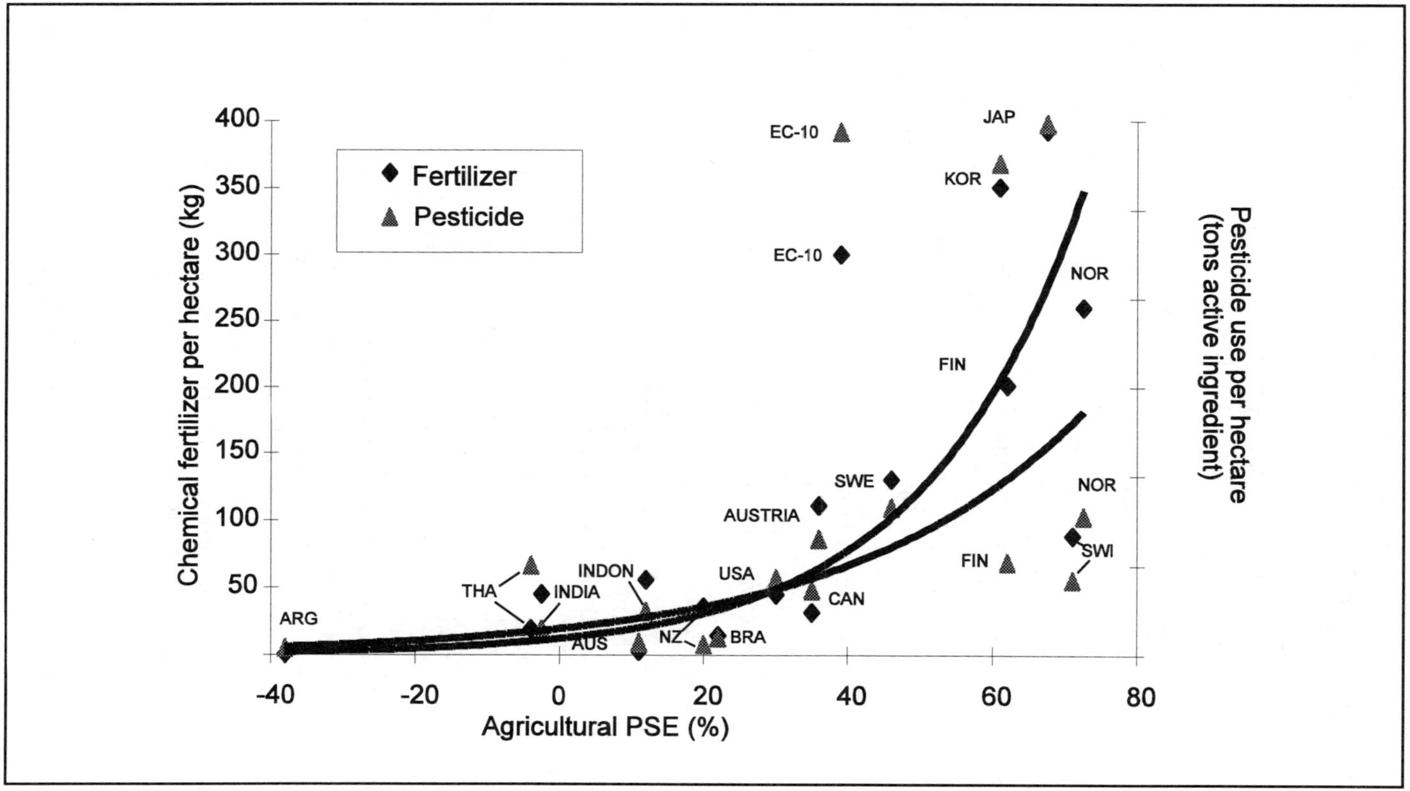

being suggested by the shape of the curve in Figure 11.4). In the absence of any environmental taxes, the economic welfare cost of the externality associated with farm chemicals in the protectionist region, net of the economic benefit of using the chemicals, would be area *abc* prior to reform, but only *def* after the reform. By contrast, if $D'$ crossed the $Sp'$ line to the left of $z$ in the non-protectionist region as shown, there would be no negative externality prior to reform abroad, nor would there be after the reform if $D'$ shifted to $Dr'$. And even if the reform shifted $D'$ as far to the right as $Dr''$, the environmental externality in the expanding region would involve a net cost of only area *hjk*, which would be small in comparison with the net cost foregone in the reforming region (of *abc-def*). Should the expanding region choose to introduce an optimal tax on farm chemical sales of *hm* per unit at the time of the food price rise following the reform abroad, it would suffer no net loss of welfare from expanding its use of farm chemicals. And if the protectionist region also introduced an optimal chemical tax (of *fg*) at the same time as it lowered its output price supports, the combined regions' economic welfare from chemical use would improve unambiguously by area *abc*. That is, if protagonists for trade liberalization and for environmental taxes were to successfully combine their efforts, the welfare benefits of reform would be amplified. Optimal environmental taxes would not remove all externalities from chemical use—the chemicals would still be imposing a cost represented by area *fgy* in the reforming region and area *hmz* in the expanding region—but they would ensure that at the margin the benefit to farmers from more chemical use just equaled the external cost to others.

What about the effect of trade policy reform on the use of inputs in the livestock sector? The relocation of meat and milk production from the most densely populated rich countries to relatively lightly populated and poorer countries would be associated with a decline in the extent to which the world's livestock is fed grain and supplements rather than pasture. With this would be a decline in the use of growth hormones and veterinary medicines, partly because animals are less valuable in less-protected economies and partly because the risk of diseases spreading is lower with range feeding than in intensively housed conditions. The greater use of less-intensive methods would reduce not only air, soil, and water contamination associated with the disposal of animal effluent, but also the chemical additives in the food produced. Moreover, insofar as this relocation leads to greater use of crop/leguminous pasture rotation methods, so there will be less need for chemical fertilizer and hence less water pollution from nitrates.

What about land degradation? In those rich countries where price supports are lowered and there are no land set-aside policies, land values would fall, which would probably further reduce the use of land substitutes such as farm chemicals, irrigation water, and feed concentrates. Much of that would happen immediately, but over time their use would fall even more as the land price decline reduced the incentive to seek land-saving technologies (Hayami and Ruttan 1985). The use of some land would switch to products whose prices had fallen little, such as the subset of fresh fruit and vegetables that are nontradable internationally because of high transport costs—products which may generate higher negative externalities than the previously produced ones. But other land might revert to recreational and other nonfarm uses, the positive externalities from which may well be more for nonfarmers than the aesthetic pleasure they derive from seeing the land being farmed.

Finally, what about land use in the nonsubsidizing countries where product prices would rise following reforms abroad? The lightly populated countries such as Argentina, Australia, and New Zealand, where most of the potential farming land is already cleared for agriculture, would see a more intensive use of that land, but from its current relatively low base. In tropical countries, some land may be attracted from plantation areas (causing more or less degradation), but conservationists are concerned that more tropical forests would be felled. How much so is an empirical question about which there is relatively little evidence at present. It is worth noting, however, that during the period 1950-90, world cereal production increased 185 percent, but the area of land devoted to cereal growing increased only 10 percent (Mitchell and Ingco 1993); elasticity of land area to farm product prices is estimated to be no more than 0.6 in the country of major concern, namely Brazil (Lopes 1977); and since international food prices are expected to be less than 1 percent higher each year as a consequence of the Uruguay Round, the annual expansion in the area used for farming in Brazil would at most be only a small fraction of 1 percent.

## Improved Modeling of the Environmental Effects of Policy Reform: Some Conceptual Issues

The above changes in the use of land and other farm inputs would not be a problem if private property rights were well established, full information was available on the environmental effects of production changes, and optimal environmental changes were in place where externalities existed that could not be resolved between private parties à la Coase (1960). The first priority of environmentalists therefore should be to encourage the establishment of the above conditions. If such efforts were made at the time of the trade liberalization, the benefits from reform would be even greater (as shown above in the discussion of Figure 11.5).

FIGURE 11.5 The Market for Farm Chemicals in a Reforming Protectionist Region and an Expanding Non-Protectionist Region.

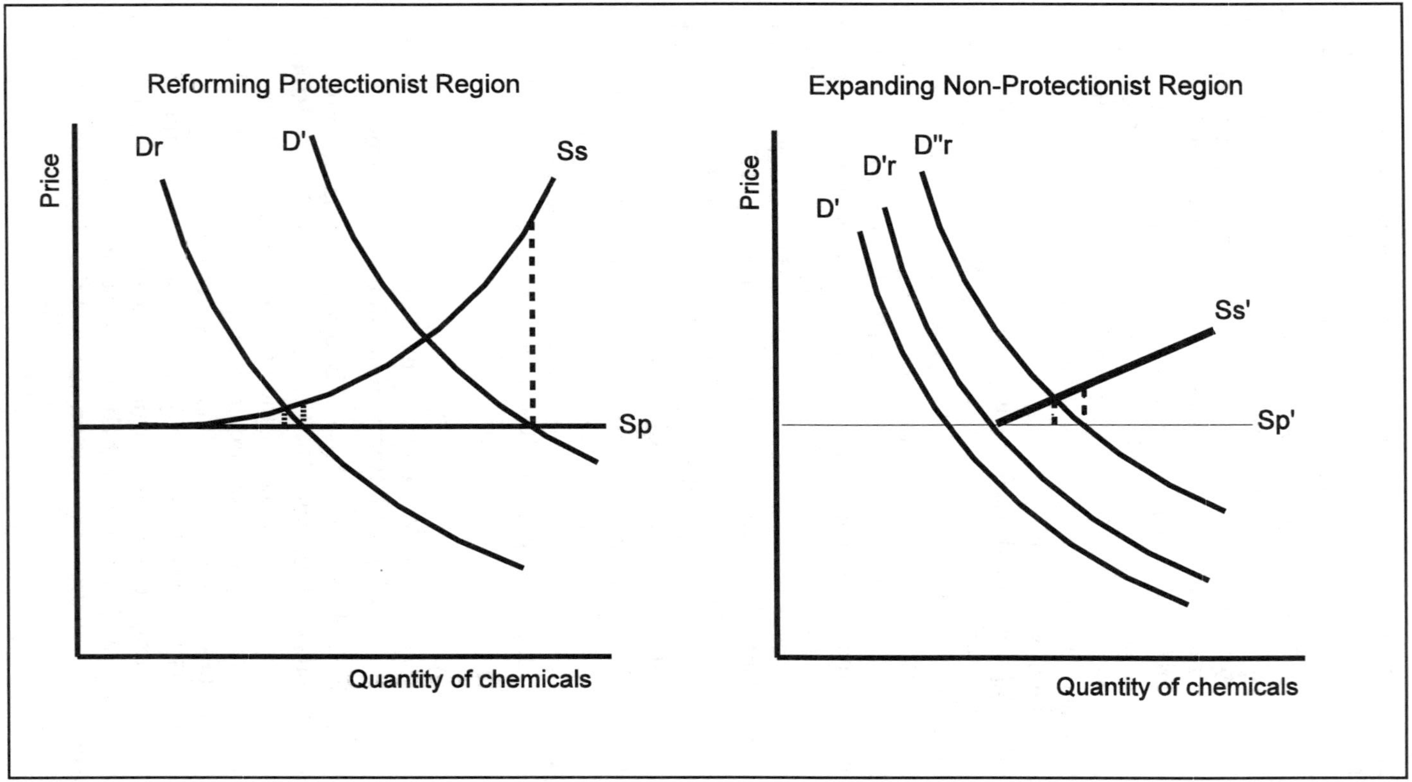

However, where that is not possible (e.g., because the damage is being done in another country with lower standards of environmental preservation and outside one's sphere of influence), it is understandable that people wish to know what the environmental costs of income-raising trade liberalization might be.

Clearly, the above model results provide only a crude beginning to an understanding of the environmental effects of trade liberalization. There are numerous directions in which modelers could go to improve that understanding at national and global levels. Even though the environmental data needed for such modeling is still scarce, explicit modeling can be useful in testing hypotheses about the relative importance of different relationships and parameter values, which will help direct the search toward the most critical environmental information needed. At a conceptual level, three types of extension for current models are discussed below by way of illustration, before turning to some practical challenges for those wishing to move ahead.

### *National Environmental/Resource Use Models*

Any country concerned about just the national environmental effects of trade liberalization could take the estimated effects of that reform on national farm production levels from an existing global trade model, and plug them into an environmental model for their country. That environmental model might relate output changes to input changes (using, e.g., input demand and supply functions) and input changes to environmental changes (using, e.g., damage functions). Once the environmental changes are quantified, market prices could then be used to obtain an estimate of the economic cost of those changes. For example, if wheat yields are expected to fall 5 percent because of extra soil erosion, then this direct cost can be calculated using the price of wheat (to which would need to be added any aesthetic value associated with the erosion and any off-site damage such as extra silting of irrigation systems). These could then be included with the other economic effects of trade liberalization to obtain a more complete estimate of the reform's consequences for real national income.

### *Adding Input Markets and Damage Functions to Models of National and Global Food Markets*

The above may be cost-effective if such environmental models already existed, but it would have only limited value because of the absence of feedback effects. A more promising approach might be to take an existing multi-commodity economic model of food markets and explicitly incorporate markets for farm inputs, equations for environmental damage, and shadow prices associated with that damage.

This approach would have several advantages over using just an environmental model on its own and treating the production changes as exogenous. First, in principle at least, it could incorporate the environmental effects in a way that enabled an economic welfare evaluation of them alongside the conventional welfare measures of the economic gains and losses from trade liberalization (or any other policy or market changes).

Second, where environmental damage from using an input to produce one agricultural product affects the resource base and inputs for, or production of, another farm product, that relationship could be included explicitly in this economic/environmental model.

Third, such a model would allow the incorporation of input price and other environmental policies and their integration with the usual output price and trade policies (see Just and Antle 1990). If (a big "if") endogenous policy equations were included to link environmental effects to input/environmental policies, which in turn had feedback effects on production, the consequences for the environment would be more accurately estimated. Typically, the estimates of the adverse environmental effects would be smaller (and aggregate economic welfare gains from trade liberalization greater) the more responsive are input/environmental policies to changes in environmental damage. For example, trade reform abroad might stimulate Asian developing countries to raise the price of farm chemicals by imposing or raising a tax on their use for reasons to do with greater off-site environmental damage as a result of output expansion. Farmers there might then be more inclined to adopt a crop rotation that involved a nitrogen-fixing legume such as soybeans after every one or two rice crops. Similarly, if water use were to be priced more appropriately, this too would encourage a switching away from the most water-intensive crops such as rice (Pingali and Rosegrant 1993). The consequences for the relative prices and quantities traded internationally of rice, soybean, and related products could be traced through with a global multi-commodity simulation model.

Fourth, insofar as consumers begin to pay significantly more for foods perceived to have fewer chemical residues (whether because of chemicals used in producing crops, in feeding animals, or in irradiating fresh produce after harvesting), so the model could be expanded to allow for products to be differentiated according to their exposure to chemicals. It might also be able to be used incidentally to evaluate the likely returns from investments in promoting foods with low chemical residues.

And finally, a model with both the input and output markets included would be better able to assess the economic and environmental effects of imminent or prospective new technologies that might be induced by trade liberalization. The use of open-economy models for evaluating agricultural research investments to assist in research priority setting is gradually expanding (see Alston, Norton, and Pardey 1994), and this tendency would strengthen if environmental effects were incorporated explicitly in such models, given that agricultural scientists are now directing much of their research towards the production of environmentally friendlier technologies (Ruttan 1991, 1994). Such *ex ante* research evaluation could be important because further subsidization of basic research to boost the production of new technologies may be a cheaper way for society to reduce environmental degradation than adding environmental damage taxes, particularly given that in most countries agricultural research is in any case grossly underfunded (Huffman and Evenson, 1993).

## Adding Damage Functions to National and Global CGE Models

The models of global food markets [e.g., the U.S. Department of Agriculture's (USDA's) SWOPSIM, the Organization for Economic Cooperation and Development's (OECD's) Mandate model, and the Tyers/Anderson model] are partial equilibrium in the sense that they typically do not include nonfood tradable agricultural goods, nontradable foods, forest products, energy, and the catch-alls of other tradables and other nontradables. It would not be difficult, again at least in principle, to add those other sectors to convert such models into general equilibrium ones. Their inclusion would add considerably to evaluating the environmental as well as economic effects of trade reform. For example, including forest products would help because agriculture competes with forests for land. This is particularly critical in tropical countries where there are still large areas of forest, and those forests are valued not only nationally but also as part of the global commons for their services as absorbers of carbon dioxide, providers of pristine wilderness, and sources of biodiversity.

The inclusion also of fruits and vegetables would be useful if one wanted to focus not just on environmental but also on food safety issues. There are at least four reasons for their inclusion: (1) even though they are not traded much (and then mainly as processed goods with a large share of nonfarm value added), fruits and vegetables are very significant contributors to the gross value of farm production; (2) they compete with tradable farm products for land, water, and other farm inputs; (3) they use those inputs very intensively, and so contribute disproportionately to environmental problems; and (4) being to a considerable extent nontradable, their prices would change less than those for tradable foods following farm trade liberalization, and so their production could expand considerably. With such goods included in sufficiently differentiated form, it would be possible also to evaluate the tradeoff for consumers in a densely populated country, where farmland is relatively expensive and so chemicals are used intensively, between consuming (1) fresh domestic produce that did not require post-harvest irradiation (because it was grown close to its market) but required heavy pesticide application during its growth; and (2) imported produce, grown in countries with lower land prices and hence with less use of farm chemicals, but which requires processing to be tradable (UHT or powdered milk; canned, frozen, or dried fruits and vegetables; irradiated "fresh" fruits, etc.).

An alternative to converting multi-commodity partial equilibrium models of farm trade into CGE models is to modify existing general equilibrium models used for trade liberalization simulations. Since these typically have input markets already included, they could be simply expanded to include environmental damage functions. They could be national or global. An early example of the simplest national model useful for this purpose is provided by Tobey and Reinert (1991), although it has only one agricultural industry and one (agricultural) environmental damage function. Another CGE model, for an archetypical developing Asian country, has two agricultural regions (upland and lowland), but only one other (tradable manufacturing) sector and no damage functions; it simply infers land degradation changes from the switching in the use of upland between food and tree crop production (Coxhead and Jayasuriya 1994a, b). Beghin et al. (1994) provide an algebraic prototype national CGE to be used in a project at the Paris OECD Development Centre, building on an earlier study of Indonesia and Japan (Lee and Roland-Holst 1993). While that work will focus on the emission of industrial pollution and at present is limited to specifying emissions (from manufacturing only) simply as proportional to output, scope exists for adding environmental damage functions for agriculture and other sectors.

Two global CGEs used to analyze the economic effects of agricultural trade liberalization that might be modified to also evaluate some environmental effects are the RUNS model of the World Bank/OECD Development Centre (see Goldin, Knudsen, and van der Mensbrugghe 1993) and the SALTER model developed in Australia and since modified and marketed as the GTAP model through Purdue University (see Jomini et al. 1991 and forthcoming; Hertel and Tsigas 1993). Likewise, the various global CGEs built to analyze global warming, which focus primarily on carbon emissions from burning fossil fuels, could be modified to include agriculture (and forestry and other sectors) more explicitly. Since agriculture and deforestation each contribute an estimated one-eighth of all greenhouse gases (World Resources Institute 1990), that extension also would enable such models to examine a wider range of options for alleviating any global warming than just taxing or otherwise reducing the use of fossil fuels.

One of the attractions of using a multi-sectoral CGE model instead of a partial equilibrium model of just agricultural markets is that it allows simulations of changes in nonagricultural policies and markets. This is important in the case of simulating Uruguay Round-type agreements, for example, since by their very nature those agreements involve reforms to policies affecting *all* sectors. It may well be that while a reform to agricultural policies alone might worsen a particular country's rural environment, the additional reduction in trade barriers in nonagricultural markets at home and abroad may have positive environmental effects that are more than offsetting (or vice versa). Even if nonagricultural policies remained unchanged, it is still an advantage to have damage functions for nonagricultural activities included in the model. This is because an expansion in farm production might cause some environmental damage, but the resources required for that expansion would have otherwise been employed in nonagricultural production that might have caused greater environmental damage. And since there are now CGE models available with considerable agricultural detail, and also models with decades-long dynamic modes (used for global warming experiments), these reasons for previously not using CGE models are now less compelling.

Even so, there are still some tradeoffs to be made in choosing between partial and general equilibrium models. Since the former are simpler, they are still able to more easily include greater commodity detail and dynamics. Also, they use supply and demand elasticities rather than elasticities of substitution and transformation, and there are much better estimates of the former than the latter. Since the required environmental damage functions for agriculture are likely to be available only at a rather disaggregated level, they will be more easily incorporated into multi-commodity agricultural models than more aggregated CGE models. The likelihood is, therefore, that both types of models will continue to be used, according to the types of issues to be analyzed and preferences of the analysts.

## Improved Modeling of the Environmental Effects of Policy Reform: Some Practical Issues

Those engaged in the economic modeling of agricultural trade liberalization were well aware of the considerable complexities involved in performing that task empirically, even before the Uruguay Round neared its conclusion. Now that the Round has concluded with an agricultural agreement, the real-world complexities of representing the *actual* policy changes to be implemented loom even larger. This is particularly so because of the uncertainty over the nature and extent of policy reinstrumentation to be undertaken over the rest of the 1990s (Tangermann 1994; Anderson 1994a, b). It will be especially important to model well the reinstrumentation towards production-limiting policies such as cropland set-asides and livestock quotas. Those instruments are likely to be used much more in conjunction with domestic price supports now that such supports—when and only when coupled with the production-limiting policies—are to be excluded in the calculation of the Aggregate Measure of Support to be reduced under the Uruguay Round agreement (see Josling et al. 1994). Does it make sense, then, to be thinking about further complicating the empirical modeling task at this time by adding an environmental dimension to conventional economic models, particularly if, as Whalley's (1994) survey suggests, the estimated economic welfare consequences of the environmental effects turn out to be small?

We believe the answer is yes, not least because, (1) the policy debate will increasingly demand informed answers to questions about the environmental effects of international trade/integration agreements; and (2) the environmental-economic interactions are too complex for adequate answers to be forthcoming *without* formal modeling. But we believe also, given the paucity of data on the environmental side, that only modest environmental modules will be appropriate until much more progress is made in estimating environmental damage functions.

So, how do we proceed? The first step has already begun to be taken: that is, simply to use existing models to generate the effects of trade reform on production, and if possible also on input use, and to infer environmental effects in a qualitative sense from those estimated production and input changes. A second step is to try to estimate physical damage functions and include them in the economic models, to get quantitative measures of the environmental effects. As Smith (1992) and others have made abundantly clear, even this step is no trivial exercise. In particular, the problems of aggregating up from very micro environmental studies are considerable (Antle and Crissman 1994). There is a great deal of scope for economists to work more closely with agricultural and other scientists to improve our understanding of the physical relationships in ways that make them usable in economic models.

Third, where the damage involves more than a change in the effective (quality adjusted) quantity of the modeled producers' available inputs and resource base (e.g., some off-site damage to other industries or consumers and perhaps aesthetic loss as well), a further step requires obtaining a shadow price for that additional damage or a Hicksian estimate of the willingness to pay to avoid that damage. This is needed so the welfare cost of that damage can be included in the estimate of the real income effect of the policy change. We know only too well how difficult it is to obtain such valuations even in a national setting; it will be far more difficult when one's focus is broadened to global environmental damage, even from the viewpoint of just one country's nationals. Thus it will be a long time before this third step is taken confidently. But, meanwhile, it would be possible to at least present the evaluation of the conventional gains to producer and consumer incomes from trade liberalization and any estimated environmental damage, and leave it to policy makers to judge whether the income gains more than compensate for the expected environmental changes.

## Conclusions

The profession has before it a fascinating area for further conceptual and empirical research and subsequent policy analysis. The directions in which it might go are numerous. They will be complemented and partly directed by (as well as simultaneously influencing) micro studies by multi-disciplinary teams of economists and agricultural and other scientists focusing on the agro-environment in various settings. True, the complexity of the models required for this research will be significantly greater than those used for *ex ante* evaluations of the Uruguay Round in the 1980s. Fortunately, though, we have substantial stocks of knowledge and models on which to build. Moreover, for *ex post* evaluations of even just the conventional economic effects of the Uruguay Round, the existing models need to be improved in any case to include input markets well enough to incorporate and evaluate better the production-limiting programs such as land set-asides and livestock quotas, given that such programs are going to be used more as a consequence of the Round. That improvement to our models alone will take us down the path of understanding better some of the environmental effects of policy changes. And, of course, once environmental policies are built into the models as well, they can also be used in reverse; i.e., to simulate the trade effects of environmental policy changes, as called for by the Commission on Sustainable Development (1994). Indeed, that may turn out to be just as important as analyses of the environmental effects of trade reform, especially if trade reforms prompt the improvement in domestic environmental policies so that the latter issue gradually dwindles in importance relative to the former.

## References

Alston, J.M., G.W. Norton, and P.G. Pardey. *Science Under Scarcity: Principles and Practice for Agricultural Research Evaluation and Priority Setting.* Ithaca, NY: Cornell University Press, 1994.

Anderson, K. "Agricultural Policies, Land Use, and the Environment." The 14th Denman Lecture, Granta Editions, University of Cambridge, Cambridge, 1992a.

_____. "Agricultural Policies and the New World Trading System." In *The New World Trading System*, G. Raby, ed. Paris: Organization for Economic Cooperation and Development (OECD), 1994a.

_____. "Agricultural Trade Liberalisation and the Environment: A Global Perspective." *The World Economy* 15(1992b):153–71.

_____. "Multilateral Trade Negotiations, European Integration, and Farm Policy Reform." *Economic Policy* 18(1994b):13–52.

Anderson, K., and R. Blackhurst, eds. *The Greening of World Trade Issues*. Ann Arbor, MI: University of Michigan Press (and London: Harvester Wheatsheaf), 1992.

Antle, J., and C. Crissman. "Empirical Foundations for Environment-Trade Linkages: Implications of an Andean Study." Paper presented to the International Agricultural Trade Research Consortium (IATRC) conference on "Trade and the Environment: Understanding and Measuring the Critical Linkages," Toronto, 17-18 June 1994.

Ballenger, N., and B. Krissoff. "Environmental Side Agreements: Will They Take Center Stage?" Paper presented to the International Agricultural Trade Research Consortium (IATRC) conference on "Trade and the Environment: Understanding and Measuring the Critical Linkages," Toronto, 17-18 June 1994.

Beghin, J., S. Dessus, D. Roland-Holst, and D. van der Mensbrugghe. "Prototype CGE Model for the Trade and Environment Programme: Technical Specification." OECD Development Centre, Organization for Economic Cooperation and Development, Paris, 1994.

Bhagwati, J.N. "The Generalized Theory of Distortions and Welfare." In *Trade Balance of Payments, and Growth: Papers in International Economics in Honor of Charles P. Kindleberger*, J.N. Bhagwati, R.W. Jones, R.A. Mundel, and J. Vanek, eds. Amsterdam: North-Holland, 1971.

Coase, R.H. "The Problem of Social Cost." *Journal of Law and Economics* 3(1960):1–44.

Commission on Sustainable Development. "Draft Decision on Trade, Environment, and Sustainable Development." Mimeo, Second Meeting of the CSD, Geneva, 16-31 May 1994.

Coxhead, I., and S. Jayasuriya. "Technical Change in Agriculture and Land Degradation in Developing Countries: A General Equilibrium Analysis." *Land Economics* 70(1994a):20–37.

_____. "Trade and Tax Policy Reform and the Environment: The Economics of Soil Erosion in Developing Countries." Paper presented at the annual meeting of the Australian Agricultural Economic Society, Wellington, New Zealand, 8-10 February 1994b.

Dean, J.M. "Trade and the Environment: A Survey of the Literature." In *International Trade and the Environment*, P. Low, ed. Discussion Paper No. 159. Washington, DC: The World Bank, 1992.

Goldin, I., O. Knudsen, and D. van der Mensbrugghe. *Trade Liberalisation: Global Economic Implications*. Paris: Organization for Economic Cooperation and Development (OECD), 1993.

Grossman, G.M. "Pollution and Growth: What Do We Know?" In *The Economics of Sustainable Development*, I. Goldin and L.A. Winters, eds. Cambridge: Cambridge University Press, 1994.

Hayami, Y., and V.W. Ruttan. *Agricultural Development: An International Perspective,* revised ed. Baltimore: Johns Hopkins University Press, 1985.

Hertel, T.W., and M.E. Tsigas. "GTAP Model Documentation." In *Handbook for the Short Course on Global Trade Analysis.* Department of Agricultural Economics, Purdue University, West Lafayette, IN, 1993.

Huffman, W., and R.E. Evenson. *Science for Agriculture.* Ames, IA: Iowa State University Press, 1993.

Jomini, P., J.F. Zeitsch, R. McDougall, A. Welsh, S. Brown, J. Hambley, and P. Kelly. *SALTER: A General Equilibrium Model of the World Economy.* Canberra, Australia: Industry Commission, 1991.

————. *The SALTER Model of the World Economy.* Canberra, Australia: Industry Commission, 1994.

Josling, T., M. Honma, J. Lee, D. MacLaren, B. Miner, D. Sumner, S. Tangermann, and A. Valdes. "The Uruguay Round Agreement on Agriculture: An Evaluation of the Outcome of the Negotiations." IATRC Commissioned Paper No. 9, International Agricultural Trade Research Consortium, Stanford, 1994.

Just, R.E., and J.M. Antle. "Interactions Between Agricultural and Environmental Policies: A Conceptual Framework." *The American Economic Review* 80(1990): 197–202.

Lee, H., and D. Roland-Holst. "International Trade and the Transfer of Environmental Costs and Benefits." OECD Development Centre Technical Paper No. 91, Organization for Economic Cooperation and Development, Paris, 1993.

Lopes, M. "The Mobilization of Resources from Agriculture: A Policy Analysis for Brazil." Ph.D. dissertation, Purdue University, West Lafayette, IN, 1977.

Mitchell, D.O., and M.D. Ingco. *The World Food Outlook.* Washington, DC: The World Bank, 1993.

Pingali, P.L., and M.W. Rosegrant. "Confronting the Environmental Consequences of the Green Revolution in Asia." Paper presented to the American Agricultural Economics Association pre-conference workshop on "Post-Green Revolution Agricultural Development Strategies in the Third World." Mimeo, International Food Policy Research Institute (IFPRI), Washington, DC, 1993.

Powell, A.A. "Integrating Econometric and Environmetric Modelling." General Paper No. G-102, Centre of Policy Studies and the Impact Project, Melbourne, Australia, 1993.

Radetzki, M. "Economic Growth and Environment." In *International Trade and the Environment,* P. Low, ed. Discussion Paper No. 159. Washington, DC: The World Bank, 1992.

Ruttan, V.W. "Challenges to Agricultural Research in the 21st Century." In *Agricultural Research Policy: International Quantitative Perspectives,* P.G. Pardey, J. Roseboom, and J.R. Anderson, eds. Cambridge: Cambridge University Press, 1991.

Ruttan, V.W., ed. *Agriculture, Environment, and Health: Sustainable Development in the 21st Century.* Minneapolis, MN: University of Minnesota Press, 1994.

Smith, V.K. "Environmental Costing for Agriculture: Will It Be Standard Fare in the Farm Bill of 2000?" *American Journal of Agricultural Economics* 7 4(1992):1076–88.

Tangermann, S. "An Assessment of the Uruguay Round Agreement on Agriculture." First draft of paper prepared for the Directorate for Food, Agriculture, and Fisheries, Organization for Economic Cooperation and Development (OECD), Paris, 4 April 1994.

Tobey, J.A., and K.A. Reinert. "The Effects of Domestic Agricultural Policy Reform on Environmental Quality." *Journal of Agricultural Economics Research* 43(1991):20–28.

Tyers, R., and K. Anderson. *Disarray in World Food Markets: A Quantitative Assessment.* Cambridge: Cambridge University Press, 1992.

Whalley, J. "Quantifying Trade and Environment Linkages Through Economy-Wide Modelling." Paper presented to the International Agricultural Trade Research Consortium (IATRC) conference on "Trade and the Environment: Understanding and Measuring the Critical Linkages," Toronto, 17-18 June 1994.

World Resources Institute. *World Resources 1990-91.* New York: Oxford University Press, 1990.

# 12

# Empirical Foundations for Environment-Trade Linkages: Implications of an Andean Study

*John M. Antle, Charles C. Crissman,*
*R. Jeff Wagenet, and John L. Hutson*

## Introduction

The Rio Summit, the Uruguay Round of the GATT negotiations, and NAFTA have all brought attention to the issue of trade and the environment. Will the movement toward trade and domestic policy liberalization in agriculture lead to environmental degradation? The location-specific nature of the interactions between agricultural production and the environment, as well as the changes in the intensity and location of production brought about by policy liberalization, suggest that the answer to this question is to be found in careful empirical research, not in stylized generalities. This study proposes a methodology for quantifying the economic and environmental impacts of trade and related policies in agriculture that accounts for the location-specific relationships between agricultural production and the environment, and illustrates this methodology in an Andean case study.

Neoclassical trade theory and its generalizations provide a link from trade to natural resource utilization in the aggregate (Kemp and Long 1984). There is also a theoretical literature that specifically addresses the linkages from agricultural and environmental policy, through the behavior of farm firms, to environmental quality (Hochman and Zilberman 1978; Antle and Just 1992). This literature demonstrates that changes in price, technology, or policy can alter patterns of production and resource utilization that may have environmental impacts. Viewed from this perspective, the existing conceptual framework that has been developed to understand linkages between domestic policies and environmental quality can be used to understand the linkages between trade and the environment. The features of the policies may differ, but the basic economic relationships do not.

What is different about the discussion of trade and the environment from other discussions of the environmental impacts of agriculture is the unit of analysis. Trade policy analysis and quantitative modeling typically are conducted at the national level, using constructs such as the representative producer and consumer, and changes in production and resource utilization are predicted at the national level. While this level of aggregation may be useful for general equilibrium analysis, it is not useful for analysis of the environmental impacts of these changes because the processes that govern environmental impact are location specific. Consequently, constructs analogous to the representative producer and consumer do not exist and are not considered useful in the physical and environmental sciences. For example, in the analysis of the impacts of pesticide use on groundwater quality, soil scientists do not use a representative soil to predict leaching of a pesticide into the groundwater of a large geographic region. Rather, soil scientists disaggregate the region into units of analysis with recognized soil types and other geophysical characteristics, and estimate leaching for each of these units. The only circumstances under which the leaching at each site could be meaningfully aggregated would be if water from a number of sites fed a common aquifer or if flows from groundwater fed a common body of surface water. From the perspective of trade policy analysis, however, environmental data at this level of disaggregation are of limited usefulness. Clearly, some way of aggregating environmental impact information is needed.

This chapter begins to address the problem of providing scientifically valid empirical foundations to analysis of the aggregate environmental impacts of policy changes, such as trade liberalization. Our approach is to define a common unit of measurement that can be used by the relevant scientific disciplines, including economics, to obtain valid predictions of the impacts of policy change. In the case of many agricultural applications, the unit of analysis is a farmer's field where a crop is produced. By describing the populations of these units in statistical terms, and estimating impacts on each unit, it is then possible to statistically aggregate impacts to a level useful for policy analysis. In cases where it is not meaningful to characterize environmental impact using summary statistics such as the population mean, it is possible to describe impacts in probabilistic terms, e.g., as the change in the probability that a contaminant exceeds some level of concentration in air, soil, or water. It is then possible to define aggregate tradeoffs between economic and environmental outcomes in the form of a transformation frontier that is analogous to a production possibilities frontier. This transformation frontier can be used in aggregate analyses of trade policy impacts.

The next section of the chapter outlines the conceptual framework at the disaggregate level where the relevant scientific disciplines can be integrated, and then describes the problems that arise in statistical aggregation for policy analysis. The remainder of the chapter illustrates the use of the approach in a case study of the effects of trade liberalization on pesticide use in the Andean region. The chapter concludes with some observations about the data needed to develop the empirical foundations for environment-trade linkages.

## Disciplinary Integration, Aggregation, and Policy Analysis

Figure 12.1 provides an overview of the conceptual framework for disciplinary integration and policy analysis developed by Antle and Just (1991). The upper part of the figure pertains to the analysis of a unit of land at the farm level. Prevailing market prices, policies, and the physical attributes of land affect farmers' management decisions in terms of both land use and input use. These decisions affect agricultural production, but also may affect the environment and human health through two distinct but interrelated mechanisms. Decisions at the extensive margin determine which particular acres of cropland are put into production. Management decisions at the intensive margin determine the application rates of chemicals, water use, and tillage practices. Physical relationships between the environmental attributes of the land in production and management practices then jointly determine the agricultural output, environmental impacts, and health impacts associated with a particular unit of land in production. Thus, the land use and input use decisions of farmers form the linkage between policy and environmental and health consequences.

Each unit of land in production has environmental and management characteristics that are functions of prices, policies, technologies and other farm-specific characteristics. As the lower part of Figure 12.1 indicates, the distribution of farm and environmental characteristics induces a joint distribution of input use, outputs, and environmental impacts. This joint distribution provides the basis for aggregation of the field-specific characteristics. These aggregate values can be utilized in welfare and policy analyses.

The construction of the disaggregate model begins by defining a population of land units (referred to henceforth as a field) in relation to an environmentally meaningful geographical unit, such as an aquifer or

**FIGURE 12.1. Conceptual Framework.**

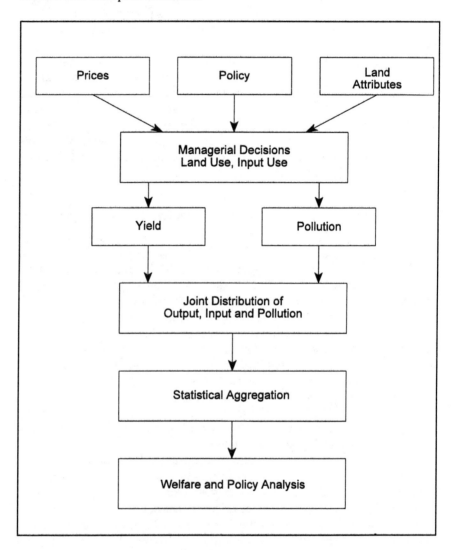

*Source*: Antle and Just (1991).

watershed. Environmental impact is represented with a stylized physical model:

$$z_{jt} = z(x_{jt}, \omega_j, \epsilon_{jt}),\qquad(1)$$

where $x_{jt}$ is a vector of management actions taken on the *j*th field at time *t*, $\epsilon_{jt}$ is a random term representing the effects of weather and climatic variation, and $z_{jt}$ is the environmental impact measured in physical terms per unit of land (e.g., per square meter). The function $z(x, \omega, \epsilon)$ is assumed to be increasing in $x$, and may exhibit certain convexity properties, depending on the type of physical process involved.

The economic model is based on the allocation of land and other inputs to maximize expected economic returns (which may be adjusted for risk attitudes in a more general presentation). All farms produce with an identical technology (more generally, the technologies may be differentiated by measurable characteristics). In the production period, the $i$th farmer manages $n^i$ fields with environmental characteristics $\omega^i = (\omega_1^i, ..., \omega_n^i)$. The indicator function $\delta_{jk}^i$ is defined to be equal to one if field $j$ is in production of crop $k$, and equal to zero otherwise. Also, let $\delta_j^i = \Sigma_k \delta_{jk}^i$, and $\delta^i = (\delta_1^i, ..., \delta_n^i)$. The vector of physical attributes of land in production is then $\omega(\delta^i) = (\omega_1^i \delta_1^i, ..., \omega_n^i \delta_n^i)$. Letting the size of the $j$th field on the $i$th farm be $a_j^i$, total land in production on the $i$th farm is $\Sigma_j a_j^i \delta_j^i$.

Production of crop $k$ on field $j$ is defined by $q_{jk}^i = q_k(a_j^i, x_j^i, \omega_j^i, \epsilon_j^i)$, where, for simplicity, the production process is represented as static. As described below, it will more generally be defined as a dynamic process. By defining suitable probability distributions for the production disturbances $\epsilon$ and for prices, the $i$th farmer's management problem is to maximize expected returns by choosing $x^i = (x_1^i, ..., x_n^i)$ and $\delta_j^i$ subject to physical attributes $\omega^i$, and price, policy, and technology parameters $\phi$. The solution to this optimization problem gives the demand functions $x_j^i = x(\phi, \omega_j^i)$ and $\delta_j^i = \delta(\phi, \omega_j^i)$. Observe that these functions are discontinuous, but under reasonable conditions the discontinuity in $x$ occurs only when $\delta$ switches from one value to the other. Otherwise, $x$ is a conventional factor demand function.

The physical characteristics $\omega_j^i$ of fields are distributed in the population according to a distribution with parameter $\Theta$. This distribution induces a joint distribution of input use $x^i$ and land use $\delta^i$ in the population, $G(x, \delta \mid \phi, \Theta)$, for given policy parameters $\phi$ and for the given distribution of physical characteristics $\Theta$. This joint distribution in turn induces distributions of the physical characteristics of land in production, crop production, and environmental impact through the relationships defined above. Thus, farmers' production decisions generate a joint distribution of land use, input, output, and environmental impact associated with the population of fields in the region. From this joint distribution, corresponding conditional and marginal distributions can be derived for these variables that can be used in policy analysis. Of particular interest for policy analysis is the joint distribution of crop production and environmental impact, $F(q, z \mid \phi, \Theta)$. Using this joint distribution, it is possible to aggregate these outcomes for use in policy analysis.

The construction of an aggregate transformation frontier can proceed in a manner similar to the construction of a conventional production possibilities frontier. Following Stoker's (1982) analysis of statistical aggregation, and its application to production analysis by Antle (1986), aggregate quantities $X$ and $\Omega$ can be interpreted as mathematical expectations of the vectors $x$ and $\omega$ taken with respect to the distribution $G(x, \delta \mid \phi, \Theta)$. Moreover, an aggregate environmental impact function of the form $Z(X, \Omega; \phi, \Theta)$ can be derived from $G$ and the field-level function (1). Similarly, using the crop production functions defined above, it is possible to construct an aggregate output function $Q(A, X, \Omega; \phi, \Theta)$, where $A$ is total land in production. The notation used here is intended to convey Stoker's (1982) basic result that the aggregate functions are defined for given parameters of the distributions of the underlying disaggregate variables. Changes in the distributions brought about by changes in the price and policy parameter vector $\phi$, or by changes in the parameter vector $\Theta$ defining the distribution of physical characteristics in the population, induce changes in the aggregate relationships.

Two fundamental problems arise in the construction of the aggregate environmental impact function $Z(X, \Omega; \phi, \Theta)$. First, even at the field level, it is unclear how one aggregates the water quality effects of different types of chemicals. This problem could be solved if damage functions were available that expressed outcomes such as human health as a function of different types of chemical contamination. Second, as mentioned in the introduction, it is unclear whether an aggregate quantity concept is meaningful, as illustrated by the discussion of the spatial aggregation of pesticide leaching to infer regional water quality changes. One approach to resolve this problem is to interpret the variable $Z$ as a probability statement based on the distribution function $F$, and then use this distribution to infer changes in contamination risks.

Interpreting $Z$ as an indicator of environmental quality, so that social welfare is increasing in $Z$, the function $Z(X, \Omega; \phi, \Theta)$ should be decreasing in the elements of $X$. If the disaggregate function is defined so that $z$ is increasing in $\omega$, then $Z$ should be increasing in $\Omega$. The curvature properties of the field-level environmental impact function (1), and of the aggregate $Z$ function, however, are not generally known. According to economic theory, $Q$ is an increasing and concave function of $A$ and $X$. Therefore, the aggregate transformation function between $Z$ and $Q$ has a negative slope, but it is necessarily concave to the origin only if $Z$ is a concave function. Antle and Heidebrink (1994) argue that as environmental resource utilization rises, beyond some point its marginal productivity becomes negative, and therefore the slope of the transformation frontier between agricultural output and environmental quality becomes positive beyond some point, as illustrated in Figure 12.2. This reasoning suggests that the transformation frontier must be concave to the origin at least in a neighborhood around the point where the frontier is vertical.

The slope of the transformation frontier provides information about the opportunity cost of environmental quality in terms of forgone output. This opportunity cost reflects the degree of vulnerability of the environment to disruptions caused by production activities. This vulnerability depends on the factors embodied in the underlying distributions of physical characteristics of the land in production, the economic and technological characteristics of the farms, and the prices and policies faced by farmers. A key empirical research question is how these underlying conditions affect the environmental vulnerability and thus the slope of the transformation frontier.

Both the transformation frontier presented in Figure 12.2 and the neoclassical transformation frontier represent the changes in outputs that are generated by varying input use for a given technology. However, there is an important difference between the two constructs. The derivation of the neoclassical transformation frontier is based on a representative

FIGURE 12.2. Transformation Frontier for Agricultural Output and Environmental Services.

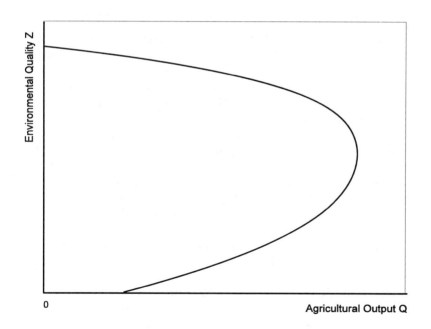

0

Environmental Quality Z

Agricultural Output Q

aggregate technology for each sector of the economy; the aggregation problem is ignored in the neoclassical derivation of the transformation frontier. In contrast, in the preceding derivation, each aggregate function, and thus each transformation frontier, is defined for given values of the parameter vectors $\phi$ (policy) and $\Theta$ (physical characteristics of land). Therefore, changes in policies that change relative prices in the economy induce movements along the frontier as input use changes, and also may induce changes in the position of the transformation frontier in the $(Q, Z)$ quadrant. Consequently, the distinction between movements along, and shifts in, the frontier may be ambiguous when policy changes occur.

In the short run, $\Theta$ is taken as given, but in analyses of long-term sustainability, $\Theta$ may be time-dependent and related to past production decisions (e.g., as in the case of soil degradation over time). These dynamic considerations also may complicate the distinction between movements along, and shifts in, the frontier.

Changes in technology with given prices and policy parameters clearly shift the frontier. Thinking in terms of the aggregate economy, the transformation frontier between $Q$ and $Z$ is a two-dimensional slice of a higher-dimensional transformation surface that includes other sectors' outputs. Intersectoral changes in resource utilization in response to trade liberalization or other policy changes also should shift the frontier.

## Trade and Economic Policy Changes in the Andean Region

The empirical analysis conducted in the following section is based on a case study of the environmental, health, and production impacts of pesticide use in potato production in Ecuador. Ecuador and other Andean countries are undergoing policy reforms, switching from protectionist, import-substituting policies toward that set of policies associated with trade and domestic policy liberalization.

Ecuador is classified as a lower-middle-income country by the World Bank and has a rapidly growing population of 10 million. It is about the size of the U.S. states of Georgia and Alabama combined, and is divided into three distinct geographic regions: the coastal plain, the sierra, and the Amazon. Population in the sierra is found in the series of inter-Andean valleys formed between the parallel ranges of the Andes.

In most of the sierra of Ecuador, the agricultural frontier has been closed. The inter-Andean valley bottoms were the traditional sites of agricultural production based on indentured labor on large farms. Valley sides were used as forest reserves or pasture. Agricultural reform broke up the large farms, with the less desirable land on valley sides going to the new class of small farmers. Rapid population growth and a low technology base resulted in area expansion, principally by moving up the valley sides onto marginal land. The result is large areas of sierra cropland under risk of environmental degradation (Southgate and Whitaker 1992). The large farms on the valley bottoms converted cropland to activities with lower labor intensity, typically pasture for dairy production. With the agricultural frontier closed, further growth in agricultural production must come from intensification of production through higher yields and shorter crop rotations.

Agricultural products are important exports for Ecuador. The traditional export crops—bananas, coffee, and cacao—are all from the coast. The principal sierra products of corn, beans, wheat, barley, potatoes, and dairy are typically for domestic consumption (Whitaker and Alzamora 1990). Though there are cross-border flows, food crops are lightly traded within the Andean region (Janssen et al. 1992). However, these patterns of regional trade are likely to change. Substantial investments in infrastructure have improved roads, reducing the isolation of sierra producers. In most locales, market information is disseminated rapidly by radio and by transporters and wholesalers.

The Andean Pact is a regional trade bloc that consists of the five tropical Andean countries: Venezuela, Colombia, Ecuador, Peru, and Bolivia. These countries, until recently, have followed the import-substituting industrialization policies common in Latin America, preventing effective economic integration. In this sense, Ecuador has been similar to many other countries in Latin America: successive governments utilized overvalued exchange rates, large fiscal deficits, price controls, subsidies to major sectors, restrictive tariffs, and nontariff barriers to trade in a matrix of inward-looking, protectionist policies. Examination of these policies shows a distinct bias against agriculture, in particular the nonexport agriculture sector (Scobie, Jardine, and Greene 1991; de Janvry, Sadoulet, and Fargeix 1991). Lee and Espinosa (1995) examined the effect of this policy matrix on agricultural pesticides and found an effective subsidy of 27 percent, mainly through the distorting effects of controlled exchange rates. Thus the Ecuadorian policy setting is similar to those of other lower-income countries documented by Schiff and Valdés (1992).

Recently, however, the Andean Pact established a process of trade reform, eliminating prohibitions and reducing tariffs and nontariff barriers on a host of products, including agricultural food crops (Ramos and Acosta 1991). The new Pact agreements, coupled with earlier reform efforts, have reduced some of the biases against sierra agriculture. Responding to an improved policy environment in Ecuador, sierra producers expanded the area of potatoes and wheat, and increased milk output, reversing downward production trends for these products and recapturing domestic markets (Whitaker and Alzamora 1990). In addition to recovering domestic markets, the regional trade reforms offer the opportunity for producers to sell into neighboring countries. Ramos and Acosta (1991) observe that relative to Peru and Colombia, Ecuadorian producers enjoy a comparative advantage in several sierra food crops.

Potato production in Ecuador is almost exclusively the domain of small farmers located on the sides of inter-Andean valleys. The data used in the case study were collected from a typical sierra potato/dairy production zone in Carchi Province in northern Ecuador, just on the Colombian border. Carchi recently has become the largest potato-producing province in Ecuador, reflecting a trend toward concentration of production in fewer locations. Improved roads reduced transportation costs to major markets and allowed production to move to more ecologically favorable areas (Crissman and Uquillas 1989). For the potato farmer, the fallow portion of the crop rotation is used as pasture for a mix of beef and dairy cows. Most milk in Ecuador is produced by large farmers in specialized dairies. Milk production for the small potato farmer is a supplementary activity for home consumption and occasional sale.

In addition to its ecological advantages, Carchi potato farmers tradition-ally have taken advantage of their frontier location to sell into both Colombian and Ecuadorian markets. Despite restrictive policies on trade, numerous observers have noted that there can be significant black- market flows of potatoes in either direction due to price differences in major markets (Barsky 1984; Crissman and Uquillas 1989). Ramos et al. (1993) examined the comparative advantage of potato production in Carchi compared to importing potatoes from the frontier market towns of Peru and Colombia. Confirming current market flows from Carchi into Peru and Colombia, in mid-1992 Carchi enjoyed a distinct comparative advantage in potato production. Trade reform will remove prohibitions on trade in potatoes, eliminating most of the transactions costs of the black market.

Potatoes are an important staple in Andean diets. Growth of potato production in Colombia has exceeded that of other Pact countries, mirroring its per capita income growth and rapidly expanding population. In addition to uses in the traditional diet, the growth of the fast-food industry has created a significant new market for potatoes in Colombia. The newly open Colombia market is thus expected to cause a significant shift in demand, putting upward pressure on Ecuadorian potato prices in the short to medium term.

Seasonality of production and lack of storage due to strong consumer preferences for a fresh product mean that potato prices cycle sharply in major urban markets in the region. Andean Pact government efforts to dampen price swings have universally failed, and presently there is no government intervention in the output market. With open access to both Colombian and Ecuadorian markets, Carchi producers can take advantage of different price cycles in their major markets, as illustrated in Figure 12.3. With options to send potatoes to the better markets, Carchi producers effectively reduce downside price risk, obtaining higher prices on average.

In addition to trade barriers, there are numerous government interventions in agricultural input and output markets. As mentioned above, an exception to the rule is the potato output market. An example of input market intervention is documented in a study of pesticide subsidies by Lee and Espinosa (1995), where a combination of overvalued exchange rates and price controls effectively lowered the price of pesticides to farmers. The removal of these subsidies can be expected to cause increases in pesticide prices.

In the output market, the case of milk contrasts with that of potatoes. All the Andean Pact countries are deficient in milk production, and all have milk price supports. In 1992, Colombian price supports were significantly higher than those of Ecuador, and mule trains taking black-market milk from Ecuador to Colombia were a common sight along the border. The support prices of the two countries are expected to converge. Whether those of Colombia will fall or those of Ecuador will rise is not

**FIGURE 12.3. Index of Monthly Potato Price in Cali and Quito.**

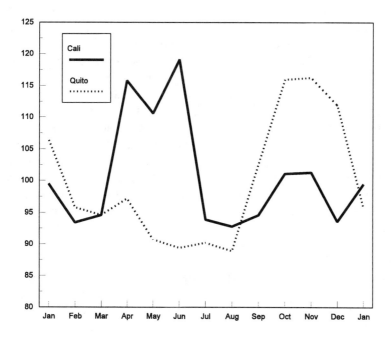

clear. Regardless, for the small potato farmer of Carchi, milk production is a minor farm activity, and the majority of any increased demand will be met by the specialized producers. Large Ecuadorian producers are rapidly improving milk yields, especially compared to the low-technology systems of smaller farmers.

## Trade Liberalization and the Environment:
## A Case Study of Pesticide Use in Ecuador

This section presents an analysis of the impacts of trade liberalization on agriculture and the environment using data obtained in a study of the economic, environmental, and health impacts of pesticide use in the potato production system of northern Ecuador. A complete description of this study is found in the book manuscript in preparation by Crissman, Antle, and Capalbo (1995). Following the approach described by Antle and Capalbo (1991), primary production data were used to estimate econometric models that represent the farmers' decisions on the extensive (crop choice) and intensive (input use) margins. These econometric models provided the parameters for construction of a stochastic simulation model of the production system, summarized in Figure 12.4. The outcomes of this economic simulation model then were input into a physical simulation model to estimate environmental impact, defined here in terms of the leaching of pesticides beyond the crop root zone (Hutson and Wagenet 1993; Wagenet, Hutson, and Ducrot 1995). These two simulation models provided the basis for construction of the distributions of land use, input use, environmental impact, and agricultural production that in turn allow the construction of the aggregate transformation frontier described above.

Potato production in the Carchi Province of northern Ecuador is concentrated in a highland zone 30 kilometers south of the Colombian border. Only half a degree north of the equator, production occurs in altitudes between 2,800 and 3,400 meters on steeply-sloped, deep volcanic soils. There are virtually no changes in day length, little seasonal temperature variation, and limited variation in rainfall. The cropping system is dominated by potatoes and pasture for dairy cattle. Because of the equatorial location and rainfall patterns, there are no distinct planting or harvesting seasons, virtually all recorded planting dates are on different days, evenly distributed throughout the months of the year. Conditions in Carchi are highly favorable to potato production, with farmers in the sample obtaining average yields of 22 metric tons (MT) per hectare (ha), as compared to a national average of 8 MT/ha and yields of around 30 MT/ha in the United States.

FIGURE 12.4. Integrated Economic/Physical Simulation Model.

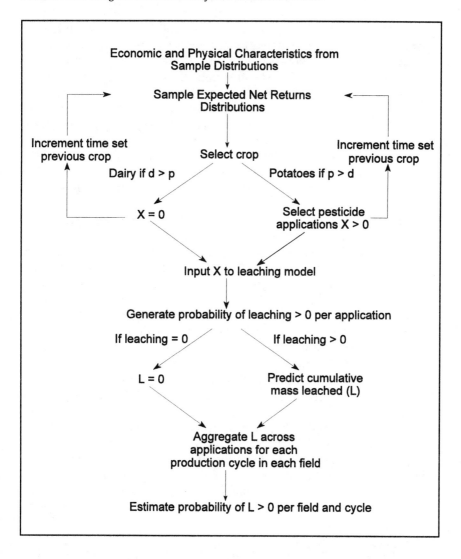

Production data were collected in a farm-level survey conducted in the Carchi region on 40 farms during 1990-92. Because crops are planted and harvested continuously throughout the calendar year, data were collected for parcels, where a parcel is defined as a single crop cycle on a farmer's field. Excluding pasture, a total of 490 parcels were registered, of which 338 were potato. From these, a total of 320 potato parcels were used in the estimation sample. The potato fields not used had incomplete harvest data due to the local practice of selling an unharvested field to third-party harvesters. The 320 parcels in the sample represent 178 different fields.

Detailed parcel-level production data were collected on a monthly basis. Potato production in Ecuador is management intensive, and there are as many as 20 distinct operations during the six-month crop cycle. Post-harvest farmer recall of detailed data on pesticide use is unlikely to be accurate. Thus, the investment in monthly visits was deemed essential to the success of the data collection effort. See Crissman and Espinosa (1992) for further details on sampling and data collection procedures.

Late blight fungus (*Phytophthora infestans*) is the principal disease, and the tuber-boring Andean weevil (*Premnotrypes vorax*) and several foliage-damaging insects are the principal pests affecting production. The control of these three threats requires distinct strategies relying primarily on chemical pesticides.

Late blight can be a devastating disease where, in a susceptible variety, entire fields can be destroyed overnight. Effective control relies on prevention. Most fungicides are contact type, killing the fungus encountered on the surface of the plant. These products typically are applied at prescribed intervals depending on the weather. During periods of rainy weather, the frequency of spraying increases as conditions for fungus development are better and the rain washes the fungicide off the foliage.

The data contain 1,881 observations on fungicide applications, where the unit of observation is a day when one or more fungicides were applied. Figure 12.5 illustrates the timing patterns of the individual applications during the production cycle. The data show that most fields were treated with fungicides at least four times. The dispersion in the timing of the applications reveals a wide range of pest management behavior that presumably reflects differing physical and economic conditions faced by farmers. The quantity data reveal that the amounts applied follow the development of the foliage, with average application amounts increasing through the first several sprays and then staying at about the same level for the remaining sprays. After plant senescence, foliage does not contribute to tuber development and farmers cease using fungicides.

### Construction of the Integrated Economic/Physical Simulation Model

The economic simulation model is built from four basic components. First, as illustrated in Figure 12.4, are the underlying distributions of economic and physical characteristics of the fields in the study watershed. The second component is the net returns distributions of the principal crops in the rotation (potatoes and milk). The net returns distribution for potatoes was estimated using restricted Cobb-Douglas revenue and cost functions, with input prices for variable inputs normalized by expected

**FIGURE 12.5. Timing of Fungicide Applications.**

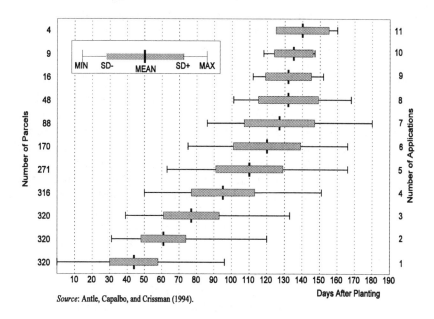

Source: Antle, Capalbo, and Crissman (1994).

output prices (labor, fertilizer, and pesticides), and with given field size and other physical characteristics. The net returns distribution for dairy was estimated as a log normal distribution. The third component of the simulation model is a system of dynamic factor demand equations for the three categories of pesticides used in potato production, as described in Antle, Capalbo, and Crissman (1994). The final component of the economic simulation model is a restricted revenue function used to predict the value of production, estimated with prices for labor and fertilizer inputs and with quantities of pesticides, land, and physical characteristics.

The leaching model is a simplified version of the LEACHM model designed by Hutson and Wagenet (1993). This is a detailed process model of pesticide leaching that was parameterized with soils and other physical data collected from the study area, and simulated with a 30-year series of weather data (rainfall and temperature). The distribution of cumulative leaching beyond the root zone was found to be positively skewed, with many observations at or near zero, but also with a long positive tail. This distribution was estimated using Heckman's two-stage econometric procedure for censored distributions, by defining a cutoff point below which all observations were interpreted as equal to zero, and above which all observations were interpreted as positive. The probit technique was used to estimate the probability that a positive amount of leaching occurred, as a function of weather and physical characteristics, and then the Heckman procedure was used to estimate a regression relating the quantity of leaching to weather and physical characteristics, corrected with the Mill's ratio for the probability of zero leaching.

### Results of the Simulation Analysis of Trade Liberalization

As described in the previous section, trade liberalization would be expected to have two significant impacts on the commercial potato production regions of Ecuador. First, it is estimated that elimination of exchange rate distortions would indirectly increase the price of pesticides, an imported good, by approximately 30 percent. Second, the price of potatoes relative to dairy products would rise, although quantitative estimates of the magnitude of this effect are not available. Therefore, to represent the possible effects of trade liberalization on the potato/dairy production system, three policy scenarios were used relative to the status quo: an increase in pesticide prices, referred to here as a tax on pesticides, ranging from 0 to 90 percent; a potato price increase, referred to here as an output price subsidy, ranging from 0 to 90 percent; and a pesticide tax of 30 percent, with a potato price subsidy ranging from 0 to 90 percent. Forty fields were sampled for each of the three policy scenarios and the four policy settings (status quo and changes of 30, 60, and 90 percent) in each scenario. Each field was simulated for 10 production cycles (a cycle is one crop from planting to harvest). Each policy setting was replicated four times. The model thus produced 1,600 observations for each policy setting. These 1,600 observations form a marginal distribution of outcomes for the variables of interest. The model produces distributions for total pesticide quantity applied to a field, total number of pesticide applications, pesticide leaching, and crop revenue.

Changes in the location and shape of the distributions make it possible to analyze the effect of the different policy settings. Leaching outcomes were estimated for each pesticide application within each production cycle. About 30,000 individual pesticide applications were simulated in the complete analysis. Though it is possible to sample from the set of environmental characteristics, for simplicity in interpretation, the simulation experiment was conducted for one set of physical conditions deemed to be representative of the land currently in production.

All else being equal, the pesticide tax scenario should reduce pesticide use, and higher potato prices should increase pesticide use; these outcomes were verified in the simulations. The third scenario, in which the pesticide tax and potato price subsidy were combined, is considered to be most representative of actual policy liberalization. Figures 12.6-12.9 show the simulated marginal frequency distributions of fungicide quantity, numbers of applications, leaching, and revenue distributions under the base case (30 percent pesticide tax, status quo potato prices) and the three levels of output price subsidy (30, 60, and 90 percent).

Recall that the model chooses between a potato crop and pasture used for dairy production. A pasture cycle receives no pesticide applications, while virtually all potato cycles are treated. Thus, the zero category in Figures 12.6-12.8 indicates the extensive margin effects on fungicide quantities, application numbers, and leaching as farmers shift from potatoes to pasture in the simulated crop rotation.

Figure 12.6 presents the simulated marginal distributions of the total mass of the fungicide Mancozeb in grams of active ingredient applied to each field. The imposition of the 30 percent pesticide tax reduces pesticide use relative to the status quo, but the higher potato prices have the opposite effect. The changes in the zero category show the extensive margin effects as pasture occurs less frequently in the rotation. The shift of the mass of the distribution to the right shows the intensive margin effects, as fields receive larger treatments. Figure 12.7 shows that the total number of applications also increases as potato prices increase.

Figure 12.8 shows the distributions of cumulative mass (mg/m²) of Mancozeb leached below the root zone on each field in production. The leaching patterns are similar to the pesticide use patterns, but are not identical. It is significant that the likelihood of a positive leaching event is not in direct proportion to pesticide use. Despite the dramatic reduction in pasture, the zero category shows numerous fields without leaching, indicating that many fields received fungicide applications in amounts or under weather conditions insufficient to cause leaching. The distributions in Figure 12.8 indicate that the probability of a positive amount leached increases substantially with a moderate increase in the price of potatoes. Thus, the change in the total mass of pesticide entering the watershed is explained by the change in area which produces potatoes, the change in quantity applied per treatment, and the change in the number of treatments.

Figure 12.9 shows the effects of the policies on the revenue distribution in millions of Ecuadorian Sucres for the sample fields. The mass of the distributions shift to the right with higher potato prices.

Figures 12.10 and 12.11 present the aggregate data from the simulation analysis for the three policy scenarios (pesticide tax, potato price subsidy, and combined tax and subsidy), with the natural logarithm of the total value of production of all fields measured on the horizontal axis. Defining $M = 50,000$ as an upper bound for total cumulative mass of Mancozeb predicted to leach beyond the root zone from all fields in the watershed over the five-year period following the crop cycle during which it was applied, and defining $L$ as the predicted total cumulative mass leached

FIGURE 12.6. Fungicide Quantity Distributions for 30% Pesticide Tax and Potato Price Scenario.

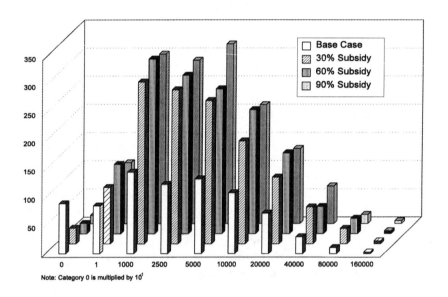

FIGURE 12.7. Fungicide Number Distribution for 30% Pesticide Tax and Potato Price Scenario.

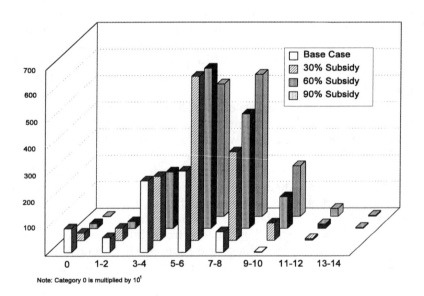

FIGURE 12.8. Fungicide Leaching Distributions for 30% Pesticide and Potato Price Scenario.

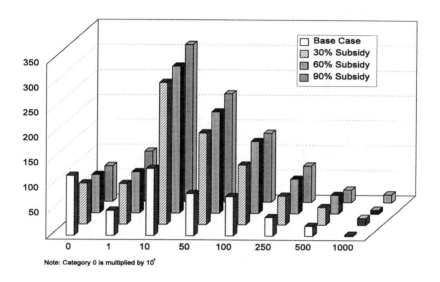

Note: Category 0 is multiplied by $10^1$

FIGURE 12.9. Revenue Distribution for 30% Pesticide Tax and Potato Price Scenario.

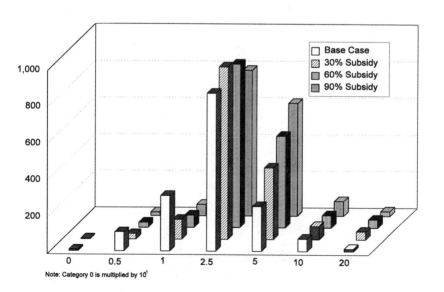

Note: Category 0 is multiplied by $10^1$

192

FIGURE 12.10. Transformation Frontiers for Trade Liberalization Scenarios.

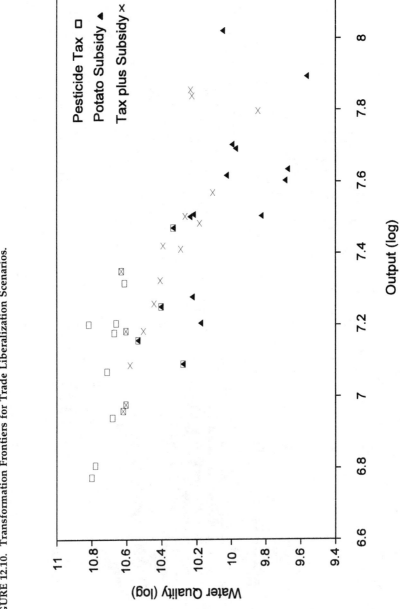

FIGURE 12.11. Transformation Frontiers for Trade Liberalization Scenarios.

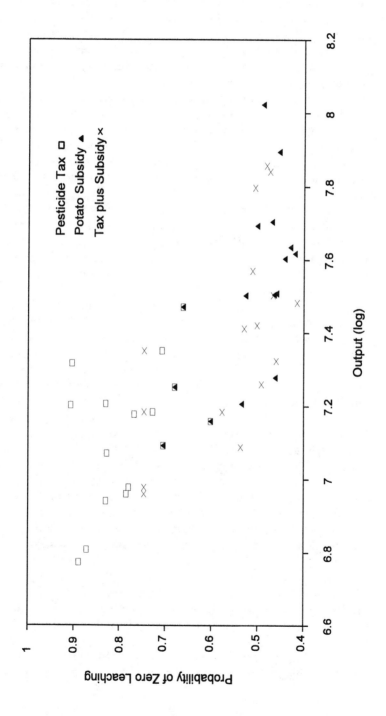

from all fields in the watershed, aggregate water quality is measured in Figure 12.10 as $\log(M - L)$. The vertical axis of Figure 12.11 measures the probability that leaching on a field in the watershed is zero, estimated as the proportion of fields in the simulation that had zero leaching. The base case (status quo) points are the four in each figure where the pesticide tax and potato subsidy scenarios coincide.

As theory predicts, the scattering of data points from the simulations imply that the transformation frontier has a negative slope, indicating the tradeoff between environmental quality and production that occurs as changes in policy induce changes in crop rotations and pesticide use. Compared to the status quo, the pesticide tax yields improvement in water quality at the cost of lower output; the increase in potato prices shows the opposite effect.

As noted in the theoretical derivation of the frontier, policy changes could induce both a movement along, and a shift in, the transformation frontier. Because these simulations were conducted holding constant the physical characteristics of land in production and the production technology, it seems reasonable to interpret these results as representing a movement along a stable frontier.

Viewed in this way, the results indicate that policy liberalization that increases pesticide prices by 30 percent, and also increases potato prices by 0-90 percent, would not necessarily have an adverse impact on either the environment or on agricultural production. Indeed, about half of the 16 policy simulations yield combinations of output and water quality that are in the same general area of Figure 12.10 as the base case. The results of the simulation also indicate, however, that because of the natural variability in both output and in the physical processes associated with leaching, a fairly wide range of outcomes is possible.

The nearly log-linear relationship in Figure 12.10, with both axes measured in logarithms, indicates that there is a tradeoff between output and water quality as theory predicts, but the transformation frontier is convex to the origin. Figure 12.11 also indicates a tradeoff that is convex to the origin. The explanation for these findings is that, as the price of potato output rises relative to dairy, the crop rotation shifts to nearly continuous potato production. Once this extensive margin substitution has occurred, the marginal impacts on water quality decline because they are caused only by increases in pesticide intensity, but potato production continues to increase in response to higher output prices. The declining groundwater quality does not feed back to adversely affect production, so there is no reason in this case for the frontier to be concave to the origin as in Figure 12.2.

Social welfare presumably depends on both the total quantity of leaching and its probability of occurring. With an appropriate welfare metric, the outcomes in Figures 12.10 and 12.11 could be summarized functionally and included in an aggregate analysis of the welfare effects of policy liberalization.

## Implications for Research on Trade and the Environment

This study proposes a methodology for establishing the linkages from the field level at which environmental impacts can be meaningfully measured and modeled, to the aggregate level at which policy analysis is conducted. The methodology was illustrated with an integrated economic/physical model that links farmers' production behavior to the leaching of pesticides to groundwater. The distribution of outcomes at the field level was used as the basis to statistically aggregate outcomes and represent them in the form of a transformation frontier that can be used in policy analysis. The resulting transformation frontier demonstrates the tradeoff between agricultural production and environmental quality that has been hypothesized in the economics literature. Several features of this tradeoff deserve further research from both theoretical and empirical perspectives, including its convexity properties, the effects of aggregation, and the factors that shift the frontier versus those that cause movements along it.

As the Andean case study illustrates, disaggregate analysis of the relationship between agricultural production and environmental quality can generate a large amount of detailed information, too much information to be comprehended and used in aggregate policy analysis. The aggregation of the detailed, disaggregate data into a transformation frontier provides a means to summarize the disaggregate data in a form that is valid from the point of view of the underlying scientific disciplines and also intuitively appealing to policy analysts.

The modeling conducted in this study is partial equilibrium, and needs to be linked to a general equilibrium model to predict long-term trends in relative prices that would be associated with policy liberalization. Most general equilibrium models in the literature, however, do not provide the necessary level of detail on the agricultural sector to be useful for this purpose. There is a need for these general equilibrium models to be further disaggregated by commodity and geographic location to facilitate the linkage to environmental impact analyses such as the one described in this study. This disaggregation will need to be done on a case-by-case basis, to match the particular economic and environmental relationships that are judged to be most important.

A key problem with environmental analysis is that it is data intensive. A critical challenge facing researchers is to discern what level of precision is required in the disaggregate economic and physical analysis to be adequate for policy analysis at the aggregate level. Knowing the level of precision required would, in turn, define the minimum data sets that are needed to provide scientifically valid inferences for the individual land units that are to be statistically aggregated for policy analysis. We hypothesize that the solution to this challenge lies in the development of geographic information systems that integrate location-specific physical and economic data.

## References

Antle, J.M. "Aggregation, Expectations, and the Explanation of Technological Change." *Journal of Econometrics* 33(1986):213–36.

Antle, J.M., and S.M. Capalbo. "Physical and Economic Model Integration for Measurement of the Environmental Impacts of Agricultural Chemical Use." *Northeastern Journal of Agricultural and Resource Economics* 20(1991):68–82.

Antle, J.M., S.M. Capalbo, and C.C. Crissman. "Econometric Production Models with Endogenous Input Timing: An Application to Ecuadorian Potato Production." *Journal of Agricultural and Resource Economics* 19(1994):1–18.

Antle, J.M., and G. Heidebrink. "Environment and Development: Theory and International Evidence." *Economic Development and Cultural Change* 43(April 1995):603–25.

Antle, J.M., and R.E. Just. "Conceptual and Empirical Foundations for Agricultural-Environmental Policy Analysis." *Journal of Environmental Quality* 21(1992):307–16.

————. "Effects of Commodity Program Structure on Resource Use and the Environment." In *Commodity and Resource Policy in Agricultural Systems*, R.E. Just and N.E. Bockstael, eds., pp. 97–128. New York: Springer-Verlag, 1991.

Barsky, O. *Acumulación Campesina en el Ecuador: Los Productores de Papa del Carchi.* Colección Investigaciones 1. Quito, Ecuador: FLACSO, 1984.

Crissman, C.C., J.M. Antle, and S.M. Capalbo, eds. *Getting Pesticides Right: Tradeoffs in Environment, Health, and Sustainable Agricultural Development.* Book manuscript in preparation, 1995.

Crissman, C.C., and P. Espinosa. "Agricultural Chemical Use and Sustainability of Andean Potato Production: Project Design and Pesticide Use in Potato Production in Ecuador." Paper presented at the Rockefeller Foundation seminar on "Measuring the Health and Environmental Effects of Pesticides," Bellagio, Italy, 30 March–3 April 1992.

Crissman, C.C., and J.E. Uquillas. *Seed Potato Systems in Ecuador: A Case Study.* Monograph, Centro Internaciónal de la Papa (CIP), Lima, Peru, 1989.

de Janvry, A., E. Sadoulet, and A. Fargeix. "Politically Feasible and Equitable Adjustment: Some Alternatives for Ecuador." *World Development* 19(1991):1577–94.

Hochman, E., and D. Zilberman. "Examination of Environmental Policies Using Production and Pollution Microparameter Distributions." *Econometrica* 46(1978):739–60.

Hutson, J.L., and R.J. Wagenet. "A Pragmatic Field-Scale Approach for Modeling Pesticides." *Journal of Environmental Quality* 22(1993):494–99.

Janssen, W., C.C. Crissman, G. Henry, M. López Pereira, L. Sanit, and T. Walker. *The Role of CIAT, CIMMYT, and CIP in Agricultural Research in Latin America and the Caribbean: Relevance and Results.* Monograph, Centro Internaciónal de la Agricultura Tropical (CIAT), Cali, Colombia, 1992.

Kemp, M.C., and N.V. Long. "The Role of Natural Resources in Trade Models." In *Handbook of International Economics, Vol. 1: International Trade,* R.W. Jones and P.B. Kenen, eds., pp. 367–417. New York: North-Holland Publishers, 1984.

Lee, D., and P. Espinosa. "Pesticide Use and Economic Policy Issues in the Andean Region." In *Getting Pesticides Right: Tradeoffs in Environment, Health, and Sustainable Agricultural Development,* C.C. Crissman, J.M. Antle, and S.M. Capalbo, eds. Book manuscript in preparation, 1995.

Ramos, H., and M. Acosta. "Impactos de la Apertura Comercial Regional en el Sector Agropecuario." Mimeo, IDEA, Quito, Ecuador, 1991.

Ramos, H.H, A. Hibon, C.C. Crissman, I. Reinoso, R. Flores, and P. Salazar. *Determinación de la Ventaja Comparativa de la Produccion de Papa en el Ecuador: Implicaciones para la Asignación de Recursos de Investigación y Transferencia de Tecnología a Traves de Regiones.* Monograph, IDEA, Quito, Ecuador, 1993.

Schiff, M., and A. Valdés. *The Political Economy of Agricultural Pricing Policy, Vol. 4: A Synthesis of the Economics in Developing Countries.* Baltimore: The Johns Hopkins University Press, 1992.

Scobie, G.M., V. Jardine, and D.D. Greene. "The Importance of Trade and Exchange Rate Policies for Agriculture in Ecuador." *Food Policy* 17(February 1991):34–47.

Southgate, D., and M. Whitaker. *Development and the Environment: Ecuador's Policy Crisis.* Monograph, IDEA, Quito, Ecuador, 1992.

Stoker, T.M. "The Use of Cross-Section Data to Characterize Macro Functions." *Journal of the American Statistical Association* 77(1982):369–80.

Wagenet, R.J., J.L. Hutson, and C. Ducrot. "Describing Pesticide Movement in Potato Production in Carchi Soils." In *Getting Pesticides Right: Tradeoffs in Environment, Health, and Sustainable Agricultural Development,* C.C. Crissman, J.M. Antle, and S.M. Capalbo, eds. Book manuscript in preparation, 1995.

Whitaker, M., and J. Alzamora. "Production Agriculture: Nature and Characteristics." In *Agriculture and Economic Survival: The Role of Agriculture in Ecuador's Development,* M. Whitaker and D. Colyer, eds. Boulder: Westview Press, 1990.

# 13

## Environmental Policies in Europe and the Effect on the Balance of Trade

*Jan C. Blom*

### Introduction

The green revolution led to considerable production increases in agriculture, but also to some negative impacts on the environment. In those areas where intensive agricultural production causes environmental stress, governments often take measures and formulate policies which constrain production practices. For most regions in the European Union (EU), environmental policies related to food and agriculture have been, or are being, formulated. This chapter discusses the possible impacts of these environmental policies on agricultural production and the balance of trade for the EU.

The GATT Uruguay Round agreement is a historical breakthrough with respect to international agreements concerning agricultural trade. It is considered a first step on the way to trade liberalization in the agricultural sector. Environmentalists claim, however, that if production and/or consumption of a food is polluting, then an expansion in global output of that good following trade liberalization would lead to greater environmental degradation (Anderson 1992). Two crucial assumptions underlying this reasoning are that no optimal environmental taxes are levied, and that less polluting production technologies are not introduced. It is on the basis of these arguments that some countries are just one step away from erecting new trade barriers in the name of environmental protection.

In a study on trade liberalization and the environment, Lutz (1992) concludes that trade liberalization will bring industrialized countries positive environmental effects, but developing countries will face negative environmental changes. Confounding the results, however, Lutz expects that developing countries will experience positive economic effects from trade liberalization; the overall welfare effects of trade liberalization are thus uncertain. He advocates empirical work to estimate the importance of the different effects and the parameters involved. Rauscher (1992) formalizes the reasoning of Lutz by developing a model in which capital is mobile and environmental resources are immobile. He concludes that under trade liberalization, countries well endowed with environmental resources tend to increase their emissions, whereas resource-poor countries tend to reduce their emissions. As does Lutz, Rauscher concludes that the overall welfare effects of trade liberalization on the different countries are indeterminate.

In another study, Anderson (1992) concludes that there are more efficient policy instruments than trade policies for preserving the natural environment. Not only should trade liberalization never be put off for environmental reasons, he argues, but the benefits of trade liberalization can be enhanced if appropriate environmental instruments are introduced at the time of liberalization. Blom (1990) and Heerink et al. (1993) come to the same conclusions as Anderson.

In Anderson's 1992 study of the effects of trade liberalization on the environment, he uses a model that abstracts from environmental policy-driven technological change. Likewise, Lutz's (1992) conclusions do not consider induced changes in technology. Rauscher (1992), too, abstracts from technological change.

Environmental policies have been shown to induce changes in technology, consumer attitudes, and institutions. So, a distinctive element of environmental policies is their potential effect on the basic supply/demand elements of the economic system. But changes in technology, consumer attitudes, and institutions normally are not captured by economic models. Consequently, conclusions from these models must be interpreted with caution. Hartmann (1993) incorporates into a partial-equilibrium model information about the changes to production methods in German agriculture, based on interviews among experts. Brouwer and van Berkum (1994) conclude that tools presently available do not allow for an analytic examination of EU sustainable agriculture. They contend that existing economic models must be improved if they are to contribute to an understanding of the linkages among agriculture, international trade, and the environment.

This chapter works from the current state of knowledge about economic linkages between environmental concerns and trade, as weak as it is. The chapter does not attempt to quantify the effects of environmental policies in the EU on the balance of trade. Instead, it analyzes the policies and their effect on the basic supply/demand elements of the economic system and broadens economic understanding about the impact of environmental concerns on the balance of agricultural trade.

EU environmental policies and their effects on the balance of trade are discussed within the framework of the excess supply (demand) function:

$$E = S(.) - D(.),$$

where $E$ is excess supply (demand), $S(.)$ is national supply, and $D(.)$ is national demand. Given trade policies, $E$ is the result of the difference between internal supply and demand. $S(.)$ is affected by environmental policies, not only due to shifting price relationships, but also due to technological and institutional changes. $D(.)$ is affected by changes in consumer preferences caused by health and environmental concerns.

The chapter starts with the EU agricultural balance of trade for some important products. An overview is given of the main environmental policies in the EU member states. This is followed by a discussion about the effects of environmental policies on the basic elements of the EU economic system and the balance of agricultural trade. Some conclusions are offered in the final section.

## EU Agriculture and Trade

Before discussing the possible trade effects of environmental policies in Europe, it is instructive to review the position of the EU on the world market, and the importance of agricultural trade for the European Union. An overview of the most important agricultural products is provided in Table 13.1. It is clear that exports are especially important for the wheat, butter, and milk-powder markets. In all the other markets, exports are less than 10 percent of EU production. In two markets, the EU is a net importer—both for feed proteins. While exports are small as a percentage of production, the EU's dominance is strong in world markets for animal products and somewhat less in markets for cereals and sugar. On the import side, only the EU position in oilseeds is important in a world trade context.

Export of the reported products has only been possible with subsidies. Only in a few instances is part of the export level based on quality consideration, e.g., cheese. Subsidies on hogs, poultry, and eggs mainly compensate for higher EU feed prices. For some products, a small change in the quantities produced can have a considerable effect on EU exports—pork, for example. When environmental policies negatively affect the production of those products, the consequence can be a significant decrease in EU agricultural exports. Therefore, the essential question for these products is whether or not the environmental policies will result in a decrease in agricultural production.

**TABLE 13.1  EU-12 Production and Trade in 1989**

| Product | EU (1,000 tons) | | Trade Share (%) | EU Share of World Trade | | |
|---|---|---|---|---|---|---|
| | Production | Net Trade | | Import | Export | Net Export |
| Wheat | 78,677 | 19,479 | 24.7 | 2.0 | 19.6 | 17.6 |
| Coarse grains | 82,366 | 7,872 | 9.5 | 4.1 | 10.1 | 6.0 |
| Oilseeds (excl. soya) | 8,500 | -1,675 | -19.7 | 28.1 | 0.6 | -27.5 |
| Soybeans | 1,959 | -12,135 | -619.4 | 48.4 | 0.1 | -48.3 |
| Sugar | 14,681 | 1,362 | 9.3 | 6.9 | 17.8 | 10.9 |
| | | | | | | |
| Milk | 109,082 | 222 | 0.2 | 1.6 | 33.1 | 31.5 |
| Butter | 1,697 | 394 | 23.2 | 8.8 | 43.7 | 34.9 |
| Cheese | 4,619 | 443 | 9.6 | 13.1 | 49.3 | 36.2 |
| Milk-powder | 2,352 | 993 | 42.2 | 1.3 | 50.6 | 49.3 |
| | | | | | | |
| Cattle | 7,461 | 517 | 6.9 | 6.6 | 23.9 | 17.3 |
| Hogs | 13,024 | 329 | 2.5 | 4.0 | 23.5 | 19.5 |
| Poultry | 6,127 | 333 | 5.4 | 5.6 | 23.8 | 18.2 |
| Eggs | 4,765 | 109 | 2.3 | 9.3 | 30.4 | 21.1 |

*Source*: Commission of European Communities, *The Agricultural Situation in the Community* (1990 and 1992).

Note: Minus indicates net import; plus indicates net export.

Two developments, one in agricultural production and another in agricultural trade, have to be considered for a meaningful answer. First, agricultural production has increased substantially in recent decades. Will strict environmental rules change this growth? Or will they only slow past trends? Could they possibly have no effect? Second, the GATT Uruguay Round agreement will change the agricultural trade balance of the EU, irrespective of any environmental policies. In nearly all reported markets, the EU likely will see a decline in exports in the coming years.

## EU Environmental Policies

This section describes the different environmental policies in the EU. Nutrient policies and policies with respect to pesticides are reported extensively. Given the fact that nutrient policies are complex and differ across, and even within, the member states of the EU, it is impossible to go into detail here. Discussion is limited, therefore, to the main features of the different measures. Additional details can be found in the referenced literature. Policies related to water and energy will be treated only marginally.

### *Nutrient Policies*

Brouwer and Godeschalk (1993) report on different measures taken to prevent ammonia emissions and an oversupply of nutrients for a number of regions in the EU [Niedersachsen (Germany), Bretagne (France), Flanders (Belgium), Denmark, and the Netherlands]. Nutrient policies aim to protect the quality of drinking and surface water, reduce the acidification of soil and water caused by ammonia emissions, and prevent accumulation of phosphate in soils. Agriculture is a leading nonpoint source of nitrate water pollution (Brouwer and Godeschalk 1993). The nitrogen in ammonia can lead to acidification in countries with concentrations of intensive livestock production. National and regional nutrient policies have several elements in common: (1) standards for the application of manure and, in some cases, fertilizer; (2) regulations restricting spreading of manure; and (3) specific measures related to the reduction of ammonia emissions.

At the EU level, the EC Nitrate Directive provides guidance on how and when member states should deal with the nitrate problem. This directive relates to the earlier EC directive that establishes drinking water quality standards (Directive 80/778/EEC), by imposing a nitrate standard of 50 mg/l. The EC Nitrate Directive calls for member states to take the following actions: monitor all waters by December 1993, identify zones vulnerable to nitrate, and formulate an action program by no later than December 1995. Rude and Frederiksen (1994) give an overview of the national nitrate policies in seven member states (Belgium, Denmark, Germany, France, the Netherlands, the United Kingdom, and Italy).

In Flanders, Niedersachsen, Denmark, and Bretagne, there is a maximum for the application of nitrogen from inorganic and/or organic sources. Flanders and Bretagne have a limitation on the total use of nitrogen from organic and inorganic sources. Table 13.2 gives a synopsis of the standards applied in different regions. In Walloon (Belgium), the standards are comparable to those in Flanders. In Schleswig-Holstein, Hamburg, Bremen,

TABLE 13.2 Standards on the Application of Minerals from Inorganic and/or Organic Sources for the Year 1992 (kg/ha utilized area)

| Region | Nitrogen (N) kg/ha | Phosphate ($P_2O_5$) kg/ha |
|---|---|---|
| Niedersachsen | 200 | |
| Bretagne | Pasture: 350<br>Pulses:   0<br>Other:  200 | |
| Flanders | 400 | Green maize:  200<br>Arable crops:  150<br>Grass:        175 |
| Netherlands | | Green maize:  250<br>Arable crops:  125<br>Grass:        200 |
| Denmark | 250 | |

*Source*: Brouwer and Godeschalk (1993).

Nordrhein-Westfalen, and Sachsen-Anhalt (Germany), measures can be compared to those in Niedersachsen. In the remaining parts of Germany, there are no restrictions on the application of manure. In the Netherlands, the limitation on manure application is based on phosphate. In Flanders, there is a limitation for both the application of phosphate and nitrogen. However, the phosphate limitation is the binding restriction. In the United Kingdom, there are no regulations with respect to manure application. Only in the so-called "nitrate advisory areas" are farmers asked to voluntarily undertake restrictions on their agricultural practices. In the "nitrate sensitive areas," it is possible to compensate farmers for adopting sub-optimal agricultural practices. These regions only cover a limited area—10,700 hectares (Rude and Frederiksen 1994). Italy faces serious problems in the Po Valley. In Lombardia and Emilia Romagna, measures are taken with respect to the application level of manure. In the other parts of Italy, policies are based on voluntary measures.

The figures in Table 13.2 are indicative of the large differences among regions of application standards for nitrogen and phosphates. In the future, national governments must develop regulations that meet the EU standard on nitrate. For this reason, the national government of Germany is considering adjusting its nitrogen standards: arable land, 170 kg N/ha; intensively-used grassland, 240 kg N/ha; and other grassland, 210 kg N/ha. In the Netherlands, the standards for application will decrease in 1995 for green maize and arable crops to 125 kg $P_2O_5$/ha. In the year 2000, the Dutch government aims for an equilibrium between supply and extraction of nutrients in agriculture. In Flanders, too, the government aims for a lower standard on the application of phosphate (125 kg $P_2O_5$/ha) by the year 2001. The measures in Denmark need only small adjustments to meet the standards of the EC Nitrate Directive. Given the farm structure in the United Kingdom, compliance with the EU standards on nitrate will not be problematic. However, the proposed changes to agri-environmental policy in Italy might be insufficient to meet the EU requirements (Rude and Frederiksen 1994).

In order to limit ammonia emissions and mineral leaching into surface and groundwater, restrictions with respect to the spreading of manure are in place for agriculture in the different regions. These restrictions detail seasons and specific conditions in which manure cannot be spread (e.g., not during the winter or on frozen land or snow). Regulations also depend on soil type. In Flanders, Denmark, and the Netherlands, there are special prescriptions for the way manure should be applied. Furthermore, in Flanders, Bretagne, Denmark, Niedersachsen, Lombardia, and Emilia Romagna, farmers are obliged to have a certain storage capacity for manure. In the Netherlands, these obligations arise from the manure-spreading restrictions.

The governments in Flanders and the Netherlands aim for a reduction in ammonia emissions. Flanders seeks a 20 percent reduction by the year 2000, and 60 percent by 2010. In the Netherlands, a reduction of 50 percent should be achieved by 2000; the long-run goal is to achieve a reduction of 70 percent. A reduction of 50 percent is considered to be technically and economically feasible. Further reductions are technically possible, but the economic costs involved would be considerable (Baltussen et al. 1990). One of the technical options to reduce the emission of ammonia is the new housing systems that are being developed for intensive livestock and cattle. The Netherlands already requires sealing manure storage facilities.

The general feature of all measures is their command and control character. Until now, Pigovian taxes and subsidies (economic incentives) have played no role in achieving an equilibrium between agricultural practices and environmental standards. The Dutch government aims for the introduction of a mineral accounting system by 1995 for all livestock farms, and by 1997 for arable and horticultural farms. The system will be combined with a prohibitive levy of about $15 per kg of phosphate surplus. It is expected that the mineral accounting system will be a better solution to the problem than the command and control measures, but a combination likely will be necessary (Baltussen, de Hoop, and van Os 1993). In Flanders, similar systems are being developed (Rude and Frederiksen 1994).

## Pesticide Policies

The use of pesticides in agriculture can lead to undesired emissions into the environment. As a consequence, soil and ground and surface water can be contaminated, which is a risk to human life and the ecosystem. Policy standards especially address quality of drinking water. The Drinking Water Directive specifies that the maximum admissible concentration (MAC) for any one pesticide is 0.1µg/l in water that is intended for human consumption, and 0.5µg/l for the total sum of pesticides (Reus, Weckseler, and Pak 1994).

In 1992, the Commission of the European Communities (CEC) launched its Fifth Environmental Action Programme (FEAP) (CEC 1992). One objective for the agricultural sector, a target sector in the FEAP, is to decrease chemical use so that the basic processes are unaffected, allowing a sustainable agricultural sector. No specific goals are defined, but the general aim is translated into three action points: (1) ongoing—registration of sales and the use of pesticides, (2) from 1992 on—promotion of "integrated control" and organic farming, and (3) starting from 1995 on—control of sales and pesticide use (Reus, Weckseler, and Pak 1994). Directive 91/414/EEC aims for the harmonization of pesticide registration schemes in the member states. Reus, Weckseler, and Pak expect this directive to have only qualitative effects.

National pesticide policies differ strongly among member states, sometimes reflecting differences in the use of pesticides. A synopsis of the main characteristics of the national policies, based on Reus, Weckseler, and Pak (1994), follows. Belgium has no national action or reduction program. Its general approach is to impose a strict registration policy and promote good agricultural practices. Denmark has specific reduction targets, formulated in 1986 (based on 1981-85 sales). The plan aimed for a reduction of 25 percent by 1990, and a reduction of 50 percent by 1997. Sales currently have been reduced 17 percent. Targets to reduce the application frequency failed. France aims for strict registration and good agricultural practices. Some applications are restricted. Germany, through strict authorization rules, has reduced the number of permitted products as well as the number of active ingredients. No specific goals or limits are reported. Greece only has policies concerning the application of pesticides. In Ireland, there is little need for a policy, since average use is only 2.2 kg of active ingredients per hectare. Italy developed a National Integrated Control and Protection Plan in 1987, which aimed for a reduction of 30-50 percent. Luxembourg has no pesticide policy, because agriculture is a minor sector and the average application dosage is relatively low (3.1 kg/ha). In the Netherlands, the Multi-Year Crop Protection Plan (1991) passed Parliament. This plan establishes reduction targets per sector and by category of pesticide. On average, a reduction of 37 percent is targeted for 1995 (compared to 1984-88), and 56 percent by 2000. In Portugal, pesticide use is low and restricted to a number of regions with intensive cropping. No policy has been reported. In Spain, measures are driven by export considerations. Although Spain has no reported policy, to meet EC standards for food residues, integrated pest control is encouraged. In the United Kingdom, the general objective is to minimize pesticide use. This is pursued by using approval mechanisms based on a statutory Code of Practice on the Safe Use of Pesticides, surveillance monitoring, and distribution of information on pesticide use.

In all countries, policies on the application of allowable pesticides, to the extent they have been developed, are voluntary. Under a voluntary approach, diffusion of information and research are important instruments to reach targets. No economic instruments, such as Pigovian taxes, are currently being used and none are foreseen. The most hazardous active ingredients are restricted or no longer admitted. Pesticide policies are thus different in character from nutrient policies, which rely on command and control mechanisms.

Brouwer, Terluin, and Godeschalk (1994) report on pesticide use in the EU. Pesticide use is relatively low in Denmark, Spain, Ireland, and Portugal (less than 3 kg active ingredients per hectare). Belgium and the Netherlands are the most intensive users, with 11 kg and 17 kg active ingredients per hectare, respectively. The remaining EU member states use between 3 and 6 kg active ingredients per hectare. Brouwer, Terluin, and Godeschalk conclude that the sales of pesticides in terms of kilograms of active ingredients have been decreasing in the EU-12 since 1985. From data for Belgium, Denmark, Germany, Greece, France, and the Netherlands (50 percent of total EU usage), Brouwer, Terluin, and Godeschalk conclude that sales of pesticides have declined by 17 percent since the mid-1980s.

## Other Environmental Policies

Two other policies are related to the environment: energy and water. Energy and water policies could also affect agricultural production. The concern with energy use at the moment is primarily its greenhouse gas effect, which is caused by $CO_2$ emissions. This is a global problem that can be redressed only by global policies. The aims of EU energy policies are to decrease energy usage and to enhance energy efficiency. Discussions in the Netherlands have led to the conclusion that taxes on energy, if initiated, should be introduced in an EU context. A general increase in the costs of energy will affect energy-intensive sectors such as greenhouse horticulture and transportation.

Nutrient and pesticide policies are strongly motivated by standards for drinking water. Therefore, there is a linkage between these policies and water policies. But there is also a water quantity problem in some EU member states. In contrast to energy, water quantity problems have a regional dimension. Policies to reduce water usage will affect agriculture across some regions. In some EU areas, irrigation is even used for the production of cereals and forage (e.g., cereals in Spain, Portugal, Greece, and France; forage in the Netherlands). The regional or national water policies, in combination with the new Common Agricultural Policy (CAP), will result in a reduction in the agricultural sector's demand for water. Gopalakrishnan (1994) stresses the strong linkage between water and energy usage in agriculture. In the United States, irrigation is the third highest (20 percent) user of energy in agricultural production, next only to field machinery (30 percent) and transportation (25 percent). So an effective water policy will also reduce the agricultural sector's demand for energy.

### Effects on the Economic System

In this section, a number of relevant changes in the basic elements of the economic system are addressed. This section draws heavily on experiences in the Netherlands. Nevertheless, similar developments would be expected to take place in comparable economic and technological circumstances where technological changes can be easily adopted. The Dutch examples refer to the nutrient policies especially, because the pesticide schemes are on a voluntary basis.

### *Institutional Changes*

New laws and regulations are the primary form of institutional change in response to environmental problems. Laws and regulations related to nutrients attempt to influence the number of animals per hectare, inducing scarcity in land. Expansion of livestock and cattle is only possible on farms with a low animal density. This is an example of Rauscher's (1992) factor endowment theory. Production rights often are based on historical grounds, which means that new production assets are created. For young farmers, it means additional costs for the establishment of a farm.

The new CAP forces arable farmers to set aside a part of their land. However, production losses caused by pesticide or nitrate policies can be compensated for by relaxing the set-aside obligation, under certain conditions. A telling example of this type of substitution is the text of Council Regulation EEC no. 1541/93, article 1.2, which states that regions which implement an action program that significantly reduces fertilizer use can relax their set-aside obligations.

## Technological Developments

The technologies discussed below are only a few of the numerous examples of the development of environmentally-friendly agricultural technology. These technologies will reduce the compliance costs of new agri-environmental regulations.

*Feeding Technology.* The feeding of animals is improved by changing the composition of the feed according to the different growth phases of the animal. Fine-tuning the composition of the feed to the needs of the animal is the first step in more efficient nutrient use and, therefore, less loss of nutrients in animal wastes. The enzyme phytase is used to improve the availability of phosphate in feed. The enzyme discloses phosphate from the phytine acid, which is available in sufficient amounts in feed. Therefore, the addition of mineral phosphate can be decreased. In another example, the availability of synthetic amino acids allows a reduction in the raw protein in feed and thereby diminishes nitrogen losses. The addition of synthetic amino acids to feeds is possible for pigs, laying hens, broilers, and other monogastric animals. For cattle, soybean meal is toasted to improve the efficiency of protein use and to reduce nitrogen levels in animal waste.

*Technology to Reduce Ammonia Emissions.* Manure storage is now sealed and housing systems are being developed to reduce ammonia emissions from manure. New spreading technologies also have been developed which bring the manure directly into the soil.

*Technology to Reduce the Water Content in Manure.* Several technologies have been developed to reduce the water content in manure, thus reducing the costs of manure transport. Research has demonstrated that water used by pigs could be reduced to 10 percent of the original usage. Manure is treated on the farm in such a way that the waste with a high dry matter content can be transported over long distances, while the liquid manure is spread in the neighborhood of the farm. Manure of laying hens and broilers is dried at the farm and transported over long distances. With the help of membrane technology, liquid manure from fattening calves is centrally treated in a cost-effective way, and in accordance with the environmental rules. So far, the development of a cost-effective treatment for manure from pigs has not been very successful.

*Technology to Reduce the Use of Pesticides.* Developments in the areas of integrated pest management and organic farming have been successful. Better pesticide management, changes in the cropping pattern, and mechanical treatment are the main features of integrated pest management. The application of pesticides has been improved by new spraying technologies, which lower emissions to the environment. Less harmful pesticides are being developed by the chemical industry. In greenhouses and fields, natural predators are used to reduce harmful insects.

*Changes in Consumer Preferences*

Consumers are concerned primarily with harmful residues in food. This creates small markets for products from organic farms. Fruit and vegetable markets are very sensitive with respect to production methods and risks of residues. Retail trade and food industries have introduced controlled production methods in order to avoid risks from food residues. In the United Kingdom, for example, wheat for bread is certified safe with respect to residues.

Consumers are now more aware of the potentially negative environmental effects from agricultural production. Even in the absence of regulations, consumer preferences for environmentally-safe foodstuffs have important market implications. Regions with environmental problems caused by agricultural production or industries may face negative consequences in the marketplace. For example, products from exporting regions with a poor environmental reputation could be in a vulnerable position in a marketplace with environmentally-conscious consumers. On the other hand, areas with little or no environmental problems can exploit the "green" label of the region. In the Netherlands, for example, one retailer is successfully selling beef from Ireland under the trademark "greenfield."

## Effects on the Balance of Agricultural Trade

It is difficult to quantify the effects of these policies on the balance of trade. Hartmann (1993) attempts to do so through an analysis of the trade effects of nitrogen fertilizer and pesticide reduction. She analyzes the effects in Germany of a 50 percent reduction in nitrogen input and a 95 percent reduction of pesticides. Hartmann concludes that these reductions have a large effect on the German balance of trade. Germany becomes a large importer of cereals and feed. In Hartmann's model, increases in manure use are not restricted. Therefore, intensive livestock production grows in order to supply nitrogen from manure, resulting in a dramatic increase in feed imports. Other reasons for these results are the rather extreme scenarios, and the fact that no institutional and technological changes are taken into account. On the basis of the environmental targets, the results of the policy changes on the nitrogen balance are worse than the existing situation, since the efficiency of nitrogen from manure is much lower than from fertilizer. Thus, the nitrogen scenario may not be consistent with German or EU environmental policy at all.

It is possible to provide some general comments about the likely effects of nutrient and pesticide policies on the EU balance of trade. However, it should be stressed that the effects of the GATT Uruguay Round agreement will overwhelm those effects due to environmental policies.

## The Effects of Nutrient Policies

Feeding technologies will partly solve the nutrient problem—phosphate will decline 15 to 20 percent and the feed protein content may decline 5 to 10 percent (Van der Veen, Blom, and Luesink 1993). Ammonia emissions will be reduced by storage, housing, and spreading technologies. Environmental concerns and the milk quota system have already reduced the use of nitrogen fertilizer in the Netherlands by 15 to 20 percent since 1988.

Institutional changes will stimulate a shift in livestock production from intensive to less-intensive regions in the EU. This shift likely will be further stimulated by CAP reform, which will reduce the competitiveness of imported feed (Blom 1992). However, it remains to be seen how the changing concentration of livestock production in the EU will affect overall trade balances.

While intensive livestock will shift from current regions of high concentration to regions with arable farming, EU production will not decline considerably. However, given the importance of the EU in the world market, there might be a relatively large effect on world trade. The EU most likely will not become a net importer of pork, eggs, and broilers as a consequence of nutrient policies.

The effect of nutrient policies on dairy production and exports will be negligible, because the production restricted by quota is rather profitable. The export of beef will be reduced considerably under the GATT agreement, but will be little affected by the nutrient policies.

The nitrogen policy will affect the feed composition in regions with a concentration of intensive livestock. The availability of amino acids will decrease the demand for protein. Protein feeds such as corn gluten feed probably will be negatively affected by this type of technological development (Van der Veen, Blom, and Luesink 1993).

## The Effects of Pesticide Policies

While nutrient policies will largely affect animal production, pesticide policies will be important for crop production. Experiences in the Netherlands have shown that the Dutch pesticide policy targets, as formulated for 1995, can be met by farmers if integrated pest management methods are adopted (Wijnands et al. 1992). The targets for the year 2000 are not yet fully met, but the results from "innovation" farms are promising. The economics of integrated farming seems to be positive, or neutral, with respect to "normal" farming practices. This is the result of slightly lower costs and steady, or only slightly lower, revenues.

Environmental policies in the different member states are reinforced by the new CAP, which will elicit a decline in the marginal revenues of major crops. In the Netherlands, CAP reform will cause a decrease in the use of pesticides and nitrogen fertilizer (Dijk, de Haan, and Hoogeveen 1994). This confirms the results reported by Lutz (1992).

Given the fact that yields are unchanged, or only slightly lower, production in the EU likely will be relatively unaffected by the restriction of pesticides, as occurs in the Netherlands. It is not clear what the effect will be on future yield increases, however. Yield increases should slow to some extent because the technical possibilities are somewhat restricted. In any case, it is expected that the EU will use the export possibilities as formulated under the latest GATT agreement. Any decrease in production caused by pesticide or nitrogen policies could be offset by lowering the set-aside obligations.

## Conclusions

Environmental policies can induce change in the basic elements of the economic system. Consequently, the economic models developed in the past to analyze and predict developments in agricultural markets have to be adapted before they can be used to analyze the impact of environmental policies. Environmental policies will affect three important economic elements: institutional change, technological development to cope with the environmental problems, and changes in consumers' attitudes. Institutional and technological change, in turn, will affect resource availability.

The GATT Uruguay Round agreement is the most important element in the determination of future EU trade. Environmental policies will only marginally change EU agricultural production. The export of cereals will develop along the lines as agreed in the Uruguay Round. Possible negative impacts of environmental policies on production likely will be compensated by adjustments in the set-aside scheme. A reduction in the export of dairy products and beef, as foreseen in the GATT agreement, allows EU farmers to employ less intensive, land-based animal production methods. The EU policy for dairy began this process. An additional reduction in exports caused by environmental policies is not expected. The production of intensive livestock will be reallocated in the EU, from areas where concentration is high, to regions with relatively few animals per hectare and a surplus of feed. This shift in animal production patterns is the result of CAP reform and heavy environmental constraints in high concentration areas. It is difficult to predict if, on balance, it will affect the EU export position in these markets. The changes in feed technology with respect to protein could reduce imports of protein feeds.

## References

Anderson, K. "Effects on the Environment and Welfare of Liberalizing World Trade: The Cases of Coal and Food." In *The Greening of World Trade Issues*, K. Anderson and R. Blackhurst, eds. New York: Harvester Wheatsheaf, 1992.

Baltussen, W.H.M., D.W. de Hoop, and J. van Os. "De as van het Milieubeleid: Fysieke of Financiële Regulering om Mineralenemissies Terug te Dringen."

Publikatie 3.153, Agricultural Economics Research Institute (LEI-DLO), The Hague, Netherlands, 1993.

Baltussen, W.H.M., P.L.M. van Horne, J. van Os, and H. Altena. "Gevolgen van Beperking van Ammoniakemissie voor Veehouderijbedrijven." Publikatie 3.147, Agricultural Economics Research Institute (LEI-DLO), The Hague, Netherlands, 1990.

Blom, J.C. "The CAP Reform and the Change in the Competitive Position of the Intensive Livestock Sector in Different Regions of the EC." Paper presented at the seminar of the Association Française de Zootechnie/Association Française des Techniciens de l'Alimentation Animale, Paris, 1992.

_____. "Europese Veevoederimporten, Graanoverschotten en Milieuproble-men." Boerengroep Wageningen, Herkomst van Het Voer, Toekomst van de Boer. Wageningen: Boerengroep Wageningen, 1990.

Brouwer, F.M., and F.E. Godeschalk. "Pig Production in the EC: Environmental Policy and Competitiveness." Publikatie 1.25, Agricultural Economics Research Institute (LEI-DLO), The Hague, Netherlands, 1993.

Brouwer, F.M., I.J. Terluin, and F.E. Godeschalk. "Pesticides in the EC." Onderzoekverslag 121, Agricultural Economics Research Institute (LEI-DLO), The Hague, Netherlands, 1994.

Brouwer, F.M., and S. van Berkum. "Agriculture, Trade, and the Environment: Models for Sustainable Development of EC Agriculture." Paper presented at the International Symposium: Models for Sustainable Development. Exclusive or Complementary Approaches of Sustainability? Paris, March 16-18, 1994.

Commission of the European Communities (CEC). *The Agricultural Situation in the Community*. Brussels and Luxembourg: CEC, various years.

_____. "Towards Sustainability—A European Community Programme of Policy and Action in Relation to the Environment and Sustainable Development." Publication No. COM(92), 23, Commission of the European Communities, Brussels and Luxembourg, 1992.

Dijk, J., T. de Haan, and M.W. Hoogeveen. "Prijsverhoudingen, Extensivering en Milieubelasting." Agricultural Economics Research Institute (LEI-DLO), The Hague, Netherlands, 1994.

Gopalakrishnan, C. *The Economics of Energy in Agriculture*. Aldershot, England: Avebury, 1994.

Hartmann, M. "Nationale und Internationale Auswirkungen einer Reduzieringdes Einsatzes van Stickstoffdünger und Pflanzenschutzmitteln in der Deutschen Landwirtschaf." In *Landwirtschaft und Chemie*, P.M. Schmitz and M. Hartmann, eds. Kiel, Germany: Wissenschaftsverlag, Vauk Kiel KG, 1993.

Heerink, N.B.M., J.F.M. Helming, O.J. Kuik, A. Kuyvenhoven and H. Verbruggen. "International Trade and the Environment." Wageningen Economic Studies Publication No. 30, Wageningen Agricultural University, 1993.

Rauscher, M. "International Economic Integration and the Environment: The Case of Europe." In *The Greening of World Trade Issues*, K. Anderson and R. Blackhurst, eds. New York: Harvester Wheatsheaf, 1992.

Reus, J.A.W.A., H.J. Weckseler, and G.A. Pak. "Towards a Future EC Pesticide Policy: An Inventory of Risks of Pesticide Use, Possible Solutions, and Policy Instruments." Centre for Agriculture and Environment, Utrecht, Netherlands, 1994.

Rude, S., and B.S. Frederiksen. "National EC Nitrate Policies: Agricultural Aspects for Seven EC Countries." Rapport No. 77, Statens Jordbrugsøkonomiske Instituut, Kopenhagen, 1994.

Van der Veen, M.Q., J.C. Blom, and H.H. Luesink. "Verlaging van Fosfor- en Stikstofgehaltes in Mengvoeders: Een Economische Evaluatie." Onderzoekverslag 107, Agricultural Economics Research Institute (LEI-DLO), The Hague, Netherlands, 1993.

Wijnands, F.G., S.R.M. Janssens, P. van Asperen, K.B. van Bon. "Innovatiebedrijven Geïntegreerde Akkerbouw: Opzet en Eerste Resultaten." Lelystad, Netherlands: PAGV, 1992.

# 14

# Environmental Regulation and the Competitiveness of U.S. Agriculture

*Bruce L. Gardner*

## Introduction

Whenever the U.S. Congress or executive agencies propose tightening environmental regulation, one of the first objections to surface is a worry about the effects upon U.S. competitiveness in export markets. This chapter considers the conceptual cogency and empirical evidence surrounding these concerns. First, the regulatory agenda for U.S. agriculture is reviewed. Then, evidence of past and prospective effects of regulation is assessed. Finally, the policy implications are discussed.

## U.S. Environmental Regulation Affecting Agriculture

Environmental regulation that affects agriculture can be separated usefully into two categories: *direct*—regulation of farm production practices, and *indirect*—regulation of nonfarm products or enterprises that affects the prices of farm inputs or outputs. In terms of the supply-demand conditions for agriculture, direct regulation changes the cost (supply) of farm output and the demand for inputs by farmers, and indirect regulation changes the demand for farm output and the supply functions of farm inputs. Both types of regulation can be economically important, but the direct regulations are usually specific to agriculture.

### Direct Regulation of Farmers' Practices

Farm practices can cause many environmental problems: nitrates and phosphates from fertilizer or animal wastes; pesticide drift (airborne) or leaching (waterborne) that claims victims beyond the targeted farm; soil erosion caused by wind or water that deposits damaging silts off the farm; overuse of antibiotics in livestock, generating microorganisms that are resistant to antibiotics; and destruction of habitat from swamp drainage or use of river water for irrigation. These are all classic externalities—unpriced technical relationships among individuals in different industries. Environmental laws also have been aimed at results of farm practices that are not, strictly speaking, externalities, e.g., pesticide residues in food products, poisoning of farm workers, and reduced future farmland value due to soil erosion. It should be noted, too, that externalities are not all negative; e.g., draining a swamp may do more good by reducing the number of mosquitoes than harm by reducing the number of ducks. The scenic value of pastures and woodlands with livestock grazing creates utility for nonfarmers.

Most U.S. regulatory activity at the federal level can be reduced to six areas of policy instruments in pursuit of the seven general goals shown in Table 14.1. In addition, policies have been enacted to promote preservation of farmland in urban areas and to regulate odors and noise from farming, but these have been predominantly local and state efforts without national significance.

The most significant direct regulatory action to date is the Conservation Reserve Program (CRP), a voluntary program that has idled 36.5 million acres, roughly 10 percent of U.S. cropland acreage. The CRP's primary goal is to reduce soil erosion on highly erodible land. Other environmental goals include reduction of sedimentation and habitat preservation. This program, however, is not aimed entirely at environmental goals; it also is intended to help support farm prices and farm incomes (by reducing output and by making annual payments to farmers in the program averaging about $50 per acre).

In the area of chemical regulation, many pesticides have been withdrawn from the market under the Federal Insecticide, Fungicide, and Rodenticide Act (FIFRA) registration requirements. Some of these pesticides were once economically important, e.g., DDT, dieldrin and aldrin (corn rootworm control), chlordane and heptachlor (for control of termites and fire ants), and mirez. A current issue involves the Environmental Protection Agency's (EPA's) ban on the soil fumigant methyl bromide, having previously banned a substitute used for similar purposes—ethylene dibromide (EDB). Entry of farm workers into fields treated with pesticides has been restricted, with tighter standards imposed in April 1994. Farmers have been required to undergo training to apply certain pesticides, and to keep records of their use.

Wetlands regulation under the Clean Water Act and the "swampbuster" provisions of the 1985 Farm Act have placed substantial penalties on

**TABLE 14.1.  Environmental Goals and Policy Instruments Intended to Affect Agriculture .**

| | Goals (and principal legislation) | | | | | | |
|---|---|---|---|---|---|---|---|
| Policy Instruments | Water Quality (Clean Water Act) | Air Quality (Clean Air Act) | Soil Conservation (Farm Acts) | Endangered Species Protection (ESA) | Food Safety (Food, Drug and Cosmetic Act) | Farm Worker Safety (FIFRA) | "Sustainable" Agricultural Production (Farm Acts) |
| Pesticide Regulation | X | X | | X | X | X | X |
| Nutrient (N, P) Regulation | X | | X | | | | X |
| Cropland Idling | X | | X | X | | | |
| Wetland Regulation | X | | | X | | | X |
| Soil Conservation | X | | X | X | | | X |
| Water (Irrigation) Regulation | X | | | X | | | |

Note: The X's indicate area regulated explicitly in an attempt to foster achievement of the goal at the top of the column. Regulation that affects the goals, but not as part of a program directly intended to attain the goal, has no X entry. For example, irrigation regulation may well affect soil conservation, but irrigation regulations are not an explicit component of soil conservation laws.

*Source:* Gardner (1993).

conversion of wetlands to cropland. The Endangered Species Act has caused some diversion of river water from irrigation, and species recovery plans have placed restrictions on farmers' land use in some limited areas. Nutrient management plans for livestock producers and taxes on chemicals have been imposed on farmers in some state and local jurisdictions.

While most environmental regulation of agriculture derives from specific environmental laws, the omnibus farm bills of recent years have incorporated an expanding environmental agenda (Table 14.2). However, these titles and subtitles have not yet imposed mandatory requirements upon farmers beyond the swampbuster, soil conservation, and pesticide recordkeeping provisions already mentioned.

No published estimates of the overall economic consequences of these regulations are available. It would be a formidable task to estimate the immediate costs, much less the ultimate effects on prices, output, and economic welfare, attributable to any of them.

### Indirect Regulations

The indirect regulations that receive the most attention are those concerning food safety and nutrition. Several processed food additives, such as coloring agents and preservatives, have been banned by the Food and Drug Administration. Federal agencies also have been responsible for labeling requirements, dietary advice, and school lunch regulations— programs that have influenced the demand for and availability of food products. The most recent changes are new regulations under the Nutritional Labeling and Education Act of 1990, implemented in April 1994.

Various environmental regulations have affected agricultural inputs. Environmental regulations of the lead content of gasoline, hormones and other additives in feed, disposal of chemical containers, licensing of pesticide applicators, and regulation of experiments in biotechnology are examples of policies that raise farmers' costs by increasing input prices.

Indirect regulations have two notable features that distinguish them from direct regulation of agricultural production. First, input cost increases often are not specific to the agricultural sector. Gasoline cost increases are shared with all other industries that use gasoline. This means that agriculture may not lose as much as other sectors, and may even gain from indirect regulation. For example, regulations that raise wage costs actually may reduce production costs in agriculture relative to the nonagricultural economy because labor is a smaller share of agriculture's costs.

Second, indirect regulation sometimes can be beneficial to agriculture, by increasing the demand for agricultural output. A notable example is

TABLE 14.2. Environmental/Food Titles of Recent Farm Legislation.

| 1977 Act | 1981 Act | 1985 Act | 1990 Act |
|---|---|---|---|
| XIV. Research, Extension and Teaching: Subtitle H, Solar Energy; Subtitle J, Sec. 1461, Organic Farming Study<br><br>XV. Rural Development and Conservation | XIV. Research, Extension and Teaching: Sec. 1434-35, Solar Energy<br><br>XV. Resource Conservation | XII. Resource Conservation: Subtitles A-C. Conservation of Highly Erodible Lands and Wetlands; Water Resource Conservation<br><br>XIV. Research, Extension and Teaching: Sec. 1410, "High Priority" to Biotechnology and Conservation Research; Sec. 1444, Pesticide Resistance Study | XII. Subtitle C, Tree Planting<br><br>XIII. Subtitle C, Cosmetic Appearance<br><br>XIV. Subtitles A-H, Highly Erodible and Wetland Conservation; Environmental Quality Council; Water Quality; Pesticide Recordkeeping; Composting Research<br><br>XVI. Research. Subtitle B, Sustainable Agriculture; Subtitle G, Alternative Agricultural Research; Subtitle H, Sec. 1668, Biotechnology Risk Assessment<br><br>Title XXI. Organic Certification<br><br>Title XXIV. Global Climate Change |

*Source*: Gardner (1993).

the oxygenate requirements of the 1990 Clean Air Act Amendments (still not fully implemented in 1994). These requirements are expected to increase the demand for ethanol as a fuel additive, by some estimates doubling ethanol demand over the next few years. This in turn would increase the demand for corn in the neighborhood of 300 million bushels. Similar regulations in pursuit of biodegradable products, such as lubricants and plastics, tend to increase the demand for agricultural products as raw materials. Over the long term, these demands are likely to be increasingly important.

## Economic Consequences of Regulation

It is important to distinguish two steps in the analysis of regulation: (1) cost increases resulting from input/output restrictions or incentive changes, and (2) the incidence of these cost increases on product and factor prices, and hence on the economic well-being of individuals. This two-step process is analogous to the analysis of a tax increase: the first step is to specify the size of the tax, and second, the incidence. Unlike the tax-analysis case, the first step is far from trivial in the analysis of regulation. It is one thing to say that restricting use of a pesticide is like an input tax, but quite another to determine the magnitude of the tax. The question involves technical issues in crop, soil, and animal science, areas with which economists need assistance. A brief review of the state of knowledge and educated guesses in the area, and the implications for U.S. agricultural trade, follows.

In the empirical economics of environmental regulation, more quantitative estimates have been published for prospective regulations than for regulations actually in place. In fact, it is difficult to detect consequences of past regulation in commodity and input market data. The existence of potentially interesting dynamics is apparent from the U.S. Department of Agriculture (USDA) data on agricultural chemical (pesticide and inorganic fertilizers) use. These chemicals are the primary target of environmental regulation. Figure 14.1 indicates that chemical use in U.S. agriculture, after rising rapidly during 1950-80, has declined in the 1980s (Figure 14.2); but the same trend of rapid increase followed by a slight decline in the 1980s is apparent for the ratio of chemicals to cropland (Figure 14.3). If the change in the 1980s is attributable to regulation, and if this regulation increased the inputs needed per unit of output (and hence raised costs), then this effect should show up in the trend of total factor productivity growth in agriculture. However, the USDA index of total factor productivity, also shown in Figure 14.3, does not suggest a decline in the rate of growth of productivity in the 1980s.

FIGURE 14.1. U.S. Agricultural Chemical Use.

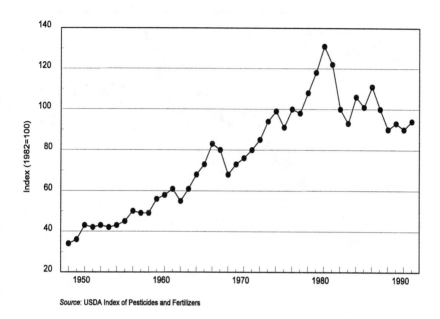

Source: USDA Index of Pesticides and Fertilizers

FIGURE 14.2. U.S. Cropland Harvested.

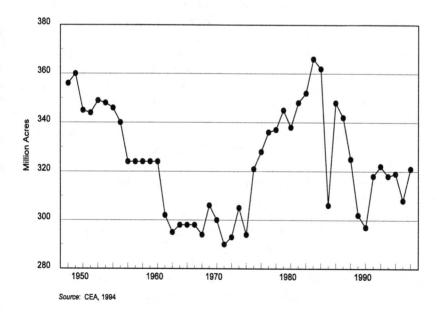

Source: CEA, 1994

FIGURE 14.3.  Total Factor Productivity and Chemicals Used per Acre.

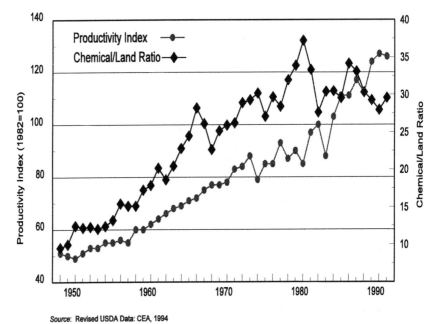

Source: Revised USDA Data: CEA, 1994

Aggregate measures of total factor productivity are subject to many important pitfalls, both conceptual and practical, which include data limitations in particular (Ball 1985). Therefore, it is helpful to consider alternative measures which may be conceptually equivalent but which use different data. In particular, price-based measures use some independent data and are equivalent under standard assumptions of convex technology and competition (López 1988). Real U.S. agricultural output prices, and the ratio of U.S. farm output to farm input prices, have continued to decline in the 1980s, but at a rate similar to that found during the 1950-70 period (Figure 14.4).

On the other hand, some individual crop yields, notably corn, wheat, and soybeans, appear to have grown at a slower rate in the 1980s than during 1950-80. Nonetheless, the U.S. data as a whole are unlikely to convince proponents of further reductions in agricultural chemical use that such reductions threaten agricultural productivity.

The strongest econometric evidence for the role of chemicals in agricultural productivity growth is provided by production function studies, notably Griliches (1964), Headley (1968), and related works. These studies suggest that in the 1950s and 1960s, purchased fertilizers and pesticides generated $3 to $5 in output for a marginal dollar spent on these inputs. These findings fit well with the rapid expansion of input

**FIGURE 14.4  Output/Input Prices.**

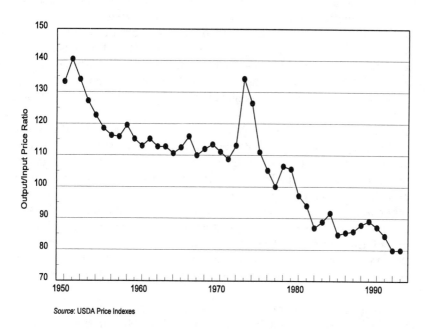

*Source*: USDA Price Indexes

use during this period. However, more recent research questions the
validity of the Griliches/Headley production function specification of
pesticides as inputs. Babcock, Lichtenberg, and Zilberman (1992)
emphasize that many pesticides, particularly in fruits, principally affect
quality rather than the quantity of output. Lichtenberg and Zilberman
(1986), and Chambers and Lichtenberg (1994) have improved the
econometric methods of estimating pesticide demand, but their dual
approach assumes that the value of marginal product equals factor price
for all producers; so they cannot find that a dollar's worth of pesticides
generates more (or less) than a dollar's worth of output. The best
evidence that farmers are no longer using too little agricultural chemicals
for purposes of profit maximization is the simple observation that
chemical use stopped expanding in the 1980s.

The most widely used approach to estimating effects of reduced
chemical use is the use of simulations based on agricultural scientists'
estimates of yield losses under various production practices. The USDA's
National Agricultural Pesticide Impact Assessment Program (NAPIAP)
provides estimates of the relationship between production and pesticides
for use in the EPA's pesticide regulatory decisions. NAPIAP polls
agricultural scientists across the country to estimate yield losses, typically
from the absence of a particular chemical. The Economic Research Service

of the USDA then estimates the economic implications. One big problem with these assessments is that it is often unclear what substitute production method the analysts have in mind when a chemical is withdrawn. Osteen and Kuchler (1986) demonstrate the importance of this consideration in a study of acetanilides, used to kill weeds in corn and soybeans. If one of them—alachlor—is banned, the estimated U.S. costs are $149 million, and if the other—metolachlor—is banned, the costs are similar. But if both are lost simultaneously, the estimated costs are $2.1 billion.

Dinan, Simons, and Lloyd (1988), in an EPA study, considered a whole set of EPA regulatory actions. Zilberman et al. (1991) summarize results of proposed multi-chemical, multi-crop regulations under the "big green" referendum in California. They estimate crop losses amounting to about 25 percent of the value of the crops.

Other analysts have considered the issue by estimating the costs of "organic" or "sustainable" crop production from experimental plots or ongoing farm enterprises. The findings are mixed. The most telling study, of Ohio farms certified as organic producers under a state-level program, estimated organic farm costs to be almost double conventional farm costs (Batte 1992).

The most wide-ranging, ambitious simulation study of chemical regulation was carried out by Knutson et al. (1990) for the American Farm Bureau Federation. They estimated crop losses from a complete ban on all pesticides. The estimated yield losses, and hence cost of production increases, are quite large. But these costs result from regulatory prohibitions more sweeping than any that the EPA or congressional committees have seriously contemplated.

Beyond the question of the magnitude of cost increases due to more stringent regulation, the economic incidence of such changes requires further analysis. However, it is often difficult to determine the portion of the regulation cost that is borne by farmers versus that borne by food and fiber consumers. Knutson et al. (1990), as well as other analysts, typically have found that consumers bear the brunt of the cost increases, essentially because the demand for agricultural output is relatively inelastic, and because restricting purchased chemical inputs may increase the demand for farmer-owned inputs (land and labor).

Commodities that are traded internationally may have different cost incidences than purely domestic goods; i.e., traded commodities will tend to have prices determined by international market conditions and hence be less sensitive to U.S. input regulations. Thus, farmers are more likely to bear the economic losses from regulation of exported and imported commodities—grains, oilseeds, cotton, tobacco, citrus, and some nuts and specialty crops.

## Regulation and Competitiveness

The concept of competitiveness refers to the domestic cost of production as compared to production costs in other countries. Competitiveness is evaluated on a product-by-product basis. Consider a regulation affecting a relatively small sector of the economy. The consequences for trade and welfare can be examined within several alternative contexts:

1. a partial equilibrium analysis in which cost increases cause exports to fall and/or imports to rise, depending on product demand and input supply elasticities;
2. a general equilibrium model in which (a) all inputs are used in all sectors (e.g., Jones 1965), or (b) some inputs are specific to agriculture.

In order to achieve concrete results, consider a specific regulatory package following Gardner (1993). Suppose there is a combination of Endangered Species Act recovery plans, further cancellations of pesticides under FIFRA and food safety laws, and nutrient regulations under nonpoint pollution provisions of the Clean Water Act and related federal and state legislation. Imagine further that this combination of policies causes a 20 to 30 percent reduction in fertilizer use, a 30 to 40 percent reduction in pesticide use, and a 3 percent reduction in cropland use. In addition, assume that biotechnology regulation slows the development of new pest control methods that could substitute for regulated chemicals. This regulatory package was estimated to raise costs of U.S. crops by 10 to 15 percent and consumer prices by 7 to 12 percent. Thus, consumers bear more than half of the regulatory burden.

To observe the more fundamental input market conditions that could generate these results, Azzam, Helmers, and Spilker (1990) use a five-input (land, labor, machinery, chemicals, and other) model to investigate the effects of 10 and 25 percent reductions in chemical use (including fertilizer) in grains and soybeans. Under the 25 percent cut scenario, they estimate that crop prices would rise about 5 percent on average, and the rental value of cropland would fall about 25 percent.

In a general equilibrium model without specific factors, the results are quite different. Assuming all sectors use regulated inputs, but that these inputs are a larger share of costs in agriculture, an increase in regulation should shift resources and output out of agriculture. In the small-country case, relative prices are unchanged and nonagricultural output increases in absolute terms (by application of the Rybczynski Theorem), even though the resource base is reduced. If factor-price equalization holds, there are no input price effects, but only production and trade flow effects. This model is not taken seriously as a practical tool because it is clear that some inputs are factors specific to agriculture.

Rendleman (1991) uses a specific-factor general equilibrium model to analyze chemical reduction. His results indicate a 25 percent chemical reduction would increase grain/oilseed prices by about 8 percent and would reduce the rental value of cropland by about 10 percent. The results are quite similar to the partial equilibrium estimate cited earlier.

Neither partial nor general equilibrium simulations have focused on the international trade effects of environmental regulation. All published studies assume U.S. commodity prices are not determined by international market prices—otherwise, U.S. consumers would bear none of the burden, all of which would be borne by U.S. farmers and input suppliers. Elasticities of foreign demand for U.S. products vary substantially from commodity to commodity, and none are known with precision. Assuming that on average, the elasticity of export demand is -3 for an intermediate-run period of three to five years, a 10 percent price rise would cause the volume of exports to fall by 30 percent and the value of exports to fall by 20 percent. With U.S. agricultural exports of $40 billion, the result would be a loss of $8 billion in export revenue.

On the import side, one would expect less quantity response to tighter environmental regulations for two reasons: (1) quantitative import barriers restrict import response, and (2) many imports are tropical products which the United States does not produce and hence on which regulations would not be placed. Nonetheless, it would be reasonable to expect U.S. agricultural imports to increase by $1 or $2 billion from the current $25 billion level.

These admittedly conjectural calculations indicate that expanded environmental regulation could plausibly eliminate two-thirds of the U.S. agricultural trade surplus. Of course, this involves two key policy assumptions—that the United States does not offset higher U.S. production costs by increased export subsidies, and that the U.S. intensifies environmental regulation while other countries do not. Thus, further attention to political issues is crucial for an economic assessment.

## Policy Issues Outstanding

When the Clinton Administration was inaugurated in January 1993, many expected a new era of environmental action. Agriculture, in particular, was held to be ripe for intensified regulation because:

- The Clean Water Act was due for reauthorization. Two of the key issues were wetlands preservation and nonpoint water pollution from agricultural sources.

- The Endangered Species Act (ESA) was up for reauthorization. Environmentalists claimed that the act was not doing enough to protect threatened wildlife, particularly in allocating fresh water for wildlife in the West.
- Secretary of the Interior Babbitt was set to raise grazing fees on federal lands, and to include requirements for environmental protection in leases for such land.
- The administration announced a campaign to reduce pesticide use by farmers. Amendments to the Food, Drug, and Cosmetics Act were expected to impose more stringent standards on pesticide residues in all agricultural products (in exchange for repealing the "Delaney Clause" of 1958, which bans any detectible trace of those processed food additives which have been shown to cause cancer in laboratory animal tests).
- Vice President Gore's preference for environmental protection, and in particular his focus upon the threat of global warming, suggested a general push for "sustainable" agricultural practices.

In mid-1994, a year and a half into the Clinton regime, U.S. politics are colored distinctly less green. Reauthorization of the Clean Water Act and the ESA has so far produced little to threaten agriculture, and indeed the dominant trend appears toward weakening environmental legislation. Grazing reforms have been stymied. A landmark case in which Florida sugar and other crop growers would have to change their water use practices and finance catchment basins to reduce phosphate concentration in water going to the Everglades turned out more favorable to agricultural interests than was expected. It is questionable whether any significant new regulatory burdens will be imposed upon farmers.

The next omnibus farm bill will be considered in 1995. Given the 1995 expiration of some ten-year contracts under the Conservation Reserve Program, and the uncertainty that the $1.6 billion annual payments will be continued under intensified budgetary pressures, both environmental and farm interests face major policy challenges. The environmental view is that there should be an extension of the approach taken in the conservation compliance provisions of the 1985 Act—requiring farmers, in exchange for price-support benefits, to undertake soil conservation, improved pesticide and nutrient management, and other steps to promote water quality and other environmental goals.

While the present political climate is not friendly for such changes, popular support for environmental protection persists. This support is evident at the state level. For example, after several years of failure, the Pennsylvania legislature enacted a nutrient management law that will impinge upon the practices of an estimated 60 to 65 percent of the state's livestock producers. Maryland has spent $30 million subsidizing farmers' practices aimed at improving water quality.

A policy issue often discussed recently is the role of environmental policy in NAFTA and GATT. NAFTA did address some environmental regulatory issues through an elaboration of dispute settlement panels. The Uruguay Round addressed these issues only in the Sanitary and Phytosanitary (SPS) Agreement. The SPS Agreement is a step toward harmonization of regulation across countries, while discouraging the use of unjustified health-related measures as disguised barriers to trade. Environmentalists, however, worry that commercial interests will use this agreement to discourage legitimate health-related trade restrictions. One unresolved issue is the authority that NAFTA or WTO institutions will have in influencing countries' environmental policies.

In general, it seems likely that the more powerful international trade institutions are, the fewer the differences between environmental regulation in different countries, and therefore the less the competitive effects of U.S. regulation. There are two distinct issues: the level of environmental protection, and differences between nations in the degree of protection and regulation needed to achieve that level. Harmonization reduces the differences, but what is the effect worldwide? Environmental interests appear quite concerned that NAFTA and GATT are poised to weaken environmental regulation on an overall basis. More important from the producers' viewpoint are intercountry differences in regulation. For example, while the U.S. is banning methyl bromide, Japan continues to require its use to kill insects in imported grain (Marchant and Ballenger 1994).

## Summary

Environmental regulation is potentially a major factor in U.S. agricultural trade; it could raise U.S. costs of production and provide justification for restrictive trade policies abroad. To date, the effects of environmental regulation on trends in U.S. productivity and costs have not been significant. But the environmental regulatory agenda is so broad and sweeping that the potential for future harm to U.S. competitiveness in agriculture is substantial. However, harmonization of environmental protection activities across countries could forestall this outcome.

More important in the short term, political forces are not strong enough at this time to enact cost-increasing regulations in the absence of strong evidence that the environmental improvements are valuable enough to justify the costs which could be achieved by such regulations. That is, implicit and sometimes explicit benefit/cost tests are now the rule in environmental legislation (whereas earlier, in the Delaney Clause and in the Endangered Species Act, such calculations were explicitly ruled out), the result is a much stricter criteria for environmental regulation, and hence a slower adoption of tighter regulations.

## References

Azzam, A., G. Helmers, and M. Spilker. "U.S. Agriculture Under Fertilizer and Chemical Restrictions." Report No. 163, Part 2, Department of Agricultural Economics, University of Nebraska, 1990.

Babcock, B.A., E. Lichtenberg, and D. Zilberman. "Impact of Damage Control and Quality of Output: Estimating Pest Control Effectiveness." *American Journal of Agricultural Economics* 74(1992):163–72.

Ball, V.E. "Output, Input, and Productivity Measurement in U.S. Agriculture." *American Journal of Agricultural Economics* 67(1985):475–86.

Batte, M.T. "Sustainable Agriculture and Farm Profitability." Paper presented at annual meetings of American Agricultural Economics Association, Baltimore, MD, August 1992.

Chambers, R., and E. Lichtenberg. "The Simple Econometrics of Pesticide Productivity." *American Journal of Agricultural Economics* 76(1994):407–17.

Council of Economic Advisors. *Economic Report of the President.* Washington, DC: U.S. Government Printing Office, 1994.

Dinan, T., C. Simons, and R. Lloyd. "The Agricultural Sector Study: Impacts of Environmental Regulations on Agriculture." U.S. Environmental Protection Agency, Office of Policy Planning, Washington, DC, September 1988.

Gardner, B.L. "The Impacts of Environmental Protection and Food Safety Regulation on U.S. Agriculture." Agricultural Policy Working Group, Arlington, VA, September 1993.

Griliches, Z. "Research Expenditures, Education, and the Aggregate Agricultural Production Function." *The American Economic Review* 54(1964):961–74.

Headley, J.C. "Estimating the Productivity of Agricultural Pesticides." *American Journal of Agricultural Economics* 50(1968):13–23.

Jones, R. "The Structure of Simple General Equilibrium Models." *Journal of Political Economy* 73(1965):557–72.

Knutson, R.D., C.R. Taylor, J.B. Penson, and E.G. Smith. "Economic Impacts of Reduced Chemical Use." Report prepared for the American Farm Bureau Federation. Knutson and Associates, College Station, TX, 1990.

Lichtenberg, E., and D. Zilberman. "The Econometrics of Damage Control." *American Journal of Agricultural Economics* 68(1986):261–73.

López, R. "Productivity Measurement and the Distribution of the Fruits of Technological Progress." In *Agricultural Productivity*, J.M. Antle and S.M. Capalbo, eds., pp. 189– 207. Washington, DC: Resources for the Future, 1988.

Marchant, M.A., and N. Ballenger. "The Trade and Environment Debate: Relevant for Southern Agriculture?" *Journal of Agricultural and Applied Economics* 26(1994):108–28.

Osteen, C., and F. Kuchler. "Potential Bans of Corn and Soybean Pesticides." Agricultural Economics Report No. 546, U.S. Department of Agriculture, Economic Research Service, Washington, DC, 1986.

Rendleman, C.M. "Agrichemical Reduction Policy." *Journal of Agricultural Economics Research* 43(1991):7–12.

Zilberman, D., A. Schmitz, G. Casterline, E. Lichtenberg, and J. Siebert. "The Economics of Pesticide Use and Regulation." *Science* 253(1991):518–22.

# 15

# Trade Implication of the EU Nitrate Directive: An Emerging Research Priority

*Dale Leuck and Stephen Haley*

### Introduction

There is a consensus that both agricultural and environmental policies affect agricultural trade, as well as the environment. Considerable research has focused on quantifying the effects that agricultural policies, including their reform, have on trade. Attempts to quantify the effects of agricultural policies on the environment, and also the effects of environmental policies on the environment and agricultural trade are fewer in number.[1] Accordingly, there is far less consensus on these latter relationships, as well as on the best policies to accomplish the dual goals of agricultural policy reform and achieving environmental objectives. This chapter contributes to the debate by discussing how the EU Nitrate Directive, intended to reduce residual nitrogen in the environment, also may affect trade. The directive is to take effect in 1999, after the Common Agricultural Policy (CAP) reforms adopted in May 1992 are implemented.

### The Nitrate Directive

Linking environmental policies to agricultural trade and the environment is a relatively new effort. As such, it offers many challenges. Environmental policies, such as the Nitrate Directive, may induce rather significant and rapid changes in the structure of production, requiring an interdisciplinary approach to understand them. The difficulties are inherent in the newness and nature of the problem, the specific requirements of the Nitrate Directive, and the many possible alternative responses to the directive.

## Nature of the Problem

Nitrate is derived from elemental gaseous nitrogen, $N_2$, through a number of chemical reactions, as part of the nitrogen cycle.[2] Nitrate is essential for plant growth, but residual nitrate leaches or runs off into water supplies, where it poses a threat to the health of both humans and animals (Follett, Murphy, and Donahue 1981). Agriculture is the main source of nitrate, with livestock manure and chemical fertilizer contributing the major portion. The symbiotic fixation of nitrogen between soil microorganisms and legumes is a minor source of agricultural nitrogen. The main nonagricultural sources of nitrate are electrical storms, automobile exhaust, and industrial emissions.

The problems posed by high nitrate levels are geographically related. Agra Europe (1991) describes current nitrate pollution in the EU as covering most of Belgium and the Netherlands, parts of (mainly northern) Germany, the Brittany region of France, the Po Valley of northern Italy, and several regions of southern England. These are all regions with high livestock intensity, where nitrate pollution often results from the disposal of manure with little or no fertilization purpose in mind. The degree of nitrate problem in any region can be fully evaluated only if all sources of nitrate are measured.

Nitrate is measurable in the water and soil. However, there are some difficulties in measuring the amount of nitrogen deposited on the land and in the waters of specific regions. The amount of nitrate from nonagricultural sources is difficult to measure accurately without monitoring stations, although some "rules of thumb" are available. Data on the amount of chemical fertilizer actually applied typically are published on the national level, but do not distinguish among crops. Regional data that are most readily available tend to be estimates of application, or uptake by crops.

Reliable estimates of the regional distribution of livestock nitrogen are especially important, since this is what the Nitrate Directive attempts to reduce. Coefficients that measure the nitrogen output of livestock must consider the amount and composition of feed that animals consume, the weights to which they are raised, and the amount of milk or eggs produced. These factors lead to variability in nitrogen output, as evidenced by the coefficients applied by researchers to beginning inventories of livestock (Table 15.1). These coefficients can be multiplied by beginning inventory data to calculate annual nitrogen output; the coefficients already include multiple-cropping practices (e.g., two crops of pigs per year).

**TABLE 15.1. Nitrogen Supply per Animal per Year (Kg/Animal/Year).**

| | Germany, U.K., and Ireland | France, Italy, Greece, Spain, and Portugal | Denmark | Belgium and Luxembourg | Netherlands |
|---|---|---|---|---|---|
| Dairy Cattle | 85.0 | 84.0 | 126.3 | 88.0 | 144.0 |
| Other Cattle | 50.0 | 50.4 | 43.8 | 61.6 | 78.0 |
| Breeding Sows | 29.0 | 39.7 | 30.9 | 27.5 | 35.0 |
| Fattening Pigs | 11.0 | 10.1 | 14.5 | 11.8 | 13.9 |
| Poultry | 0.5 | 0.6 | 0.7 | 0.6 | 0.6 |

*Source:* Brouwer et al. (forthcoming); Schleef and Kleinhanse (1994).

Nitrogen that is actually delivered to the surface environment may return to the atmosphere before it is taken up by crops or enters the water supply as nitrate. Depending upon soil and weather conditions, and the method of application, up to 50 percent of the nitrogen in manure may reenter the atmosphere through a process called volatilization (AgraEurope 1991). Volatilization may occur after deposition of the manure by the animal, during storage and transport to the field, and after it is applied. Nitrate in the soil also may reenter the atmosphere through a process known as denitrification.

One is tempted to hope that the need to more fully understand the nitrogen cycle could be avoided by simply measuring the nitrate levels in local ground or surface waters. However, the leaching process may take years or even decades, depending upon soil conditions. Therefore, these measurements would underestimate the problem. In any event, a connection must be made to the source of the nitrate.

## The Nitrate Directive and Possible Farmer Response

The Nitrate Directive requires member countries to plan programs that will reduce manure nitrogen to 170 kilograms (kg) per hectare (ha) in certain designated "vulnerable zones," after the directive takes effect in 1999 (Commission of the European Communities 1991). Manure is considered to be the major source of nitrate pollution in the vulnerable zones. However, the directive allows consideration to be given to crop uptake of nitrogen and nitrogen from all sources. Therefore, the 170 kg/ha criterion may be interpreted as a maximum annual residual (MAR), inclusive of nitrogen from commercial fertilizer and other sources. Countries are to meet a timetable for designating the vulnerable zones, drawing up "codes of good conduct," and establishing systems to monitor nitrogen application in these zones.

The Nitrate Directive implies that livestock density may have to be reduced in the vulnerable zones, but it also specifies certain actions that farmers may take to reduce the amount of nitrogen contributing to nitrate contamination of water supplies. These actions include restrictions on the time when manure may be applied to fields and requirements for manure storage.

There are a number of ways that the livestock sector of the EU may adjust to the Nitrate Directive. Farmers may, of course, reduce the number of animals they keep. They may also transport the surplus to manure-deficit areas. The governments of both Denmark and the Netherlands have established programs to facilitate the transport of surplus manure to deficit areas and to pelletize manure for export. However, these programs alone will not solve the nitrate problem in most areas.

CAP reform also offers some possibility for reduced nitrogen levels in manure. This nitrogen reduction will occur because farmers will switch livestock feed away from imported protein meals, with their relatively high nitrogen content, toward grains and their lower nitrogen content, as grain prices fall under CAP reform. Some research suggests that the nitrogen levels in manure could fall by 10 to 25 percent as a result of CAP reform. The nitrogen coefficients in Table 15.1 offer support for this assertion. The nitrogen content of livestock in Denmark and the Netherlands is in general much higher than that in the other EU countries, where a greater proportion of livestock are grain fed.

Despite the benefits from CAP reform, it is doubtful that nitrogen levels can be reduced to desired levels without some reduction in livestock production in the vulnerable zones. Some of this production, however, may simply shift to other areas in the EU, which are currently less intensive in animal production and more intensive in grain production. Estimating the magnitude of such a shift is difficult.

### Implications for Livestock Production and Fertilizer Use

The possible reductions in livestock production implied by the Nitrate Directive are calculated in Leuck et al. (1995), using coefficients from Koopmans' (1987) study. These coefficients measure the amount of nitrogen contained in different types of livestock manure and are taken up by different kinds of crops. A nitrogen balance is calculated for each EU country using 1986 as the base year. Belgium, Denmark, and the Netherlands are the only countries that exceed the 170 kg/ha MAR, with residual nitrogen levels of 240 kg/ha, 187 kg/ha, and 480 kg/ha, respectively (Leuck et al., Table 6).

These balances are used to calculate the reduction in livestock production and fertilizer use needed to reduce residual nitrogen to the MAR. A comparison of the amounts of nitrogen from fertilizer and manure is presented in Figure 15.1. The amount of nitrogen from livestock manure is roughly equal to the amount from commercial fertilizer, on a metric ton basis. The amount of nitrogen taken up by crops is roughly equal to the nitrogen content of commercial fertilizer. Therefore, approximately all of the nitrogen from manure is residual.

The choice of how much to reduce the production of different kinds of livestock, or the amount of nitrogen to be used on crops, is ultimately a political choice. In this chapter, reductions to reduce residual nitrogen to the MAR are assumed, which may be viewed as a standard by which to judge the need for possible additional policies. In order to reduce residual nitrogen to the MAR, the required reductions in livestock production are assumed to be equal to the proportion of livestock nitrogen in the total nitrogen residual, with any remainder of the reduction coming from fertilizer cutbacks. Veenendaal and Brouwer (1991) suggest that in the Netherlands, farmers could significantly reduce fertilizer use without affecting yields. These reductions may be viewed as a standard by which to judge the need for possible additional policies.

**FIGURE 15.1. Nitrogen from Livestock Manure and Commercial Fertilizers.**

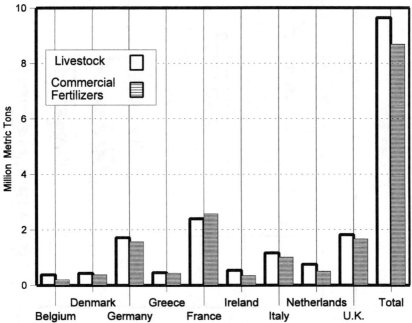

Large reductions in livestock are calculated for Belgium/Luxembourg (28 percent), Denmark (9 percent), and the Netherlands (65 percent), and a large reduction in fertilizer use (28 percent) also may have to occur for the Netherlands (Leuck et al. 1995, Table 7). These reductions are more moderate when expressed as a percentage of EU production, however: 1 percent for sheep, 8 percent for dairy, 5 percent for beef, 10 percent for poultry, and 12 percent for pigs (Figure 15.2).

A wide confidence interval may surround these calculations because they contain significant measurement errors, although these are offsetting to some extent. Nonagricultural sources of nitrogen are not measured, and the magnitude of problems in parts of Germany, the United Kingdom, the Brittany region of France, and the Po Valley of Italy are lost in aggregation. On the other hand, some double counting exists in the calculations because slaughtered livestock were included, instead of only inventories (Leuck et al. 1995, Table 5). Finally, the losses of nitrogen (nitrate) to the atmosphere from volatilization and denitrification are not measured, but the directive may ultimately regulate them because they contribute to acid rain. Any net error at the EU level may be relatively small, since the EU-wide calculations are not unreasonable, although the calculated reductions for the Netherlands and Belgium seem high.

FIGURE 15.2. E.U. Supply Changes Under Selected Policies.

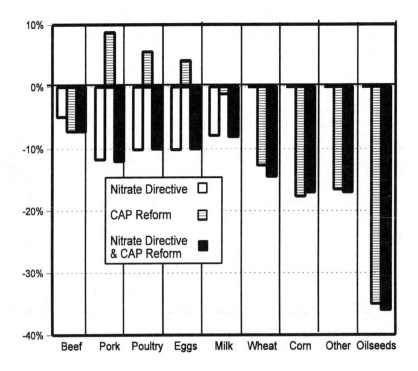

## Possible Effects on EU Agriculture and Trade

A CAP reform scenario is run as a basis for comparing the possible effects of the Nitrate Directive.[3] This reform package, planned for implementation over three years starting in 1993-94, has many specific features (Madell 1992). The most important features affecting prices are an elimination of oilseed price supports, a reduction of grain intervention prices by 30 percent, a decrease in beef intervention prices by 15 percent, and an implied reduction of 3 percent in the price of cow's milk. Governments will compensate farmers for price reductions through direct payments. Farmers who produce more than 92 tons of grain are required to set aside 15 percent of their arable crop base.

The Nitrate Directive and CAP reform have different effects on production. The Nitrate Directive essentially affects only livestock production. Under CAP reform, crop production declines while livestock production grows, with two exceptions. The livestock product-to-feed price ratio is increased because livestock prices decrease less than grain and oilseed prices. However, among all livestock, this ratio increases the least for beef, causing substitution away from beef production. Dairy production does not increase because it is bound by the milk quota.

Under the combination of the Nitrate Directive and CAP reform, livestock production decreases by the amounts implied by the Nitrate Directive, while crop production decreases by the amounts implied by CAP reform. Livestock production is bound by the reductions implied by the Nitrate Directive, while crops are free to decline in response to CAP reform.

### The Effects on the Nitrogen Balance

Both policies reduce residual nitrogen by similar amounts: nitrogen levels fall 4 percent under the Nitrate Directive and 5.5 percent under CAP reform. In the case of the Nitrate Directive, residual nitrogen levels decline because of reduced livestock numbers. Under CAP reform, the decline in residual nitrogen levels occurs because of reduced crop production and fertilizer use, and is offset somewhat by increases in all livestock except beef and dairy. However, this decline is spread throughout the EU, while the problem of nitrate pollution is centered in Belgium, Denmark, and the Netherlands. CAP reform alone is unlikely to reduce residual nitrogen in these polluted areas. Therefore, under the combination of policies, it is the constraints imposed by the Nitrate Directive that reduce nitrogen pollution in the regions of intensive livestock production.

### Net Trade Effects for the European Union

The changes in EU net trade reflect the shifts in EU production that occur under each scenario (Figure 15.3). Under CAP reform, the net exports of all livestock products increase, except beef, whose production decreases, and dairy products, for which production is bound by the milk quota. The same amount of milk is used to produce slightly more cheese exports and slightly less butter and milk powder exports. The EU shifts from a net exporter of beef to a net importer.

Under the combination of CAP reform and the Nitrate Directive, the net exports of all livestock products are reduced, because livestock supplies are reduced by the amounts implied by the Nitrate Directive, instead of being allowed to react to the prices under CAP reform. The EU becomes a net importer of all livestock products, rather than a net exporter as in the base. The EU is not as large a net importer of beef as under CAP reform alone, because the supply of beef does not decline as much under the combined scenarios. Net trade for the other livestock products is similar in magnitude to the beef net trade numbers.

Under CAP reform, the changes in net trade for crops occur because more grain is fed to livestock and less is produced under CAP reform

FIGURE 15.3 Net Trade Effects for EU Livestock Under Selected Policies.

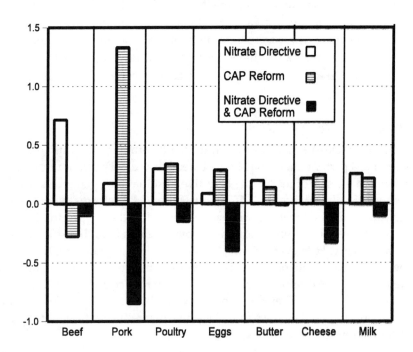

Figure 15.4. Net Trade Effects for EU Crops Under Selected Policies.

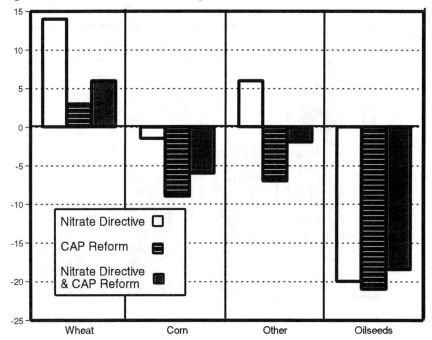

(Figure 15.4). The net exports of wheat decrease about 80 percent, and the net imports of corn and oilseed meal increase by about 300 percent and 5 percent, respec-tively. The EU shifts from exporting five million tons of other coarse grains to importing about eight million tons.

The net trade effects arising from the combination of CAP reform and the Nitrate Directive are the result of decreases in grain supply because of CAP reform and decreases in feed demand from lower livestock production imposed by the Nitrate Directive. The decrease in crop supply exceeds the decrease in feed demand, however. Therefore, net exports of wheat and coarse grains decrease and net imports of corn increase. The EU again becomes a net importer of coarse grains, but not by as much as under CAP reform alone. For oilseed meal, net imports decrease slightly, because the decrease in oilseed supply is less than the decrease in feed demand.

### Net Trade for the United States

Net U.S. trade generally benefits from CAP reform and the Nitrate Directive; i.e., net exports increase while net imports decline (Figures 15.5 and 15.6). Under CAP reform, net beef imports decline by 50 percent, and net imports of pork more than double. Exports of poultry meat decline,

*240*

FIGURE 15.5. Net Trade Effects for U.S. Crops Under Selected Policies.

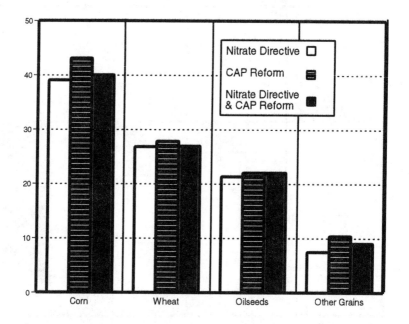

FIGURE 15.6. Net Trade Effects for U.S. Livestock Products Under Selected Policies.

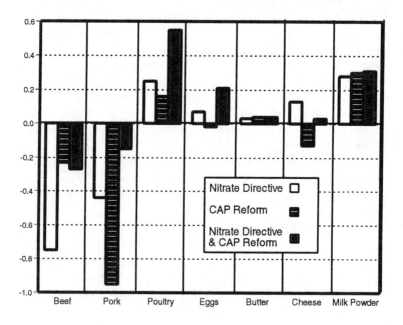

and the United States shifts from being a net exporter of eggs and cheese to a net importer. Other dairy products are not affected. The net exports of all grains and oilseeds increase under CAP reform.

The combination of the Nitrate Directive and CAP reform again causes net beef imports to decline, but also causes pork imports to decline. In the combined scenario, exports of poultry products increase, but dairy product exports are relatively unchanged. Net exports of grains and oilseeds are up only slightly above their base levels.

## Conclusions

The Nitrate Directive implies possible reductions in EU livestock production ranging from 1 percent for sheep to 12 percent for pigs. The reductions are likely to be most significant in Belgium, Denmark, and the Netherlands. Several caveats apply to these predictions. Farmers in Belgium, Denmark, and the Netherlands may alter production practices in ways that would safeguard some livestock production. While these responses by farmers may cause the estimates to be overstated, regional aggregation can hide localized areas with excessive amounts of residual nitrogen, causing the estimates to understate the reduction in livestock numbers that may be required.

Three main conclusions nevertheless emerge from the analysis. First, CAP reform is not successful at reducing residual nitrogen levels in intensive livestock areas, because, in general, livestock production increases. Only a targeted policy, such as the Nitrate Directive, reduces nitrate pollution to desired levels where needed. Finally, the increases in livestock production that would occur because of CAP reform may not materialize because they conflict with the reductions in manure nitrogen required by the Nitrate Directive.

## Notes

1. See, for example, Abler and Shortle (1992); Becker (1993); Hartmann (1994); Leuck et al. (1995); and Veenendaal and Brouwer (1991).
2. For a full discussion of the nitrogen cycle, see Follett, Murphy, and Donahue (1981).
3. See Leuck et al. for details of the modeling exercise.

## References

Abler, D., and J. Shortle. "Environmental and Farm Commodity Policy Linkages in the U.S. and the EC." *European Review of Agricultural Economics* 19(1992):197-217.
Agra Europe. *Agriculture and the Environment: How Will the EC Resolve the Conflict?* July 1991.

Becker, H. "Attaining Sustainable Regional Production Structures Through Taxes and Quotas on Pesticides and Fertilizers." In *EC Agricultural Policies by the End of the Century*, F. Soares, F. da Silva, and J. Espada, eds. Kiel, Germany, Wissenschafts- verlag Vauk Kiel KG, 1993.

Brouwer, F., F. Godeschalk, P. Hellegers, and G. Kelholt. *Mineral Balances at Farm Level of the European Union*. The Hague, Netherlands: Agricultural Economics Research Institute (LEI-DLO), forthcoming.

Commission of the European Communities (CEC). *Official Journal of the European Communities*. No. 375, Brussels, 31 December 1991.

Follett, R., L. Murphy, and R. Donahue. *Fertilizers and Soil Amendments*. Englewood Cliffs, NJ:Prentice-Hall, Inc., 1981.

Hartmann, M. "The Effects of EC Environmental Policies on Agricultural Trade and Economic Welfare." In *Agricultural Trade and Economic Integration in Europe and in North America*, M. Hartmann, P. Schmitz, and H. von Witzke, eds. Kiel, Germany, Wissenschaftsverlag Vauk Kiel KG, 1994.

Koopmans, T. "An application of an Agro-Economic Model to Environmental Issues in the EC: A Case Study." *European Review of Agricultural Economics* 14(1987):147-59.

Leuck, D., S. Haley, P. Liapis, and B. McDonald. "The EU Nitrate Directive and CAP Reform: Effects on Agricutlural Production, Trade, and Residual Soil Nitrogen." Publication No. FAER 255, U.S. Department of Agriculture, Economic Research Service, Washington, DC, 1995.

Madell, M.L. "CAP Reform." *Western Europe Agriculture and Trade Report: Situation and Outlook Series*. Publication No. 92-4, U.S. Department of Agriculture, Economic Research Service, Washington, DC, 1992.

Schleef, K., and W. Kleinhanse. "Mineral Balances in the EU: The Regional Level." Institute of Farm Economics, Federal Agricultural Research Centre (FAL), Braunschweig, Germany, February 1994.

Veenendaal, P., and F. Brouwer. "Consequences of Ammonia Emission Abatement Policies for Agricultural Practices in the Netherlands." In *Environmental Policy and the Economy*. The Hague, Netherlands: Elsevier Science Publishers B.B., 1991.

# 16

## International Environmental Indicators: Trade, Income, and Endowments

*Robert E. B. Lucas*

### Introduction

The "new" economic growth theory focuses upon positive production externalities generating multiple, potential, steady-state growth paths. In contrast, the environmental literature frequently suggests the possibility that growth itself may exhibit negative externalities, though these may be imposed upon the production process, upon human consumers, or upon nonhuman life forms. Whereas the new economic growth theory has generated a spate of empirical testing, largely founded upon cross-country comparisons, potential environmental effects remain largely neglected in the empirical literature. One reason for this contrast is the paucity of data pertaining to potential environmental effects.

Environmental measures are very limited in scope. Moreover, a number of the existing measures stem from simulations rather than direct observation. Nonetheless, given the importance and neglect of the topic, it seems worth exploring these data while bearing in mind their limitations. To the extent that the issue of reliability amounts to errors in measurement in the dependent environmental variables, discerning the statistical patterns is made more difficult by the additional noise in the data. On the other hand, any patterns which do emerge are likely to be biased only if the errors in measurement are correlated with our explanatory terms.

The objective of this study is therefore to examine some international indices of environmental impact in relation to both macroeconomic indices and information about the nature of each country. The chapter is divided into six main sections, followed by a summary section. The first section briefly describes the macroeconomic measures adopted as explanatory variables. The next two sections examine pooled time-series, cross-country data on industrial carbon dioxide ($CO_2$) emissions and on manufacturing emissions of toxins, water, and air pollutants, respectively. The remaining sections each deal with cross-country data at one point in time. In particular, the fourth section addresses some issues of land use (including wilderness preservation and deforestation) and water use; the following section takes up threats to various animal species (number of species threatened, pesticide use, and marine fishing). The final section returns to several aspects of emissions (methane and CFC emissions, nuclear power, and municipal waste). Discussions of the particular environmental measures and of the specific approaches are taken up within each section.

## The Macroeconomic Measures

In this initial exploration, the focus falls upon two sets of issues with respect to economic measures. First, although it is commonly suggested in the environmental literature that an inverse U-shaped relationship exists between environmental degradation and level of income per capita, this idea actually has not been subjected to much systematic testing. The source of data for the macroeconomic, explanatory variables explored in this study is the World Bank's "World Tables" data disks. These files contain a number of measures of income. The Summers-Heston data on income per capita are no doubt the best international comparisons. However, this measure is only available for a limited set of countries and years, and indeed it seems likely that this selectivity is not random (a point scarcely recognized in testing the new economic growth literature). For present purposes, the measure of income adopted is gross domestic product (GDP) at factor cost, measured at constant prices in local currency units and expressed in U.S. dollars using the 1987 conversion factor.[1] To a large extent, this choice is influenced by its availability for a wide range of countries. To test for inverse U-shaped patterns, income per capita obviously is included in quadratic form. In addition, at least in the pooled time-series, cross-country investigations, growth in income per capita also is included.[2]

The second macroeconomic theme explored here is the consequence of outward orientation in trade. Many environmental lobby groups oppose progress toward free trade on the assumption that trade liberalization accelerates environmental damage. There is little evidence either way on this issue, despite the critical nature of the topic both for the environment and for trade policy. For present purposes, openness is simply represented by the ratio of exports of goods and services to GDP. Since it is well known that this ratio tends to be larger for small countries, simply by virtue of their size, this same measure is also included as an interaction with size of population (and population included as a separate control).

## Industrial Carbon Dioxide Emissions

The Oak Ridge National Laboratory produced estimates of $CO_2$ emissions from fossil fuel burning and from cement manufacturing for 113 countries in each year from 1970 through 1989. These estimates were generated from apparent consumption of fossil fuels and of cement production, using global average fuel chemistry data. Table 16.1 examines these data using a fixed-effects model (incorporating a dummy variable for 112 of the 113 countries represented in the sample). Estimation of the fixed-effects models in this study is by ordinary least squares; *t*-statistics for a zero null hypothesis are shown in parentheses beneath coefficient estimates.

Total annual $CO_2$ emissions from these sources indeed at first rise with GDP per capita, then subsequently tend to decline (both effects being statistically significant on a one-tailed, 95 percent confidence level test). However, the implied turning point occurs at a GDP per capita of 24,568 1987 US$, which is well beyond the actual income of any country at the time. In other words, $CO_2$ emissions are estimated to continue to rise with income per capita over the range of existing incomes, though to rise less rapidly at higher incomes.

A similar pattern is estimated with respect to each of the component sources, with the exception of liquid fuels. In the case of burning liquid fuels, projected $CO_2$ emissions are estimated to decline with income per capita, though the rate of decline diminishes at higher incomes. It also should be noted that the $CO_2$ emissions from cement manufacture, according to these estimates, peak at an income of some 9,250 1987 US$ and decline thereafter.

More rapid growth in GDP per capita is not bought at a cost of higher $CO_2$ emissions, given income level, according to these estimates. This is true both of total emissions and of emissions from each of the separate sources.

Not surprisingly, the countries with larger populations are estimated to have significantly greater total $CO_2$ emissions. On the other hand, any statistical association between export to GDP ratio and $CO_2$ emissions is statistically very weak. If anything, the estimates for total emissions suggest that a greater openness to trade is associated with smaller emissions up to a population level of just over 9 million and increase thereafter, though confidence levels in this pattern are not high. The only context in which more confidence may be expressed in the association between exports and $CO_2$ emissions is with respect to gas flaring, which is the practice of burning off gas released during petroleum extraction. The clear positive association between export performance and $CO_2$ emissions from gas flaring may

**TABLE 16.1. Industrial $CO_2$ Emissions: Fixed-Effects Time-Series Model.**

Dependent Variable: Annual $CO_2$ Emissions (1,000 tonnes)

|  | Total | Solid Fuels | Liquid Fuels | Gas Fuels | Gas Flaring | Cement Manuf. |
|---|---|---|---|---|---|---|
| Intercept | 4,428,022 | 1,070,871 | 2,335,096 | 672,597 | 358,997 | -9,983 |
|  | (15.03) | (4.16) | (9.25) | (4.42) | (12.22) | (1.00) |
| GDP/Capita (Y) | 5.061 | 7.711 | -6.260 | 2.360 | 1.129 | 0.111 |
| (1,000 1987 US$) | (2.32) | (4.04) | (3.35) | (2.09) | (5.19) | (1.51) |
| $Y^2/1,000,000$ | -103.0 | -78.00 | 60.00 | -72.10 | -7.800 | -5.710 |
|  | (1.70) | (1.46) | (1.16) | (2.30) | (1.29) | (2.79) |
| Growth in Y (%) | 39.48 | -21.00 | 70.96 | -21.39 | 12.41 | -1.888 |
|  | (0.30) | (0.18) | (0.63) | (0.32) | (0.95) | (0.43) |
| Exports/GDP (X) | -8,323 | -16,510 | 10,161 | -3,534 | 1,321 | 255.4 |
|  | (0.72) | (1.63) | (1.02) | (0.59) | (1.14) | (0.65) |
| X*N interact. | 880.9 | 524.9 | -334.1 | 179.6 | 534.4 | -23.82 |
|  | (1.66) | (1.13) | (0.74) | (0.66) | (10.10) | (1.33) |
| Population (N) | 1,533 | 1,341 | 283.5 | -105.9 | -45.09 | 59.41 |
| (millions) | (16.49) | (16.49) | (3.56) | (2.21) | (4.86) | (18.92) |
| Time (yrs.) | -155.7 | -20.73 | -118.3 | 153.2 | -185.4 | 15.77 |
|  | (1.01) | (0.15) | (0.39) | (1.92) | (12.02) | (3.02) |
| Country dummies | 112 | 112 | 112 | 112 | 112 | 112 |
| F-statistic | 5,253 | 736 | 1,552 | 860 | 62 | 764 |
| No. observations | 1,649 | 1,651 | 1,650 | 1,650 | 1,651 | 1,651 |
| $R^2$ | 0.99 | 0.98 | 0.99 | 0.99 | 0.83 | 0.98 |

Data source: World Resources Institute.

well reflect the rising export performance of oil exporters, during the 1970s in particular.

The time trend variable included in Table 16.1 clearly shows the downward trend in the practice of gas flaring during these two decades. Conversely, the projected $CO_2$ emissions from burning of gas fuels and from cement manufacturing have both risen through time (even given population and any rises in income per capita). The result is, on balance, that total $CO_2$ emissions from all sources in Table 16.1 exhibit only a very weak downward trend.

## Manufacturing Toxic and Pollutant Emissions

The U.S. Environmental Protection Agency (EPA) collects (self-reported) information on releases of toxic and other emissions from U.S. manufacturing plants. The World Bank Industrial Pollution Projections Project team has used these data to compile average intensities of emissions per dollar's worth of output for three-digit and four-digit manufacturing industries. In this section, these intensities are applied to the pattern of manufacturing output, from 1970 through 1990, for 96 countries. Obviously this approach, as in the prior section on $CO_2$ emissions, relies upon applying common intensities to production structures, regardless of the vintage and style of technology applied and irrespective of variations in abatement procedures. Nonetheless, these are the only international data available on manufacturing emissions and consequently deserve analysis until better information is collected.

As in the previous section, a fixed-effects model, with an annual time trend plus dummy variables representing 95 of the 96 countries in the sample, is applied to these data. The results are presented in Tables 16.2A and 16.2B. Three classes of emission measures are available: total toxin releases (of which bioaccumulative metals are a subset), two types of water pollutants, and seven air pollutants. Each of these is examined separately in Tables 16.2A and 16.2B using a common simple model identical to that applied in the previous section.

In the cases of total toxic releases, bioaccumulative metals, and suspended solid water pollutants, emission intensities at first rise with the level of income per capita, then decline at higher incomes (given other factors in the model held constant). The estimated turning points in these patterns range from some 10,500 1987 US$ per capita in the case of total toxins to 6,300 1987 US$ in the case of suspended water pollutants. Among the air pollutants, volatile organic compound releases also initially rise with income per capita and then tend to decline, but in this case, the estimated turning point is not reached until an income per capita of over 20,000 1987 US$—which is beyond the range of any country at that time. Nitrogendioxide emissions exhibit the opposite pattern, initially declining with income per capita and then rising,

248

TABLE 16.2A. Manufacturing Toxic and Pollutant Intensity: Fixed-Effects Time-Series
Model.

Dependent Variable: Emissions Flows (lbs. per year per US$million of
manufacturing output)[a]

|  | All Media | | Water Pollutants | |
|---|---|---|---|---|
|  | Total Toxic Release | Bioaccumulative Metals | Biochemical Oxygen Demand | Suspended Solids |
| Intercept | -20,422 | 45.91 | -42.70 | -569.1 |
|  | (2.97) | (0.04) | (0.46) | (5.24) |
| GDP/Capita ($Y$) | 87.31 | 20.57 | 0.284 | 2.954 |
| (1,000 1987 US$) | (1.75) | (2.78) | (0.43) | (3.76) |
| $Y^2/1,000,000$ | -4.140 | -1.643 | -0.008 | -0.165 |
|  | (2.50) | (6.69) | (0.38) | (6.31) |
| Growth in $Y$ (%) | -3.914 | -0.144 | -0.003 | 0.015 |
|  | (1.32) | (0.33) | (0.08) | (0.32) |
| Exports/GDP ($X$) | 641.7 | -54.78 | -7.412 | -8.138 |
|  | (2.49) | (1.43) | (2.15) | (2.00) |
| $X*N$ interact. | 37.77 | 3.967 | 0.070 | 0.207 |
|  | (3.46) | (2.45) | (0.48) | (1.20) |
| Population ($N$) | 0.094 | 0.070 | -0.020 | -0.027 |
| (millions) | (0.05) | (0.27) | (0.86) | (0.99) |
| Time (yrs.) | 12.23 | 0.207 | 0.033 | 0.310 |
|  | (3.39) | (0.39) | (0.68) | (5.44) |
| Country dummies | 95 | 95 | 95 | 95 |
| $F$-statistic | 220 | 429 | 50 | 3,523 |
| No. observations | 1,249 | 1,249 | 1,249 | 1,249 |
| $R^2$ | 0.95 | 0.97 | 0.82 | 0.86 |

Data source: World Bank estimates.

[a]Water pollutant emissions are measured per day.

**TABLE 16.2B. Manufacturing Toxic and Pollutant Intensity: Fixed-Effects Time-Series Model.**

Dependent Variable: Emission Flows (lbs. per year per US$1,000 of manufacturing output[a])

| | Air Pollutants | | | | | | |
|---|---|---|---|---|---|---|---|
| | Suspended Particles | $SO_2$ | $NO_2$ | Fine Particles (PM10) | Lead | Volatile Organic Compounds | $CO_2$ |
| Intercept | -8.369 | -53.39 | 6.487 | -5.625 | 10.97 | -0.827 | -15.48 |
| | (1.49) | (5.95) | (0.80) | (1.98) | (3.64) | (0.17) | (1.29) |
| GDP/Capita ($Y$) | -0.053 | -0.072 | -0.264 | -0.011 | -0.034 | 0.082 | -0.040 |
| (1,000 1987 US$) | (1.29) | (1.11) | (4.48) | (0.53) | (1.54) | (2.36) | (0.46) |
| $Y^2/1,000,000$ | -0.000 | -0.004 | 0.007 | -0.000 | -0.001 | -0.002 | -0.007 |
| | (0.10) | (1.63) | (3.45) | (0.00) | (0.66) | (1.58) | (2.55) |
| Growth in $Y$ (%) | -0.001 | 0.003 | 0.003 | -0.001 | 0.000 | -0.002 | -0.004 |
| | (0.35) | (0.71) | (0.73) | (0.52) | (0.24) | (1.07) | (0.74) |
| Exports/GDP ($X$) | -0.541 | -0.490 | -0.678 | -0.376 | -0.103 | 0.650 | 0.026 |
| | (2.57) | (1.45) | (2.22) | (3.54) | (0.91) | (3.61) | (0.06) |
| $X*N$ interact. | -0.003 | 0.018 | -0.003 | -0.002 | 0.014 | 0.005 | 0.026 |
| | (0.34) | (1.28) | (0.24) | (0.41) | (2.87) | (0.67) | (1.37) |
| Population ($N$) | 0.001 | -0.002 | -0.004 | 0.001 | 0.000 | 0.001 | 0.001 |
| (millions) | (0.75) | (0.68) | (1.85) | (0.75) | (0.22) | (1.17) | (0.46) |
| Time (yrs.) | 0.006 | 0.032 | 0.001 | 0.003 | -0.005 | 0.002 | 0.012 |
| | (1.90) | (6.71) | (0.23) | (2.11) | (3.11) | (0.77) | (1.85) |
| Country dummies | 95 | 95 | 95 | 95 | 95 | 95 | 95 |
| F-statistic | 38 | 126 | 80 | 36 | 366 | 116 | 181 |
| No. observations | 1,249 | 1,249 | 1,249 | 1,249 | 1,249 | 1,249 | 1,249 |
| $R^2$ | 0.77 | 0.92 | 0.88 | 0.76 | 0.97 | 0.91 | 0.94 |

Data source: World Bank estimates.

[a]Lead emissions are measured in lbs. per year per US$million.

though again the implied turning point is beyond the sample range; similarly, carbon monoxide emission intensities decline significantly across the entire income range. Suspended particles in the air, sulphur dioxide emissions, and releases of lead into the atmosphere all tend to decline in intensity as income per capita rises, though statistical confidence in these effects is somewhat weaker. On the other hand, these data do not indicate any clear tendency for more rapidly growing economies to exhibit more emission-intensive manufacturing sectors, given income levels.

Do more open economies possess more emission-intensive manufacturing sectors? The results are mixed, based upon the measure of openness adopted here, namely the ratio of exports to GDP and its interaction with population size. Total toxic release intensity is estimated to rise significantly with respect to export propensity, irrespective of population size.[3] Volatile organic compound air pollutants also tend to rise with export propensity, and carbon monoxide displays a similar, though statistically much weaker, pattern. Bioaccumulative metals, sulphur dioxide, and lead released into the atmosphere all tend to decline with export propensity among countries with smaller populations, then tend to rise with export intensity after a critical population size of 14, 27, and 7 million people, respectively. In contrast, the remaining five releases (both water pollutant categories, suspended and fine particles in the air, plus nitrogen dioxide) all decline significantly as export propensity rises, irrespective of population size. Population size itself has little direct effect upon emission intensities other than through any interactions with export propensity already discussed. However, it is disturbing to see the statistically significant, positive trend effect estimated on six of the emission intensities.[4]

### Land and Water Use

The remaining indices of environmental impact examined in this study are available at one point in time for a subset of countries. So far, the effects of individual countries upon the outcomes have effectively been buried in the fixed-effects approach of representing each country with a dummy variable. In the remainder of the chapter, this is no longer the case. Instead, the association between environmental outcomes and the various characteristics of the sampled countries will be examined directly. In particular, the results are typically presented in at least two steps. At first, the association between the environmental measure and the economic measures (already adopted in the prior two sections) is estimated without controlling for country endowments, geography, or other characteristics.[5] In the second step, these latter measures are also included, to estimate the extent to which associations with the economic measures may simply reflect a common correlation with the underlying country characteristics. In a number of instances, it proves instructive to present results introducing the country characteristics in stages, in some cases to bring out important interactions between the characteristics themselves, and in other cases because limited data availability on some of the characteristics severely alter the sample size.

In this first section based on cross-sectional results, some measures of land and water use are examined, turning first to preservation of wilderness areas.

## Wilderness

The World Resources Institute data set reports the result of examining aerial photographs for wilderness areas. For this purpose, a wilderness area is defined as a minimum area of 4,000 square kilometers showing no evidence of human development. These measures are examined in Table 16.3. All cross-country results reported in this study are obtained by ordinary least squares; $t$-statistics for a zero null hypothesis are again reported in parentheses, and these are derived using White's, heteroskedasticity robust measure of standard errors.

Total wilderness area in each country at first rises, then declines with income per capita, with an estimated turning point at 11,738 1987 US$, if no country properties are included in the regression. In other words, it is the middle-income countries which possess the largest wilderness areas. In the first equation in Table 16.3, it is also found that wilderness area declines across countries as the propensity to export rises—suggesting that outward orientation in exports is associated with smaller areas of wilderness preserved.

However, it must be remembered that these initial results reflect nothing of the geography of the countries in question. The second equation in Table 16.3 includes the total land area of each country in question, as well as some aspects of the nature of that land plus population density measures.

The inverse U-shape of wilderness area with respect to income level is robust to inclusion of these country characteristics, though the turning point is considerably lower once the country characteristics are incorporated (1,715 1987 US$). However, the pattern with respect to export propensity alters in a critical way once these country characteristics are incorporated. In particular, in the second equation in Table 16.3, the area of wilderness actually rises with overall export propensity. Only for more populous countries, with more than 30 million people, do these results now indicate declining wilderness preservation as export orientation increases.

Turning to the country characteristics themselves in Table 16.3, not surprisingly it is found that countries with larger land areas preserve the most wilderness, other things being equal.[6] Two measures of the nature of the land/climate are available for present analysis. The World Resources Institute data base reports the fraction of land area which is arid, semi-arid, humid, and cold (based on length of growing period). In addition,

252

**TABLE 16.3. Wilderness.**

Dependent Variable: Wilderness Area (1,000 ha)

| Regression | (1) | (2) | (3) | (4) | (5) |
|---|---|---|---|---|---|
| Intercept | 41,542 | -584,860 | -474,780 | -533,120 | -232,590 |
| | (3.37) | (9.36) | (6.72) | (5.47) | (3.67) |
| GDP/Capita (Y) | 10.40 | 31.55 | 29.58 | 59.98 | 20.33 |
| (1,000 1987 US$) | (1.49) | (3.24) | (2.95) | (3.41) | (2.71) |
| $Y^2/1,000$ | -0.443 | -9.197 | -7.817 | -16.75 | -5.045 |
| | (1.61) | (3.17) | (2.62) | (3.36) | (2.31) |
| Exports/GDP (X) | -103,690 | 93,311 | 94,951 | 71,962 | 42,534 |
| | (1.99) | (3.79) | (3.39) | (4.91) | (3.08) |
| X*N interact. | -1,528 | -3,067 | -3,419 | -2,296 | -2,613 |
| | (1.12) | (3.04) | (2.16) | (2.11) | (6.65) |
| Population (N) | 73.61 | -56.15 | 7.292 | -306.2 | -64.44 |
| (millions) | (0.69) | (1.45) | (0.05) | (1.57) | (4.47) |
| Total land area | | 0.725 | 0.774 | 0.741 | 0.290 |
| (1,000 ha) | | (9.09) | (6.35) | (7.91) | (4.96) |
| Frac. area arid | | 6,092 | 9,122 | 13,658 | 5,759 |
| | | (0.98) | (0.83) | (1.72) | (1.87) |
| Frac. semi-arid | | -15,335 | 9,384 | -4,547 | -982.7 |
| | | (0.38) | (0.16) | (0.06) | (0.02) |
| Frac. cold | | 89,507 | 93,999 | 34,412 | 53,088 |
| | | (3.09) | (2.25) | (0.46) | (1.70) |
| Portion tropical | | 539,610 | 423,220 | 475,410 | 208,860 |
| | | (8.69) | (5.22) | (5.30) | (3.63) |
| Portion subtropical | | 510,410 | 395,180 | 447,230 | 194,040 |
| | | (7.51) | (4.24) | (5.60) | (3.68) |
| Closed forest (1,000 ha) | | -0.977 | -1.011 | -0.499 | -0.270 |
| | | (5.89) | (5.86) | (2.52) | (2.64) |

*(continues)*

**TABLE 16.3.** (*continued*)

| Regression | (1) | (2) | (3) | (4) | (5) |
|---|---|---|---|---|---|
| Pop. density (no./ha) | | 34,625 (3.02) | 45,244 (2.76) | 32,940 (1.62) | 16,126 (1.98) |
| Pop. urban (%) | | -153.1 (2.47) | -127.1 (1.76) | -179.4 (1.50) | -23.19 (0.54) |
| Arable area (1,000 ha) | | | -0.279 (0.40) | | |
| No. cattle (1,000) | | | 0.009 (0.02) | | |
| No. sheep (1,000) | | | -0.936 (1.48) | | |
| No. goats (1,000) | | | 0.234 (0.35) | | |
| Roads (km/1,000 sq. km land) | | | | 0.592 (1.11) | |
| Rail (km/1,000 sq. km land) | | | | 286.1 (0.25) | |
| No. cars (1,000) | | | | -11.62 (3.73) | |
| Roundwood production (1,000 cub. mt) | | | | | 0.380 (2.43) |
| Roundwood export (1,000 cub. mt) | | | | | -0.947 (4.93) |
| Sum sq. res. (E10) | 46.1 | 0.367 | 0.327 | 0.140 | 0.090 |
| No. observations | 69 | 39 | 38 | 25 | 31 |
| Adjusted $R^2$ | -0.00 | 0.91 | 0.90 | 0.91 | 0.95 |

Data source: World Resources Institute.

the same data base reports portion of land area which is tropical, subtropical, and temperate (depending upon monthly mean temperature). In both cases, one category is dropped (humid from the former and temperate from the latter) as the reference point in Table 16.3. Countries with a larger fraction of their land which is arid or semi-arid are found to have neither more nor less wilderness preserved than are humid areas, given the other factors included in the regressions. However, countries with a larger fraction of their land reported as cold do tend to preserve more wilderness. Countries which are more tropical or subtropical possess substantially larger wilderness areas than do the temperate areas, given their income levels.

Possessing larger areas of closed forest is found to be associated with less preservation of wilderness area, other things being equal. It is not altogether clear what this result reflects, but it suggests that forestry activities commonly are not consistent with wilderness preservation—a point to which we shall return in a moment.

One might think that it is the pressure of human population on the land which results in loss of wilderness. It is therefore intriguing to find that countries with higher population relative to land area actually preserve larger areas of wilderness. On the other hand, where this population pressure translates into a larger fraction of the population in urban areas (definition of which unfortunately varies from country to country), smaller areas of wilderness do remain.

Agricultural activities may well be thought to threaten the wilderness. To examine this, the third equation in Table 16.3 adds in measures of total arable land in each country as well as the numbers of cattle, goats, and sheep kept as livestock. None of these has a significant effect in reducing the extent of wilderness, given the other variables included. Nor does the inclusion of these measures reduce the effect of greater population density being associated with larger extent of wilderness.

Another hypothesis explored in Table 16.3 is that transportation pressures result in loss of wilderness. However, the inclusion of road and rail density measures proves largely irrelevant to the extent of wilderness in the fourth regression in Table 16.3. In contrast, it is interesting to note that more automobiles are associated with significantly less wilderness preservation. Obviously, the wealthier countries have far more cars, yet the observed decline in wilderness at higher income levels is (if anything) greater with the inclusion of cars.

In the final equation in Table 16.3, some additional measures of forestry as a threat to wilderness preservation are examined. Countries with higher total roundwood production actually tend to possess larger areas of wilderness (though this effect is insignificant unless roundwood exports are also included). On the other hand, countries which export large amounts of roundwood (whether given roundwood production as in Table 16.3 or not), retain significantly smaller areas of wilderness. One cannot discern causality from such studies, but these results at least suggest that roundwood export industries may pose a significant threat to the survival of the wilderness.

## Deforestation

Closely connected to the survival of the wilderness is the rate of deforestation occurring. The World Resources Institute data relating to average annual deforestation from 1981-85 are largely derived from Food and Agriculture Organization (FAO) data which frequently have been disputed. Nonetheless, once again, these are the best data available, and they are therefore examined in Table 16.4 with perhaps a special word of caution with respect to reliability.

Whereas the extent of wilderness preserved at first rises with income per capita and then declines at higher income levels, the reverse is true with respect to forest preservation. Deforestation here refers to complete transfer from forest cover to alternative use, and does not include partial logging. This rate of deforestation initially increases with income levels, then declines at higher incomes. This is true whether country characteristics are included or not in Table 16.4, with an estimated peak of deforestation at an income level of 1,956 1987 US$ in the first regression.

The results in Table 16.4 indicate a rate of deforestation which declines with general openness with respect to exports, at least among countries with smaller populations. For instance, in the first regression, in which no country characteristics are incorporated, the decline in deforestation with respect to export propensity continues up to a population level of some 88 million, thus excluding all but the largest countries (such as Brazil and Indonesia). This pattern proves robust once other country characteristics are included, though the turning point occurs at somewhat lower population levels (at 31 million in the second regression, for instance).

Countries with more arid land have smaller areas of ongoing deforestation than do the more humid areas, while semi-arid lands exhibit a greater extent of deforestation. (Both of these differences are statistically significant on a 90 percent confidence level, two-tailed test, at least in the second regression in Table 16.4.) Conversely, cold zones do not differ significantly from humid areas. Whether the tropical and subtropical zones are deforesting more rapidly, as in the second equation, depends to some extent upon what else is held constant. In particular, once arable and livestock measures are incorporated in the fourth equation, the signs on these latter differences reverse. In other words, this suggests that the extent of agriculture (and perhaps cattle in particular, rather than arable activities, from the results in Table 16.4) may be a critical factor in why the rate of deforestation in the tropics is greater.

**TABLE 16.4. Deforestation.**

Dependent Variable: Total Annual Average Deforestation (1,000 ha)

| Regression | (1) | (2) | (3) | (4) | (5) | (6) |
|---|---|---|---|---|---|---|
| Intercept | 108.0 | -6,180 | -7,037 | 10,181 | 5,378 | -3,672 |
| | (2.25) | (1.76) | (1.60) | (1.95) | (1.12) | (0.67) |
| GDP/Capita ($Y$) | 0.532 | 0.174 | 0.166 | 0.083 | 0.243 | 0.348 |
| (1,000 1987 US$) | (1.75) | (2.07) | (1.83) | (1.76) | (2.03) | (3.11) |
| $Y^2/1,000$ | -0.136 | -0.048 | -0.047 | -0.026 | -0.100 | -0.110 |
| | (1.80) | (2.04) | (1.87) | (1.87) | (2.40) | (3.08) |
| Exports/GDP ($X$) | -833.8 | -366.3 | -278.7 | -164.6 | -387.4 | -576.7 |
| | (1.72) | (3.36) | (2.23) | (2.98) | (1.93) | (3.61) |
| $X*N$ interact. | 9.499 | 11.94 | 9.176 | 34.14 | 8.712 | 10.61 |
| | (1.01) | (2.22) | (1.59) | (4.85) | (0.89) | (1.41) |
| Population ($N$) | -0.348 | -1.219 | -1.178 | -5.670 | 1.214 | -1.931 |
| (millions) | (0.38) | (3.23) | (3.07) | (8.96) | (0.90) | (7.26) |
| Frac. area arid | | -67.70 | -158.0 | 19.57 | -30.26 | -143.1 |
| | | (1.89) | (2.95) | (0.57) | (0.46) | (2.69) |
| Frac. semi-arid | | 377.4 | 269.7 | -93.16 | -184.4 | 199.2 |
| | | (1.81) | (1.00) | (0.38) | (0.74) | (0.65) |
| Frac. cold | | 8.567 | 110.0 | 35.55 | 68.00 | -161.6 |
| | | (0.05) | (0.60) | (0.16) | (0.24) | (0.72) |
| Portion tropical | | 6,247 | 7,060 | -10,135 | -5,191 | 3,745 |
| | | (1.78) | (1.61) | (1.94) | (1.20) | (0.69) |
| Portion subtropical | | 6,232 | 7,022 | -10,145 | -5,277 | 3,813 |
| | | (1.77) | (1.59) | (1.95) | (1.22) | (0.69) |
| Closed forest | | 6.446 | 4.467 | 2.393 | 6.745 | 4.811 |
| (million ha) | | (14.92) | (3.04) | (5.90) | (3.43) | (3.36) |
| Land area (million ha) | | | 0.872 | | | |
| | | | (1.54) | | | |

*(continues)*

**TABLE 16.4.** (*continued*)

| Regression | (1) | (2) | (3) | (4) | (5) | (6) |
|---|---|---|---|---|---|---|
| Pop. density (no./ha) | | | -7.697 (0.91) | | | |
| Pop. urban (%) | | | 0.506 (0.63) | | | |
| Arable area (1,000 ha) | | | | -0.001 (0.20) | | |
| No. cattle (1,000) | | | | 0.018 (4.39) | | |
| No. sheep (1,000) | | | | -0.007 (1.18) | | |
| No. goats (1,000) | | | | -0.004 (0.74) | | |
| Roads (km/1,000 sq. km land) | | | | | -0.007 (1.22) | |
| Rail (km/1,000 sq. km land) | | | | | -4.905 (1.72) | |
| No. cars (1,000) | | | | | -0.016 (0.30) | |
| Roundwood production (1,000 cub. mt) | | | | | | 0.003 (1.17) |
| Roundwood export (1,000 cub. mt) | | | | | | 0.000 (0.00) |
| Sum sq. res. (E10) | 5.571 | 0.823 | 0.775 | 0.430 | 0.351 | 0.588 |
| No. observations | 64 | 61 | 60 | 58 | 32 | 44 |
| Adjusted $R^2$ | 0.19 | 0.86 | 0.86 | 0.92 | 0.91 | 0.88 |

Data source: World Resources Institute.

Not surprisingly, it is the countries which possess larger closed forests that are experiencing the largest extent of deforestation. However, at least in the results from this simple additive specification, each additional million hectares of closed forest adds far less than 10,000 hectares of average annual deforestation (other things constant). More generally, it seems that countries with larger land areas are experiencing more extensive deforestation, even given the extent of closed forest, though the statistical confidence in this pattern is weaker.

Interestingly, there is no sign in these data that population pressure on the land, either in general or in the form of urbanization, has any significant consequence for deforestation. Moreover, this remains true through any indirect effect of population on the extent of arable farming or even the various transport measures explored in the fourth and fifth regressions, respectively.

Most importantly, there is no sign in these data that either the extent of roundwood production or its export has any detrimental effect upon the extent of deforestation (other things equal).[7] Presumably, this is largely a consequence of the definition of deforestation adopted in these data, namely the total deforestation of an area, whereas logging activities must typically result in partial deforestation only. Combined with the results on the wilderness, this finding indicates that roundwood export may pose a threat to virgin forest and to the wilderness more generally, but not to the total extent of forest survival.

## Freshwater

Freshwater resource diminution is a topic of particular environmental concern. The data on freshwater use in various countries are partly a result of direct reporting and partly a result of simulated use. Their analysis is taken up in Table 16.5.

Not surprisingly, total annual withdrawal of freshwater is greater the larger the population of a country. Freshwater use also rises with income per capita, though the estimates in Table 16.5 also show a declining absolute use at very high income levels, at least after controlling for water availability in the second and third equations.

The economies with greater export propensities generally tend to use lesser amounts of freshwater, according to the estimates in Table 16.5.[8] The data offer no sign that greater concentration of the population in urban centers or in cities (urban areas of more than 2 million people) places any greater pressure on freshwater use. If anything, there is very weak evidence here to suggest that urbanization (though not cities) may offer some scale economies in freshwater use.

It seems an important source of the global pressures on freshwater is the concentration of greater use in areas with smaller endowments. This turns

**TABLE 16.5.  Water Withdrawal.**

Dependent Variable: Total Annual Water Withdrawal (km$^3$)

| Regression | (1) | (2) | (3) | (4) |
|---|---|---|---|---|
| Intercept | -16.68 | -5.202 | -4.214 | 33.25 |
| | (2.16) | (0.58) | (0.61) | (1.49) |
| GDP/Capita ($Y$) | 2.195 | 3.907 | 2.007 | 0.519 |
| (1,000 1987 US$) | (2.04) | (2.91) | (1.72) | (0.49) |
| $Y^2$ | -0.057 | -0.146 | -0.083 | -0.030 |
| | (0.87) | (2.73) | (1.68) | (0.76) |
| Exports/GDP ($X$) | 22.67 | 18.68 | -1.593 | -43.80 |
| | (1.37) | (0.94) | (0.16) | (1.44) |
| $X*N$ interact. | -4.219 | -5.298 | -1.937 | -1.995 |
| | (1.79) | (2.40) | (1.63) | (3.79) |
| Population ($N$) | 1.681 | 2.125 | 1.006 | 1.014 |
| (millions) | (2.63) | (3.34) | (3.93) | (6.93) |
| Pop. urban (%) | | -0.171 | 0.025 | -0.136 |
| | | (1.47) | (0.37) | (1.02) |
| Frac. population cities | | 0.012 | 0.072 | -0.065 |
| | | (0.22) | (1.21) | (0.49) |
| Internal water available | | -0.022 | | |
| (cub. km) | | (1.40) | | |
| Total water available | | | -0.013 | -0.018 |
| (cub. km) | | | (3.79) | (2.59) |
| Arable area (million ha) | | | | 0.503 |
| | | | | (1.14) |
| No. cattle (millions) | | | | 0.056 |
| | | | | (0.12) |
| No. sheep (millions) | | | | -0.092 |
| | | | | (0.91) |
| No. goats (millions) | | | | -2.106 |
| | | | | (4.87) |
| Sum sq. res. (E05) | 0.611 | 0.489 | 0.049 | 0.025 |
| No. observations | 78 | 70 | 36 | 29 |
| Adjusted $R^2$ | 0.72 | 0.76 | 0.66 | 0.75 |

Data source: World Bank estimates.

out to be true in Table 16.5 no matter whether a measure of only nationally available renewable water resources is adopted, or a measure of total water resources available, the latter including reported river flows from abroad.

International estimates of freshwater use show two-thirds of this being for agriculture and one-quarter for industry. However, when total arable area and number of livestock are included in the fourth regression in Table 16.5, no evidence is found supporting pressure on water use from agriculture on average, though the role of irrigation remains to be examined in this context.

## Threats to Species

This section examines international data on three aspects of threat to species: marine catch, the use of pesticides, and direct indicators of the numbers of various species threatened.

### Marine Catch

In general, the extent to which marine fishing poses an immediate threat to marine species is not obvious, though whaling certainly appears to do so, and tuna fishing has been deemed a threat to some marine mammals. Examination of specific types of fishing is not possible here, but a more general look at total marine catch is taken up. The World Resources Institute data on average annual marine catch are derived largely from FAO data. These data refer to the total weight of fish and other marine life caught by a country's fleet anywhere in the world. Some results based on these data are presented in Table 16.6.

Unlike many of the other measures examined in this study, the total marine catch tends to show a weak U-shape with respect to income per capita. In other words, the marine catch is lowest among the middle-income countries, turning upward at an income level of about 5,500 1987 US$ according to the first regression formulation reported in Table 16.6 (though statistical confidence levels in these patterns is not high).

Unfortunately, data on fish exports are not readily available for present purposes. However, any association between marine catch and exports more generally proves to be statistically fairly weak, though the association does tend to be positive.

All but the first regression in Table 16.6 include the area of the exclusive economic zone attributed to each country. In the various specifications, this tends to have a positive coefficient—larger zones generate larger catches—but the association is quite weak, no doubt in part because of fishing in international waters.

The data on meat output, freshwater catch, and aquaculture production (available for only a subset of countries) are examined in the third and fourth regressions in Table 16.6. There is no systematic evidence that any of these

**TABLE 16.6.  Marine Catch.**

Dependent Variable: Total Average Annual Marine Catch (1,000 tonnes)

| Regression | (1) | (2) | (3) | (4) | (5) |
|---|---|---|---|---|---|
| Intercept | 267.1 | 154.7 | 128.8 | 549.1 | 90.09 |
| | (1.47) | (0.90) | (0.84) | (1.11) | (0.60) |
| GDP/Capita ($Y$) | -0.240 | -0.311 | -0.294 | -0.564 | -0.344 |
| (1,000 1987 US$) | (1.41) | (1.80) | (1.62) | (2.03) | (1.87) |
| $Y^2/1,000$ | 0.022 | 0.024 | 0.023 | 0.042 | 0.026 |
| | (1.70) | (1.92) | (1.75) | (1.94) | (1.97) |
| Exports/GDP ($X$) | -392.0 | -8.348 | 78.00 | -574.7 | 63.77 |
| | (1.03) | (0.02) | (0.26) | (0.55) | (0.17) |
| $X*N$ interact. | 74.31 | 58.97 | 53.15 | 52.13 | 54.48 |
| | (1.78) | (1.69) | (1.30) | (1.24) | (1.59) |
| Population ($N$) | -1.154 | -1.037 | -1.894 | 2.076 | -1.243 |
| (millions) | (0.35) | (0.38) | (0.85) | (0.54) | (0.46) |
| Exclusive economic zone | | 0.219 | 0.151 | 0.142 | 0.214 |
| (1,000 sq. km) | | (1.68) | (0.86) | (0.71) | (1.84) |
| Meat output (1,000 tonnes) | | | 0.061 | 0.014 | |
| | | | (0.79) | (0.12) | |
| Average annual freshwater | | | 0.615 | 0.722 | |
| catch (1,000 tonnes) | | | (0.74) | (0.75) | |
| Aquaculture production | | | | -5.003 | |
| (1,000 tonnes) | | | | (1.07) | |
| Dummy if offshore | | | | | 411.1 |
| oil/natural gas production | | | | | (1.40) |
| Sum sq. res. (E08) | 0.998 | 0.868 | 0.851 | 0.684 | 0.844 |
| No. observations | 81 | 78 | 76 | 52 | 78 |
| Adjusted $R^2$ | 0.40 | 0.46 | 0.45 | 0.48 | 0.46 |

Data source: World Resources Institute

alternatives offer a significant reduction in the level of marine catch. Perhaps this is to be expected to the extent that these protein sources are all tradable; consequently, enhanced production of one need not alter local consumption and production of the other.

Last, Table 16.6 reports a regression incorporating a dummy variable for whether the country has offshore production of either oil or natural gas. This measure offers no evidence that these offshore activities result in any reduction in the rate of marine catch, but rather the reverse.

### Pesticide Use

Pesticide use poses an obvious threat to species deemed to be pests. To what extent pesticide use poses a threat to other species (including mankind), both directly and through the mutation of pests, remains controversial. All we are able to examine here are the reported data on pesticide use for each country, with results presented in Table 16.7.

The first regression again presents an estimate of the basic economic model without inclusion of any country characteristics. Once again, an inverse U-shaped pattern with respect to income per capita is found, with pesticide use rising up to an income of 13,750 1987 US$, and then declining. Pesticide use also declines significantly among countries with higher overall export propensity (with only a very weak tendency to rise beyond a population level of 100 million). Similar patterns are found even when selected country characteristics are included in the second regression, though the estimated turning points alter (to 1,715 1987 US$ in income and to a population level over 700 million).

Not unexpectedly, pesticide use is influenced by climatic zone, with somewhat greater use in arid areas and lower use in cold zones relative to the humid regions. Given these zones and other factors held constant in the second equation in Table 16.7, the tropics and subtropics do not differ significantly in their use of pesticides relative to temperate zones. On the other hand, countries with large, closed forest areas do apply significantly larger amounts of pesticides.

Any evidence that agricultural activities increase pesticide use on average, given our economic controls and geographic factors, is very weak at best. There is a slight positive association with the extent of arable area in the specification reported in Table 16.7, though no positive association is found with size of cattle herd (nor with sheep or goats—a result not reported in the table).

Some uses of pesticides are in urban areas, and a positive association does tend to emerge between proportion of the population residing in urban areas and total pesticide use, but this association is again statistically relatively weak.

**TABLE 16.7. Pesticide Use.**

Dependent Variable: Active Ingredients in Pesticide Used (tonnes)

| Regression | (1) | (2) |
|---|---|---|
| Intercept | 11,199<br>(2.20) | -23,188<br>(0.88) |
| GDP/Capita ($Y$)<br>(1,000 1987 US$) | 8.304<br>(4.06) | 13.29<br>(2.45) |
| $Y^2/1,000$ | -0.302<br>(4.46) | -3.874<br>(2.04) |
| Exports/GDP ($X$) | -71,742<br>(2.64) | -11,127<br>(1.79) |
| $X*N$ interact. | 728.9<br>(0.93) | 14.59<br>(0.46) |
| Population ($N$)<br>(millions) | 75.76<br>(0.51) | -20.60<br>(0.49) |
| Frac. area arid | | 5,701<br>(1.56) |
| Frac. semi-arid | | -9,057<br>(0.98) |
| Frac. cold | | -28,159<br>(1.64) |
| Portion tropical | | 18,775<br>(0.73) |
| Portion subtropical | | 17,388<br>(0.63) |
| Closed forest (1,000 ha) | | 0.069<br>(2.57) |
| Arable area (1,000 ha) | | 0.348<br>(1.32) |
| No. cattle (1,000) | | -0.084<br>(0.56) |
| Pop. urban (%) | | 53.59<br>(1.46) |
| Sum sq. res. (E09) | 107.5 | 0.565 |
| No. observations | 66 | 37 |
| Adjusted $R^2$ | 0.26 | 0.77 |

Data source: World Bank estimates.

## Species Threatened

Biodiversity is an important component of the environmental dialogue, including issues of implied threat from international trade, though little systematic evidence seems to have emerged in this regard to date. The World Resources Institute reports the number of full species globally threatened (including endangered, vulnerable, and rare species) by major species class, as of 1990. These data form the dependent variables studied in Tables 16.8A-16.8E.

The number of reptile species threatened shows no particular pattern in connection with the economic measures included in Tables 16.8A-16.8E. For the other groups of species, an inverse U-shape with respect to income levels does tend to emerge, though in the case of freshwater fish, this result is quite sensitive to inclusion of other country characteristics. The implication of the first estimate in each category, which includes no country characteristics, is that the threat to freshwater fish and amphibians achieves no meaningful turning point, but continues to rise with incomes, albeit at a diminishing pace. For birds and mammals, however, the threat indeed at first rises, then declines beyond an income level of roughly 9,000 1987 US$ in both cases.

The pattern with respect to general export propensity is sensitive to inclusion of country characteristics in the case of freshwater fish and mammals. However, at least the basic economic model suggests a negative association between general export propensity and threat to each group of species, among countries with smaller populations. This pattern reverses, according to these estimates, for countries with larger populations, except in the case of amphibians. The turning point in pattern with respect to export propensity is estimated to occur at around 30 million people in the case of freshwater fish, 40 million for reptiles and birds, and 15 million for mammals. However, only in the case of mammals is there strong statistical confidence in both components of this export pattern.

In general, the results in Tables 16.8A-16.8E indicate that it is the countries possessing a larger variety of species within each category which also threaten more species. This should, of course, be expected on a random basis. However, it does mean that the largest absolute global threat to species is in those countries with greatest biodiversity within the group (other things equal). For the most part, the foregoing observations about economic patterns are not affected with inclusion of this measure of the number of species (except in the case of freshwater fish) and threats to mammals are now clearly, positively associated with general export propensity. This robustness in the economic results is despite confinement of the extended results to a much smaller set of countries, owing to lack of data on known species for many countries.

**TABLE 16.8A.  Species Threatened: Freshwater Fish.**

Dependent Variable: Number of Species Threatened

| Regression | (1) | (2) | (3) |
|---|---|---|---|
| Intercept | 2.819 | -6.301 | -46.17 |
| | (1.67) | (1.92) | (1.70) |
| GDP/Capita ($Y$) | 0.849 | -0.816 | 12.22 |
| (1,000 1987 US$) | (1.16) | (1.69) | (4.00) |
| $Y^2$ | -0.010 | 0.034 | -3.000 |
| | (0.28) | (1.89) | (3.35) |
| Exports/GDP ($X$) | -16.38 | 16.65 | -17.40 |
| | (1.56) | (2.70) | (3.81) |
| $X*N$ interact. | 0.550 | -2.567 | 0.058 |
| | (1.19) | (4.53) | (0.23) |
| Population ($N$) | 0.010 | 0.800 | 0.040 |
| (millions) | (0.12) | (5.55) | (0.66) |
| No. species known | | 0.011 | 0.000 |
| | | (2.02) | (0.05) |
| Frac. area arid | | | -0.852 |
| | | | (0.50) |
| Frac. semi-arid | | | -22.34 |
| | | | (2.03) |
| Frac. cold | | | 44.61 |
| | | | (2.45) |
| Portion tropical | | | 47.39 |
| | | | (1.76) |
| Portion subtropical | | | 65.22 |
| | | | (2.39) |
| Average annual freshwater | | -0.053 | -0.006 |
| catch (1,000 tonnes) | | (1.35) | (0.89) |
| Sum sq. res. | 31,700 | 3,954 | 108 |
| No. observations | 102 | 44 | 27 |
| Adjusted $R^2$ | 0.10 | 0.83 | 0.74 |

Data source: World Resources Institute.

**TABLE 16.8B. Species Threatened: Amphibians.**

Dependent Variable: Number of Species Threatened

| Regression | (1) | (2) | (3) | (4) |
|---|---|---|---|---|
| Intercept | 0.467 | 0.085 | -0.385 | -0.003 |
| | (1.80) | (0.08) | (0.61) | (0.00) |
| GDP/Capita (Y) | 0.247 | 0.351 | 0.240 | 0.100 |
| (1,000 1987 US$) | (2.42) | (2.10) | (1.79) | (0.56) |
| $Y^2$ | -0.007 | -0.010 | -0.008 | -0.002 |
| | (1.60) | (1.90) | (1.41) | (0.34) |
| Exports/GDP (X) | -2.525 | -3.545 | -1.064 | -1.320 |
| | (1.90) | (2.53) | (0.72) | (0.80) |
| X*N interact. | -0.001 | 0.014 | 0.022 | 0.008 |
| | (0.01) | (0.24) | (0.33) | (0.12) |
| Population (N) | 0.009 | 0.007 | -0.024 | -0.015 |
| (millions) | (1.00) | (0.85) | (4.07) | (1.85) |
| No. species known | | 0.006 | 0.004 | 0.002 |
| | | (0.86) | (1.64) | (1.00) |
| Arable area (million ha) | | | 0.092 | 0.088 |
| | | | (3.85) | (3.45) |
| Closed forest (million ha) | | | -0.028 | -0.014 |
| | | | (4.35) | (3.64) |
| Roundwood production | | | 0.026 | |
| (million cub. mt) | | | (2.19) | |
| Roundwood export | | | | 0.382 |
| (million cub. mt) | | | | (1.98) |
| Sum sq. res. | 428.9 | 384.2 | 91.9 | 91.0 |
| No. observations | 102 | 46 | 43 | 40 |
| Adjusted $R^2$ | 0.20 | 0.17 | 0.78 | 0.77 |

Data source: World Resources Institute.

**TABLE 16.8C.  Species Threatened: Reptiles.**

Dependent Variable: Number of Species Threatened

| Regression | (1) | (2) | (3) | (4) |
|---|---|---|---|---|
| Intercept | 3.269 | -0.675 | 0.330 | 0.613 |
| | (4.17) | (0.62) | (0.25) | (0.41) |
| GDP/Capita (Y) | -0.098 | 0.028 | -0.051 | -0.160 |
| (1,000 1987 US$) | (0.58) | (0.17) | (0.48) | (0.90) |
| $Y^2$ | 0.001 | 0.001 | -0.001 | 0.004 |
| | (0.07) | (0.13) | (0.18) | (0.60) |
| Exports/GDP (X) | -2.683 | 0.091 | -0.887 | -0.727 |
| | (1.14) | (0.41) | (0.32) | (0.26) |
| X*N interact. | 0.064 | 0.012 | -0.123 | -0.070 |
| | (0.57) | (0.16) | (1.56) | (0.80) |
| Population (N) | 0.022 | 0.015 | -0.007 | -0.003 |
| (millions) | (1.65) | (1.99) | (0.86) | (0.39) |
| No. species known | | 0.021 | 0.018 | 0.016 |
| | | (6.10) | (4.95) | (4.30) |
| Arable area (million ha) | | | 0.085 | 0.090 |
| | | | (1.84) | (2.93) |
| Pop. density (no./ha) | | | 0.101 | 0.067 |
| | | | (5.37) | (1.73) |
| Exports rep. skins | | | -0.995 | -1.445 |
| (million skins) | | | (0.67) | (1.49) |
| Closed forest (million ha) | | | -0.015 | -0.005 |
| | | | (2.04) | (1.07) |
| Roundwood production | | | 0.021 | |
| (million cub. mt) | | | (1.17) | |
| Roundwood export | | | | 0.247 |
| (million cub. mt) | | | | (1.48) |
| Sum sq. res. | 1,127 | 390.2 | 135.9 | 134.0 |
| No. observations | 102 | 50 | 44 | 42 |
| Adjusted $R^2$ | 0.31 | 0.64 | 0.85 | 0.84 |

Data source: World Resources Institute.

**TABLE 16.8D. Species Threatened: Birds.**

Dependent Variable: Number of Species Threatened

| Regression | (1) | (2) | (3) |
|---|---|---|---|
| Intercept | 17.77 | -9.967 | -1.657 |
| | (4.53) | (1.60) | (0.20) |
| GDP/Capita (Y) | 1.259 | 2.612 | 0.384 |
| (1,000 1987 US$) | (1.47) | (2.71) | (0.36) |
| $Y^2$ | -0.067 | -0.094 | -0.008 |
| | (1.38) | (1.89) | (0.22) |
| Exports/GDP (X) | -23.59 | -11.33 | -11.52 |
| | (2.55) | (1.59) | (1.36) |
| $X*N$ interact. | 0.591 | 0.027 | 0.653 |
| | (1.37) | (0.06) | (1.77) |
| Population (N) | 0.053 | 0.053 | -0.042 |
| (millions) | (1.19) | (1.63) | (1.14) |
| No. species known | | 0.038 | 0.027 |
| | | (4.01) | (3.19) |
| Arable area (million ha) | | | -0.130 |
| | | | (0.81) |
| No. cattle (millions) | | | 0.786 |
| | | | (6.87) |
| No. sheep (millions) | | | 0.168 |
| | | | (3.87) |
| No. goats (millions) | | | -0.982 |
| | | | (3.60) |
| Exports live parrots | | | -53.38 |
| (million birds) | | | (2.75) |
| Closed forest (million ha) | | | -0.010 |
| | | | (0.50) |
| Roundwood export | | | -2.508 |
| (million cub. mt) | | | (2.86) |
| Sum sq. res. | 21,253 | 11,194 | 3,138 |
| No. observations | 102 | 75 | 50 |
| Adjusted $R^2$ | 0.30 | 0.59 | 0.83 |

Data source: World Resources Institute.

**TABLE 16.8E. Species Threatened: Mammals.**

Dependent Variable: Number of Species Threatened

| Regression | (1) | (2) |
|---|---|---|
| Intercept | 12.01 | -12.78 |
| | (4.78) | (1.73) |
| GDP/Capita (Y) | 3.135 | 2.861 |
| (1,000 1987 US$) | (2.11) | (1.69) |
| $Y^2$ | -0.183 | -0.143 |
| | (2.14) | (1.69) |
| Exports/GDP (X) | -19.56 | 20.80 |
| | (2.36) | (1.82) |
| X*N interact. | 1.297 | 0.952 |
| | (2.33) | (2.28) |
| Population (N) | -0.064 | -0.228 |
| (millions) | (1.69) | (6.03) |
| No. species known | | 0.106 |
| | | (4.10) |
| Arable area (million ha) | | 0.238 |
| | | (1.18) |
| No. cattle (millions) | | 0.559 |
| | | (4.79) |
| No. sheep (millions) | | -0.129 |
| | | (1.44) |
| No. goats (millions) | | -1.048 |
| | | (2.85) |
| Dummy for mammal export | | -6.601 |
| | | (3.32) |
| Closed forest (1,000 ha) | | -0.438 |
| | | (4.32) |
| Roundwood production | | 0.481 |
| (million cub. mt) | | (4.43) |
| Roundwood export | | 2.716 |
| (million cub. mt) | | (2.33) |
| Sum sq. res. | 6,122 | 1,261 |
| No. observations | 64 | 36 |
| Adjusted $R^2$ | 0.34 | 0.74 |

Data source: World Resources Institute.

In the case of freshwater fish, the number of species threatened is sensitive to climatic zones. In particular, the freshwater fish threatened are fewer in semi-arid areas and significantly greater in cold zones, relative to humid areas. The threat to fish is also greater in the tropics than in temperate areas, even given income levels. In fact, once these geographical components are included, the inverse U pattern with respect to income and the negative association with exports become much clearer. In the context of the other four major species groupings, the climatic zones matter far less according to our data, and these measures are therefore omitted from the results shown.

In the case of the (partially) land-based animals, the association with agriculture is explored. Among amphibians, reptiles, and (statistically weaker) mammals, more species are threatened where arable farming is more extensive. More birds and mammals are also found to be threatened where the numbers of cattle are greater, though this is not the case for amphibians and reptiles. More generally, the number of reptile species threatened proved larger where population pressure on the land is greatest, though no such clear pattern emerged for any of the other major groups.

Beyond the broad issue of whether more export-oriented economies pose a greater threat to biodiversity (perhaps through general orientation of production), there is an important issue with respect to trade in and hunting of specific species themselves. The data available to explore this latter topic are very limited in scope. Moreover, especially where trade is supposedly restricted, official data underreport actual trade. Nonetheless, Tables 16.8A-16.8E explore some of the reported data, such as they are. In no case is any positive association found. *Reported* exports of reptile skins, of live parrots, and of raw ivory, cat skins, or live primates (the last three being represented by a dummy variable in the mammal regression) tend to occur from countries with smaller numbers of species threatened, if anything. Moreover, the average annual freshwater catch of fish also has a weak negative association with the number of freshwater fish species threatened.

However, the effects of forestry upon land-based species survival prove clearer. Among amphibians, reptiles, and mammals, the number of species threatened is significantly less where the extent of surviving closed forest is greatest. The corollary is that forest destruction may well pose a significant and major threat, though data on the change in number of species threatened are not available to test directly the association with rate of deforestation. Moreover, among amphibians, reptiles, and mammals, the number of species threatened is positively associated with the rate of roundwood production and/or export (though in the first two cases these two measures are highly collinear and their separate effects cannot be distinguished). Among birds, a similar effect from forest survival and wood production is not found, which is somewhat surprising given the consistency of the other results.

### Emissions and Waste

Some aspects of industrial and manufacturing emissions have already been explored in earlier sections. In this final section, some additional measures are examined. In particular, data on chlorofluorocarbon (CFC) and methane ($CH_4$) emissions from various anthropogenic activities, data on municipal waste in Organization for Economic Cooperation and Development (OECD) countries, and on nuclear power are each analyzed in turn.

### Chlorofluorocarbon and Methane

Besides carbon dioxide, CFC and methane are the most important greenhouse gases. Data on their annual emissions as of 1989, reported by the World Resources Institute, are largely simulated from various underlying sources. Given this, there is little point in examining any association with the sources themselves, and so the analysis in Table 16.9 is therefore confined to our basic economic factors considered throughout this study.

Both CFC and total methane emissions are estimated to rise initially with income per capita, and then to decline. However, the latter effect is very weak statistically in both cases, and any implied turning point is projected to be somewhat beyond the income of the richest nations. In other words, both emissions rise with income level, albeit at perhaps a diminishing rate.

CFC emissions tend to decline with export orientation up to a population level of around 18 million, and to rise thereafter. Methane emissions, on the other hand, tend to decline with export propensity irrespective of population level (though the decline is not strong statistically).

The total methane emissions are the sum of simulated emissions from five sources, and the same analysis is reported for each component separately in Table 16.9. The patterns vary. The inverse U pattern with respect to income levels emerges clearly only for methane emissions from domestic livestock, and more weakly in the case of municipal solid waste. However, the negative association with export propensity generally holds up more or less strongly in the components. The only exception to the latter is in the case of wet rice cultivation, where more export-oriented countries tend to produce more wet rice. To a large extent, this exception no doubt reflects the export orientation of the East Asian nations in particular, though it should be noted that in several of these countries rice production is heavily protected, despite the more general outward orientation.

### Municipal Waste

The World Resources Institute reproduces the OECD data on total municipal waste. The basis of these data differs by member country and the

272                                                                    R.E.B. Lucas

TABLE 16.9. Chlorofluorocarbons and Methane from Anthropogenic Sources.

Dependent Variable: Annual Emissions (1,000 tonnes)

| | CFC | CH4 Total | CH4 Solid Waste | CH4 Coal Mining | CH4 Oil/Natural Gas | CH4 Rice | CH4 Live-stock |
|---|---|---|---|---|---|---|---|
| Intercept | -2.052 | 109.5 | 27.12 | 318.3 | 194.2 | -303.2 | 307.0 |
| | (0.72) | (0.50) | (0.20) | (0.61) | (1.05) | (1.38) | (1.98) |
| GDP/Capita (Y) | 0.002 | 0.238 | 0.139 | 0.070 | 0.023 | -0.111 | 0.120 |
| (1,000 1987 US$) | (2.11) | (1.87) | (1.69) | (0.47) | (0.36) | (1.09) | (2.65) |
| $Y^2$/1,000,000 | -0.045 | -6.153 | -2.261 | 2.230 | 0.163 | -1.690 | -5.946 |
| | (0.76) | (1.04) | (0.53) | (0.18) | (0.06) | (0.22) | (2.18) |
| Exports/GDP (X) | -18.01 | -1,553 | -1,095 | -2,650 | -703.3 | 947.6 | -749.0 |
| | (1.91) | (1.38) | (1.58) | (1.37) | (0.92) | (1.65) | (1.92) |
| X*N interact. | 0.977 | -35.91 | 12.57 | 18.80 | 41.07 | 12.70 | -52.58 |
| | (2.62) | (0.65) | (0.51) | (0.77) | (1.06) | (0.22) | (3.30) |
| Population (N) | -0.016 | 56.58 | 6.194 | 1.887 | -0.788 | 23.17 | 19.11 |
| (millions) | (0.27) | (4.86) | (0.88) | (0.76) | (0.25) | (5.49) | (7.38) |
| F-statistic | 6.39 | 60.70 | 6.44 | 2.36 | 1.65 | 78.40 | 65.64 |
| No. observations | 64 | 98 | 98 | 30 | 43 | 72 | 97 |
| $R^2$ | 0.30 | 0.75 | 0.22 | 0.19 | 0.07 | 0.84 | 0.77 |

Data source: World Resources Institute.

measures are therefore not strictly comparable. Nonetheless, some patterns do emerge in Table 16.10.

Municipal waste per (urban) capita, even among these richer OECD nations, initially rises and then declines, with income per capita reaching a peak at around 13,000 1987 US$. On the other hand, no stark pattern emerges with respect to export orientation among this set of countries, though there is a hint of a negative association.

Municipal waste per capita rises with the absolute size of population. The U.S. is the most populous of the OECD nations and also generates the greatest municipal waste per capita. However, it is interesting to see that waste per capita tends to be negatively associated with urban and metropolitan concentration of the population, perhaps suggesting some scale economies in waste.

## Nuclear Power

The last topic addressed in this chapter is nuclear power. In a way, it is different from many of the other measures considered. Nuclear power need not pose a threat if appropriately designed and operated. However, no indications of the potential for leaks are available, and only some measures are available of the extent of power generated by nuclear means. Table 16.11 therefore examines the proportion of electric power generated from nuclear sources across countries.

TABLE 16.10. Municipal Waste: OECD Countries.

Dependent Variable: Annual Municipal Waste Relative to Urban Population (tonnes per person)

| Regression | (1) | (2) |
|---|---|---|
| Intercept | 0.227 | 5.966 |
| | (0.31) | (3.31) |
| GDP/Capita ($Y$) | 0.309 | 0.234 |
| (1,000 1987 US$) | (2.48) | (1.55) |
| $Y^2$ | -0.012 | -0.009 |
| | (2.35) | (1.28) |
| Exports/GDP ($X$) | 0.300 | -2.016 |
| | (0.13) | (1.12) |
| $X^*N$ interact. | -0.059 | -0.008 |
| | (1.07) | (0.14) |
| Population ($N$) | 0.010 | 0.006 |
| (millions) | (1.99) | (1.12) |
| Pop. urban (%) | | -0.053 |
| | | (2.87) |
| Frac. population cities | | -0.114 |
| | | (1.69) |
| Sum sq. res. | 34.60 | 28.17 |
| No. observations | 22 | 22 |
| Adjusted $R^2$ | -0.10 | -0.02 |

Data source: World Resources Institute.

**TABLE 16.11. Nuclear Power.**

Dependent Variable: Nuclear Production of Electricity Relative to Total Electricity Production
(GWH/1,000 tonnes oil equiv.)

| Regression | (1) | (2) | (3) |
|---|---|---|---|
| Intercept | -0.172 | -0.157 | 0.011 |
|  | (1.47) | (1.33) | (0.11) |
| GDP/Capita ($Y$) | 0.213 | 0.196 | 0.214 |
| (1,000 1987 US$) | (2.39) | (2.12) | (2.31) |
| $Y^2$ | -0.007 | -0.006 | -0.007 |
|  | (1.52) | (1.38) | (1.43) |
| Exports/GDP ($X$) | -0.826 | -0.726 | -0.880 |
|  | (2.61) | (2.18) | (2.96) |
| $X*N$ interact. | 0.133 | 0.130 | 0.109 |
|  | (2.53) | (2.46) | (2.25) |
| Population ($N$) | -0.008 | -0.009 | -0.006 |
| (millions) | (2.30) | (2.41) | (1.66) |
| Energy consumption |  | 0.629 | -0.513 |
| (billion tonnes coal equiv.) |  | (1.78) | (0.70) |
| Electricity generation |  |  | 0.070 |
| (million tonnes oil equiv.) |  |  | (2.53) |
| Hydroelec. installed |  |  | -0.112 |
| (1,000 MW) |  |  | (2.69) |
| Sum sq. res. | 95.37 | 93.77 | 83.33 |
| No. observations | 76 | 75 | 75 |
| Adjusted $R^2$ | 0.33 | 0.33 | 0.39 |

Data source: World Bank estimates.

Once again, the now familiar inverse U pattern with respect to income per capita emerges with nuclear power relative to total power generation, peaking at 15,200 1987 US$ per capita according to the first equation in Table 16.11. The proportion of power derived from nuclear sources initially declines with overall export propensity, then rises among the more populous countries, reaching a turning point at 6.2 million people according to our first regression. Given these factors, it is the less populous countries which rely more heavily on nuclear power. Of course, this is not necessarily heartening in terms of the potential effect from fallout which readily transgresses international boundaries.

Since, for many nations, electricity is largely nontraded, power consumption and production are highly correlated. It is the high producers/consumers that tend to rely more heavily upon nuclear power, even given their income level. On the other hand, where hydroelectricity potential is exploited in installed capacity, reliance on nuclear power is significantly reduced. Presumably, the implication is that if nations well endowed with potential hydro capacity were better able to exploit and to export this resource, world reliance on nuclear power could be reduced (but even hydro-generation can have negative environmental consequences in its own right).

## Summing Up

Some lobbyists oppose freer global trade, because of its potential harm to the environment. Expanded trade in ivory presumably would pose an even greater threat to elephant herds, (though, as with narcotics, whether expanded legal trade and reduction in illegal activities would prove harmful is less clear). But opposition to expanded trade is frequently posed in more general form.

This study has taken a wide range of international environmental indicators, such as they are, and asked whether those countries which are more outward oriented in exports show less respect for the environment. In the first two sections, it was also possible to ask whether greater outward orientation within any given country, on average, proves environmentally damaging with respect to certain industrial emissions. As one might expect, the evidence is mixed. Nonetheless, it is probably fair to say that most of the estimates presented indicate less harm to the environment as export orientation increases, especially among smaller countries—though there are notable exceptions to this.

One might oppose trade liberalization on the grounds that it can raise incomes and hence indirectly impact the environment. In fact, a remarkably consistent pattern emerges from the results presented here, of accelerating harm to the environment as income rises among lower-income countries; then this effect either tapers off or reverses at higher income ranges. Again, there are exceptions to this inverse U-shaped pattern, but not as many. To argue that incomes of the poorer nations should be restrained in order to sustain the global environment poses a fundamental moral dilemma. It is therefore important to note that, in examining these data, no evidence at all is found that more rapid growth harms the environment in any way, given income levels. In other words, even if it proves true that the transition of the poorer nations into greater affluence damages the environment, a more rapid transition does not seem to worsen the process.

Selected aspects of expanded trade probably would prove harmful to the environment. Several results in this study point to the importance of the survival of forests. However, the results also suggest that although roundwood trade may be limiting the survival of wilderness, there is no evidence in the data (given their severe limitations) that roundwood trade or production is resulting in permanent deforestation. Perhaps it is the change in the nature of the forest from roundwood production and trade which results in our finding that roundwood trade poses a direct threat to certain amphibians, reptiles, and mammals.

Much remains to be done with these data. Several alternative specifications are reported in most contexts and reference is made to yet others, but further exploration of the sensitivity of results to specification is required. The results presented here can all be viewed as essentially being in reduced form: environmental outcomes or correlations are related to endowments of the individual countries and to our economic measures, treating the latter as predetermined. More structural forms may warrant exploration, for some interdependence in our environmental indicators is probable. For example, pesticide use may well affect the number of bird species threatened, but this kind of interdependence remains to be explored. This may be important precisely because of the highly integrated and interdependent nature of ecosystems.

## Notes

1. In the cross-country analyses, income per capita for 1987 is adopted, since data for more recent years still frequently are missing.

2. In the subsequent cross-country analyses, this growth measure is generally excluded since, for instance, including average growth from 1980 to 1987 would have meant a significant (and probably biased) reduction in sample size as a result of missing data.

3. This result contrasts with earlier results obtained by the author in conjunction with David Wheeler and Mala Hettige, in which the dollar index of price distortion was adopted as a measure of openness and an earlier set of estimates of toxic emission intensities deployed. The reason for this contrast requires further investigation.

4. This is based upon a five percent, one-tailed test. The six are total toxic release and suspended solids in water, plus suspended particles, sulphur dioxide, fine particles, and carbon monoxide air pollutants.

5. The rate of economic growth is omitted from the cross-sectional results for two reasons: in general, if these measures are included they prove to have effects statistically indistinguishable from zero; second, the measure of growth adopted is the average annual growth from 1980 through 1987, and this is not available for a substantial subset of the countries because of missing income data in some portion of the period.

6. The magnitude of this estimated association is surprisingly large, and in future work one may wish to allow for more nonlinearity in this association. Future work also should include an analysis of the fraction of land area preserved as wilderness, and not merely the absolute amount as here.

7. These observations remain correct if production and export are entered individually within the last regression in Table 4, though the effect of production in increasing deforestation does become somewhat stronger statistically in this specification.

8. The only exception is in the first equation, which does not allow for water availability, wherein there is a weak tendency for water use to rise with export propensity up to a population level of about 5.4 million, and declining thereafter.

PART FIVE

# Key Questions and Research Needs

# 17

BK Title

## Key Questions

*David E. Ervin and Vivian Noble Keller*

### Introduction

Most of the research that has already been done on the relationship between expanded agricultural trade and environmental protection is theoretical, incomplete, and lacks sufficient empirical content. Nonetheless, workable hypotheses about the direction and general magnitude of possible effects can be formed to guide fruitful research and formulate policy options while accumulating better evidence.

Current and future research efforts should focus on three key questions. First: *Can existing national programs adequately address the likely environmental effects of expanded agricultural trade?* Thus far, the answer seems to be no. Most current programs rely on voluntary/subsidy measures that are neither comprehensive nor effective, and will dwindle with continued budget pressure. In particular, these programs do not adequately address the most troubling risk that expanded trade may pose to the environment: the introduction of harmful nonindigenous species. Further, their incompleteness may expose specific areas to excessive environmental stress from trade surges and shifts, for example, along border zones.

The second question researchers must explore is: *How much do environmental programs adversely affect trade?* Available evidence does not show that environmental programs significantly affect trade flows in industries outside production agriculture. Given that environmental programs affecting agriculture are primarily voluntary and implemented with education, technical assistance, and subsidies, production agriculture in an aggregate sense is not likely affected by environmental regulations in any meaningful way. Some specific sectors subject to strong and inflexible regulation may suffer a competitiveness drag. Inappropriate environmental subsidies, such as for large land setasides, may be the bigger risk. The advent of stricter and more comprehensive regulations may change the aggregate effect, but at this writing, governments' use of environmental measures as nontariff barriers to trade is probably the most potent threat.

Finally, researchers must ask: *How should transboundary or global environmental problems be addressed—through trade or other measures?* Existing institutions, including international environmental agreements and multilateral trade pacts, generally do not do the job and, in some instances, pose risks to the global environment and to trade. Alternative mechanisms and concepts for coping with transboundary or global environmental dilemmas are sorely needed.

As international trade and environmental agreements proliferate, advocates of freer trade and environmental protection clash more frequently and with greater vehemence. Many free-trade devotees fear that excessive environmental regulation will jeopardize world economic growth; many environmentalists fear that increased international trade may contribute to degrading the earth's natural resource base enough to threaten sustainability.

In the case of agriculture, each of these positions is extreme and the current evidence supporting them is quite weak. To begin with, agricultural trade has only recently been liberalized, so there are no concrete historical examples to support one position or another. Similarly, our understanding of the environmental links to agriculture is embryonic and hence unreliable. Only strong empirical work, which is scant, can yield firm insights. Finally—despite the recent GATT and North American Free Trade accords—governments still intervene considerably in agricultural production and agricultural trade. As a result, estimates of production and trade responses must rely primarily on theoretical arguments and simulation analyses of second-best situations. Indeed, given political realities, agricultural production and trade probably will continue to be distorted, second-best puzzles for the foreseeable future.

This is not to say that current predictions are little better than mere guesswork. Current theory can help us to anticipate the general directions of adjustment, and the data that we have, although meager, can help us to determine the general pattern and magnitude of possible effects. Even rudimentary analyses will help avoid large potential losses to the environment or to trade. The research agenda should therefore focus on high-priority policy targets (perhaps a strategy geared to minimize the maximum possible loss) until more complete data are at hand. In the following sections, the three fundamental questions that we feel can best guide present and future research are addressed.

## Can Existing National Programs Adequately Address the Likely Environmental Effects of Expanded Agricultural Trade?

Over the years, many environmental groups have argued that liberalized agricultural trade may cause profound environmental degradation. To support this view, they often cite the fragile farmlands that were ravaged in the early 1970s, after foreign demand for U.S. agricultural exports expanded suddenly and dramatically. Such an argument implies a simplistic understanding of the issues involved. Although the two terms are often confused in the literature, trade liberalization and trade expansion are not synonymous—and agricultural trade expansion will likely proceed with or without liberalization.

Further, such an argument does not take into account the institutional setting under which agricultural trade expansion takes place, which is key to anticipating environmental effects. Three factors—trade policies, production programs, and environmental programs—will determine what happens to the environment as trade expands. For example, many free traders claimed that liberalizing agricultural trade would enhance the quality of the environment through reduced chemical use and other beneficial developments, based on the assumption that production support programs would be reformed. Unfortunately, trade liberalization does not necessarily lead to meaningful reform of domestic agricultural policy.

The environmental effects of expanded agricultural trade fall into three categories: (1) production effects, (2) introduction of harmful nonindigenous species, and (3) "bootstrapping" of environmental standards due to income growth. The most commonly perceived impacts stem from *production effects*. These production effects can be further broken down into scale, composition, and technique components (Grossman and Krueger 1992), which are determined both by the general pressure from expanded trade and the specific economic forces and institutions shaping production responses. For example, the crop rotations used to fill export demand are influenced by commodity program incentives, and the degree of fertilization or pesticide use may be restricted by federal or state environmental controls.

### Production Effects

How does production shift as trade grows? Although we do not have complete data, initial estimates for increased land use under the NAFTA and URA pacts are not large compared to the total natural resource base. In the United States, cropland in production is estimated to expand from a low of 1 percent to a high of 3 percent after full NAFTA and GATT implementation [U.S. Department of Agriculture (USDA) 1994]. These are optimistic projections compared to other sources (e.g., International Trade

Commission). In any event, land use likely will increase as acres that are currently set aside under the Acreage Reduction Program (ARP) or the Conservation Reserve Program (CRP) are released.

When set-aside land returns to production, the general effects include more substitution of land for chemicals (although we are uncertain of the rates of substitution), more erosion, and more damage to wildlife habitat. The overall national effects are nonetheless small (Miranowski, Hrubovack, and Sutton 1991; Tobey and Reinert 1991). Shifts in crop composition and rotation depend heavily on agricultural program reforms that change the relative returns for different crops. Similarly, shifts resulting from lower barriers to trade depend on potential land use and changes in production techniques.

The small overall national effect is composed of positive and negative effects that are spread unevenly across regions. In some areas, for example, farmers will use crop rotations that require fewer chemicals and lead to less soil erosion; in others, farmers may use rotations that result in more erosion and more chemical use. An important question is whether some pockets of land will be subject to extreme stress or uncertain and irreversible damage as a result of trade shifts and surges. For the uncertain/ irreversibility cases, applying normal benefit-cost tests may be inappropriate, and using the safe-minimum standard approach may be warranted (Castle and Berrens 1993). The Antle et. al. analysis (in this volume), and others like it, can help to assess such high-risk situations. Clearly, a key research priority is identifying the most important environmental problems associated with agriculture in specific geographic areas, so that governments can directly address these problems and avoid imposing unnecessary restrictions in unaffected areas.

In general, the increased environmental stress stemming from expanded trade yields the same results as increased production for domestic consumption. Possible program responses will differ only if foreign markets demand products that require special production processes involving different environmental stresses. Accordingly, a major order of business for trade and environmental management is to assess current environmental programs in agriculture. How might they handle additional production in certain areas?

In the United States, a wide variety of programs are aimed at controlling environmental degradation and enhancing the environmental benefits of production agriculture. Most of these programs are voluntary, using education, technical assistance, and cost-sharing monies, or are linked to voluntary participation in the commodity programs (compliance schemes). A careful review of the literature evaluating the voluntary education/ subsidy programs indicates that they generally are not cost effective and were not targeted to areas with the highest environmental values [U.S.

Congress, Office of Technology Assessment (USC/OTA) 1995]. A good illustration is the repeated renting of erosive croplands over the past sixty years to stem recurring erosion problems.

Subsidies generally are effective only as long as they are offered; the vast majority do not purchase long-term or permanent control, although some enduring structures and wetlands protection efforts are exceptions. Further, they do not satisfy the polluter-pays principle, which, through increased costs, signals producers and consumers that they are using scarce environmental resources. The same difficulties pertain with compliance schemes, which depend on continuing commodity program benefits that are large enough to induce program participants to meet conservation standards. Because federal finances are so strained, it is hard to imagine large commodity or conservation subsidies continuing indefinitely. Moreover, the voluntary approaches do not ensure that all environmental problems will be addressed—especially those associated with growing crops that are not part of any government program.

Some aspects of agricultural production that cause environmental problems are regulated. Certain pesticides must be registered, point-source water pollution from confined-animal feeding operations must be controlled, and endangered species must be preserved. Nonpoint source water pollution will be partially "regulated" under the Coastal Zone Act Reauthorization Amendments in that producers will be required to choose from a list of acceptable practices to control water pollution. Unfortunately, these programs often lack flexibility across technologies and sources to meet the standards, which implies that the regulations are not least-cost solutions. Moreover, the regulations may penalize innovative producers who upgrade environmental performance by neglecting to reward the innovator and requiring all farmers to adopt the new technology.

Anderson (1992) has shown that optimal environmental policies must exist before it can be said that increased agricultural trade truly enhances welfare. Clearly, existing environmental programs for U.S. agriculture are a far cry from the nearly optimal policies needed to include accurate costs and benefits in producer and consumer decisions. Unfortunately, most other developed countries also rely on subsidies, or a variation thereof, to achieve most environmental goals, and thus suffer the same shortcomings [Organization for Economic Cooperation and Development (OECD) 1993a][1].

Another class of production-related environmental problems—transboundary and global externalities—stem from or are increased by expanding trade. This can render national approaches largely ineffective. Examples include water and air pollution that migrate across borders, depletion of the ozone layer, and reductions in global biodiversity. Existing mechanisms to deal with these phenomena are inadequate and immature.

Some, such as the Montreal Protocol on Ozone Depletion and the Convention on International Trade in Endangered Species (CITES), appear sustainable, but their long-term efficacy is uncertain. In short, to the extent expanded agricultural trade increases these transboundary problems, existing mechanisms cannot ensure that full environmental costs are paid. International arrangements will be addressed further in the last section.

## Introduction of Harmful Nonindigenous Species

The second category of environmental impacts from expanded agricultural trade, and particularly imports,[2] is the *introduction of harmful nonindigenous species* (HNIS). A recent study has estimated the cumulative economic losses to date from selected past introductions (seventy-nine cases) at nearly $97 billion. Future losses between $66 and $134 billion are estimated for just fifteen cases of the very harmful NIS plant and animal diseases (USC/OTA 1993). What is more, these estimates do not fully capture nonmarket environmental damage, much of which will affect agriculture and forestry. Russian wheat aphids, kudzu, gypsy moths, and water hyanciths have all been culprits in the past. Most recently, concern has focused on the zebra mussel, which has destroyed vegetation and aquatic life in many eastern U.S. lakes and rivers, and is currently poised to invade many western U.S. irrigation systems.

Expanded and liberalized agricultural trade, especially in biological organisms, will open up new pathways for HNIS and likely will increase damages. It is not technically or economically possible to eliminate new HNIS, but thwarting their entry and limiting their spread is essential. The task is not an easy one, however, because of the great uncertainty about the nature and degree of introductions, and about which measures may be most cost effective. The current U.S. response is a patchwork of incomplete and ineffective programs that result in substantial underestimates of HNIS' economic and environmental costs (USC/OTA 1993). International measures are even more incomplete and probably less effective, due to the substantial transaction costs of achieving effective international protocols. In this regard, efforts to create a World Trade Organization committee that would establish international guidelines to control HNIS without relying on nontariff barriers, such as health and safety regulations, might be extremely useful.

## "Bootstrapping" of Environmental Standards Due to Income Growth

The final potential environmental effect of expanded trade is the *"bootstrapping" of environmental standards due to income growth*. Eminent economists have argued that increased economic prosperity will improve overall environmental health. This argument is based on the positive income elasticity of demand for environmental quality and the built-in tendency to raise environmental standards as economic growth proceeds. A so-called "hump" effect is posited whereby poor countries experience degradation of environmental quality up to certain income levels (about $5,000 per capita), and then improvement is experienced. The forces of industrial composition and technique also work with income growth in this process.

The "hump" effect was widely cited during the NAFTA and GATT debates, and was presumed to exist. Unfortunately, the evidence for it is incomplete, so a firm conclusion is not possible. Grossman and Krueger (1991) found support for the hypothesis in their analysis of sulfur dioxide and smoke emissions across forty-two countries. However, other results, from an investigation of eighty countries, found that toxic industrial pollution invariably increased over existing per capita income levels (Lucas, Wheeler, and Hettige 1992; Lopez 1992). Lucas' further analysis (in this volume) adds important new evidence supporting the existence of the "hump" effect for several environmental performance variables.

By the authors' admissions, these tests are preliminary and incomplete. Comprehensive evidence on overall environmental quality in relation to economic growth is required. All demands on nonmarket environmental resources must be accounted for to capture the full demand and supply effects. The studies to date are reduced-form in nature and are merely suggestive of the economic mechanism at work. Whether increased incomes bootstrap all environmental quality dimensions is still an unanswered question. Omitted from testing for the "hump" effect are impacts on transboundary and global environmental resources. Given the high transaction costs of negotiating and sustaining international agreements, effective mechanisms to incorporate transnational and global environmental effects are more difficult than domestic programs. The recent evidence on the decline of ocean fisheries suggests that increased world incomes may be insufficient to reverse the process of depletion to global open-access resources. We need to investigate policies that protect valuable environmental resources so that the growth process automatically treats these resources as scarce and engenders low-cost conservation technologies—in effect a global polluter-pays approach.

Current evidence indicates that the domestic environmental impacts of trade expansion will be small. Much depends on the character of agricultural and environmental policies that accompany the trade expansions. In our view, the domestic wild card is the potential increase in HNIS. Also, foreign countries with ineffectual environmental programs who are likely to increase production significantly will cause resource degradation, some with transboundary or global consequences.

## How Much Do Environmental Programs Restrict Trade?

Like the effects of trade on the environment, the effects of environmental programs on trade fall into three categories. First, environmental regulations can *raise production and marketing costs*. Second, environmental requirements may *induce firms to migrate overseas* to avoid the costs of complying with regulations. Both effects fall under the general category of *reduced competitiveness*. The third effect on potential trade performance is the *use of nontariff trade barriers*.

Reduced competitiveness due to regulation has not been an issue for agriculture because most conservation and environmental programs are voluntary and subsidized. Two prominent exceptions are the registration/cancellation of pesticides and the control of point sources of water pollution, such as confined-animal operations and nurseries. The prospect of broader regulation has, however, increased concern in the production agriculture industry that trade opportunities may be lost or diminished. For example, recent endangered species cases have fueled concern. Some studies have attempted to estimate what increased costs might be, but their data have been scant and their methodologies incomplete (e.g., Gardner 1993). In particular, no studies have attempted to estimate comprehensively the *net* costs of environmental programs in agricultural production.

Absent reliable information for production agriculture, it is instructive to examine how environmental regulations appear to have affected the competitiveness of other industries. We must first note that pollution abatement and control (PAC) costs in public and private sectors ranged from a low of 1 percent to a high of 1.6 percent of 1990 gross domestic product for the United States, Japan, France, West Germany, and the United Kingdom (OECD 1993b). These estimates doubtless contain errors, but even if they underestimate PAC costs by 50 percent, the costs are not large compared to other production factors such as labor, materials, and energy. Not surprisingly, most evidence indicates that environmental regulation has not exerted a significant effect on industrial trade flows (Dean 1992; Tobey 1990). Similarly, attempts to discern if environmental requirements encourage industries to migrate overseas have yielded similar findings (e.g., Low and Yeats 1992). Whalley's analysis (in this volume) arrives at the same conclusion, but notes that a large-scale global environmental initiative—say, for greenhouse gas reductions—would likely cause significant economic adjustment.

It is important to qualify such broad statements by noting that some industrial subsectors may face very high environmental compliance costs, and so become less competitive abroad. Copper and steel production are two potential cases (USC/OTA 1992). Because agricultural production is not covered by the PAC survey, comparative data are not available to judge the potential trade distortion for the sector as a whole or for specific subsectors. However, as argued above, there is little reason to believe, based on current environmental programs affecting agriculture, that it faces large costs. Indeed, the industry may actually be enjoying a net subsidy to meet conservation and environmental requirements, when we consider programs such as the CRP. However, the CRP, by retiring land from production through subsidies (rental payments), may reduce overall competitiveness if it more than reduces excess production capacity caused by commodity programs.

The third effect on potential trade performance, the use of nontariff trade barriers (NTBs), is a matter of market access. The issue is crucial, given the NAFTA and GATT moves to phase out other NTBs. Two questions underlie the issue: (1) *Which criteria and standards justify imposing environmental controls?*[3] and (2) *How can the effects of legitimate NTBs on trade be minimized?* Regrettably, data detailing the breadth and scope of environmentally-related NTBs are not available. More important is the potential for new NTBs as others are phased out. Several cases of product and production process method (PPM) standards related to environmental goals have already surfaced (e.g., returnable container requirements and tuna-dolphin disputes), and their number likely will grow. Possible agricultural examples include genetically-engineered organisms and organic farm products.

Research on the economics of discerning and correcting NTBs should be a high-priority endeavor. Runge (1990) has begun the discussion, but much more needs to be done. We know from ample experience that the world trading system is constantly hindered by national protectionism, and we should not expect protectionist tendencies to disappear with the new trade accords. Conversely, we cannot automatically throw away environmental quality regulations. Dealing with environmental NTBs is particularly challenging because science alone is not a sufficient basis for determining their legitimacy—as it is for most sanitary-phytosanitary (SPS) issues.[4] Obviously, environmental standards vary across countries for more than biological and technical reasons. Preferences for the composition and level of environmental quality depend on cultural traditions and national values. Efforts to protect rural landscapes in densely populated European countries are good examples of legitimate environmental initiatives that are not based in science. Costs and benefits must be considered.

Esty (1994) has proposed a new international trade and environment test based on a balancing test using the commerce clause standard for judging whether state actions unnecessarily restrict interstate commerce. The test asks and answers three questions in legalistic fashion:

1. What is the intent and effect of the challenged regulation? (i.e., to unmask hidden trade barriers, etc.)

2. What is the legitimacy of the underlying environmental policy or claim of environmental injury? (i.e., to determine the presence of bona fide environmental harm)
3. What is the justification for the disruption to trade? (i.e., to determine whether disruption is clearly disproportionate)

Obviously, these are nontrivial questions for most disputes, but the test is operational in a domestic context, so the potential is there. Ideally, a body composed of trade and environmental experts would comprise the panel and sort out the facts and judgments. Esty notes that for now, GATT may have to assume leadership for that role because no international environmental organization is available.

Ultimately, the effects of environmental programs on trade appear to be small. Most of the evidence does not support arguments that environmental measures reduce competitiveness by increasing production costs unduly or causing firms to migrate abroad. In our view, the unknown factor here is the possible emergence of environmental NTBs that could impede trade.

## How Should Transboundary or Global Environmental Problems Be Addressed?

The discussion thus far has centered on the national implications of expanded agricultural trade and increased environmental regulation. Obviously, some pollution and resource problems are transboundary or global in nature. Pesticides and waste products may contaminate rivers crossing country borders, losses in biodiversity may affect future food or fiber plant gene pools, and releases of chlorofluorocarbons deplete the ozone layer. Such problems have been responsible for the creation of hundreds of international environmental agreements. The result, however, has been an uncoordinated, overlapping, and inefficient regime that cannot guarantee adequate coverage or protection (Esty 1994). Chichilnisky (this volume) reminds us that there are substantial problems in defining and enforcing property rights to incorporate the environmental effects in private or public transactions. With a rapidly growing world population, integration of the global economy, and improved understanding of the interrelationships of ecological systems, pressure to implement more international environmental agreements likely will increase. The basic question is whether trade or other measures should be used to remedy problems that transcend borders.

In the past, trade sanctions have been incorporated into international environmental agreements to address transboundary or global environmental problems. GATT lists seventeen international environmental agreements that contain trade sanctions (USC/OTA 1992). CITES and the Montreal Protocol are relevant examples. Without using trade sanctions as a lever, it is clearly difficult to implement multilateral agreements effectively, because there are few alternative means of addressing multinational environmental problems. Further—and even if actions to date suggest the CITES and CFC agreements can be successful—the overall effectiveness of using trade sanctions to implement international environmental agreements has not been conclusively determined (Barrett 1994b). The conventions on biodiversity and climate change, approved at or after the Rio conference, are only framework agreements, so their potential is as yet undefined. Esty (1994) proposes creating a Global Environmental Organization (GEO) to define the global environmental agenda and coordinate programs across countries. Two major research questions emerge from the current picture. First, under which conditions can we expect nations to cooperate voluntarily to solve transboundary or global environmental problems?[5] Second, which arrangements are likely to provide adequate incentives for cooperation without unduly hindering trade flows?

Another international approach is to pursue environmental management objectives in concert with multilateral trade agreements. NAFTA and GATT each address environmental concerns, albeit to different degrees. Both the Uruguay Round text establishing the World Trade Organization (WTO) and NAFTA make general overtures to protect and preserve the environment in tandem with promoting trade, and both, with some qualifications, generally allow members to set their own environmental standards. NAFTA goes further to exhort members to enforce their own environmental laws and to refrain from attracting foreign investment by lowering their environmental standards. It also allows members to impose some environmental requirements on foreign investors and, under certain circumstances, to refrain from granting patents for inventions that might harm the environment. GATT, for its part, permits subsidies to industries that are adapting existing facilities to new environmental requirements. In addition, the WTO is establishing a permanent committee on trade and the environment.

The NAFTA accord, which was accompanied by a side agreement that creates a North American Agreement on Environmental Cooperation (NAAEC), appears "greener" than the GATT Uruguay Round agreement. But there are serious questions about the ability of either agreement to provide environmental protection (Ballenger and Krissoff, this volume). GATT's provisions mostly enable or encourage national action (provided that it restricts trade as little as possible), while offering only a symbolic tip of the hat to transnational and global problems. NAAEC's agenda encompasses the full range of national and transboundary problems and, consequently, may be too ambitious and broadly focused for the current administrative and financial resources of the United States, Canada, and particularly Mexico to handle. Because there is no compelling evidence to suggest that Mexico might become a "pollution haven" for U.S. and Canadian industries if it did not adequately enforce its own environmental laws, limiting NAAEC's agenda to transboundary environmental problems would seem more practical. Institutions such as the North American Development Bank (NAD Bank) may also prove more useful than overarching mandates. NAD Bank's mission is to target and solve border-related environmental problems. Subsidized bank loans that address transboundary problems would not, of course, conform to the polluter-pays principle. Regrettably, without multilateral agreements that impose costs on polluters across borders, some form of subsidy will be necessary.

International cooperation is essential for negotiating standards and regulations that protect nations from importing and exporting harmful nonindigenous species (HNIS) as they trade. Such collaboration may not only reduce the incidence of HNIS, but also alleviate fears that measures used to combat HNIS are actually disguised nontariff trade barriers. Article XX(b) of GATT permits the imposition of trade restraints "necessary to protect human, animal, or plant life and health" by its members, but uncoordinated individual action may ultimately be more expensive and less successful than multilateral cooperation.

## Notes

1. Though not discussed here, the environmental programs to control externalities from increased production of processed products for sale abroad are deficient as well. Agricultural processing operations are regulated as water and air point source polluters, and usually do not have sufficient flexibility to always achieve low-cost solutions (e.g., tradable pollution permits). Also, the domestic and international transport industry has not incorporated all environmental costs (e.g., air pollution and ocean spills).
2. Increased imports, like production effects, can have positive and negative environmental impacts. Enhanced trade in "clean" technologies will accompany expanded trade (and firmer environmental controls in agriculture), but those technologies do not suffer high trade barriers at present and are not discussed as problems (USC/OTA 1992).
3. Runge (1990) suggests three criteria for determining the legitimacy of an environmental measure: (1) its estimated cost, (2) identification of who bears the costs, and (3) whether such a measure would have been imposed if trade were not an issue. Consideration of the origin, nature, and distribution of environmental benefits stemming from the measure also would seem appropriate.
4. SPS provisions overlap somewhat with environmental issues, mainly through nonindigenous species imports and exports, but are not mainly environmental in nature. Therefore, they are not treated in detail here.

5. Barrett (1994a) has developed theoretical arguments outlining the necessary conditions for these agreements to hold.

## References

Anderson, K. "The Standard Welfare Economics of Policies Affecting Trade and the Environment." In *The Greening of World Trade Issues*, K. Anderson and R. Blackhurst, eds., pp. 25–48. Ann Arbor, MI: University of Michigan Press, 1992.

Barrett, S. "International Environmental Management: North-South Implications." Paper presented at the Resource Policy Consortium symposia on International Environmental Management and National Policy, The World Bank, Washington, DC, 16–17 May 1994a.

_____ . "Self-Enforcing International Environmental Agreements." *Oxford Economic Papers* (forthcoming, 1994b).

Castle, E.N., and R.P. Berrens. "Endangered Species, Economic Analysis, and the Safe Minimum Standard." *Northwest Environmental Journal* 9(1993):108–30.

Dean, J.M. "Trade and the Environment: A Survey of the Literature." In *International Trade and the Environment*, P. Low, ed. World Bank Discussion Papers 159. Washington, DC: The World Bank, 1992.

Ervin, David E. "Soil and Water Conservation Down on the Farm: A Changing Economic Landscape." *Journal of Soil and Water Conservation* 49(3):232-234, May-June, 1994.

Esty, D. *Greening the GATT: Trade, Environment, and the Future.* Washington, DC: Institute for International Economics, 1994.

Gardner, B.L. "The Impacts of Environmental Protection and Food Safety Regulation on U.S. Agriculture." Agricultural Policy Working Group, Arlington, VA, September 1993.

Grossman, G.M., and A.B. Krueger. "Environmental Impacts of a North American Free Trade Agreement." Working Paper No. 3914. National Bureau of Economic Research, 1991.

_____ . "Environmental Impacts of a North American Free Trade Agreement." Discussion Paper (revised), John M. Olin Program for the Study of Economic Organization and Public Policy, Woodrow Wilson School, Princeton University, Princeton, NJ, 1992.

Lopez, R. "Discussion: Economic Development, Environmental Regulation, and the International Migration of Toxic Industrial Pollution: 1960–1988." In *International Trade and the Environment*, P. Low, ed. World Bank Discussion Papers 159. Washington, DC: The World Bank, 1992.

Low, P., and A. Yeats. "Do Dirty Industries Migrate?" In *International Trade and the Environment*, P. Low, ed. World Bank Discussion Papers 159. Washington, DC: The World Bank, 1992.

Lucas, R., D. Wheeler, and H. Hettige. "Economic Development, Environmental Regulation, and the International Migration of Toxic Industrial Pollution: 1960–1988." In *International Trade and the Environment*, P. Low, ed. World Bank Discussion Papers 159. Washington, DC: The World Bank, 1992.

Miranowski, J., J. Hrubovcak, and J. Sutton. "The Effects of Commodity Programs on Resource Use." In *Commodity and Resource Policies in Agricultural Systems*, R.E. Just and N.E. Bockstael, eds. New York: Springer-Verlag, 1991.

Organization for Economic Cooperation and Development (OECD). "Agricultural and Environmental Policy Integration: Recent Progress and New Directions." Paris: OECD, 1993a.

_____. "Pollution Abatement and Control Expenditures in OECD Countries." Environment Monograph No. 75. Paris: OECD, 1993b.

Runge, C.F. "Trade Protectionism and Environmental Regulations: The New Nontariff Barriers." *Northwestern Journal of International Law and Business* 11, No. 1(Spring 1990).

Tobey, J. "The Effects of Domestic Environmental Policies on Patterns of World Trade: An Empirical Test." *Kyklos* 43, No. 2(1990):191–209.

Tobey, J. A. and K. A. Reinert. "The Effects of Domestic Agricultural Policy Reform on Environmental Quality." *The Journal of Agricultural Economics Research* 43(1991)20-28.

U.S. Congress, Office of Technology Assessment (USC/OTA). *Agriculture, Trade, and Environment: Achieving Complementary Policies* (forthcoming, 1995).

_____. "Harmful Nonindigenous Species in the United States." Publication No. OTA-F-566. Washington, DC: U.S. Government Printing Office, September 1993.

_____. "Trade and Environment: Conflicts and Opportunities." Publication No. OTA-BP-ITE-94. Washington, DC: U.S. Government Printing Office, May 1992.

U.S. Department of Agriculture (USDA). "Effects of the Uruguay Round Agreement on U.S. Agricultural Commodities." Staff Report, Office of Economics and Economic Research Service, Washington, DC, 1994.

295-99

Global
Q20
F10

# 18

BK Title.    **Research Needs**

*Gerald C. Nelson*

### Introduction

The trade and the environment literature in this chapter is composed of two parts. One part focuses on how environmental policies affect international trade flows; the other examines how changes in trade policy affect the environment. The comments here are directed mainly to the second set of issues, that is, how trade policy changes affect the environment.

Within the scope of this focus, there appear to be three fruitful areas for research: (1) more direct analysis of the environmental consequences of trade (and other) policies, (2) incorporation of the spatial nature of the environment, and (3) greater attention to data needs.

### Greater Direct Attention Paid to the Environment

A standard approach in much of the literature is to posit a policy change, predict the behavioral responses, and infer an effect on the environment. Anderson and Strutt (this volume) provide an example of this approach. They begin with results from an earlier study that estimated the production effects (and inferred changes in farm chemical use) of complete removal of all farmer support policies. They then draw tentative conclusions about possible environmental consequences in several groups of countries.

This approach suffers from at least two potential problems. First, changes in input use suggest the potential of an environmental problem, but do not demonstrate its existence. For example, doubling the nitrogen applied to crops in the Netherlands will undoubtedly have a negative impact on that country's groundwater quality; yet it would have little effect in Nepal. Second, in partial equilibrium models there is the possibility that important environmental effects from other sectors will be ignored, and that important effects on other environmental resources will be left out. Computable general equilibrium models can address some of these concerns, but suffer from problems of their own.

A complementary approach, which draws inspiration from work by Chichilnisky (this volume) and suggestions made by Anderson and Strutt, would focus on the essence of environmental problems. The following definitions are useful for this discussion. An "environmental problem" is a negative externality arising from the overuse of an environmental resource. An "environmental resource" is a resource that has at least one attribute that is open access. An environmental resource is overused when more than one economic agent uses services from the resource, and the use of one agent affects the use of another agent. In the remainder of this discussion, the terms "environmental problem" and "environmental resource" are as defined here.

Most economists agree that environmental problems are conceptually the same as negative externalities. They arise because control rights for resource attributes are not fully (and effectively) allocated. This approach would begin by making explicit the externalities inherent in environmental problems and then modeling the impacts of economic policies, trade or otherwise, on the use of the environmental resources (see Nelson, forthcoming, for an extended presentation of this approach). Anderson and Strutt call such an approach a "national environmental/resource use model" and suggest marrying it with existing multi-commodity economic models.

A focus on externalities has several advantages. First, it suggests an explanation for the "inverted U curve" relationship between environmental quality and income, popularized by Grossman and Krueger (1991). As incomes grow, the use of open-access resources becomes more profitable, and environmental problems arise. As the external effects become larger, affected users of the resource lobby for control, and property rights are allocated. The downward sloping part of the U depends on a political process that internalizes the externalities.

In this context, rent-seeking issues are important. There is a useful parallel between the gains from trade and the gains from internalizing externalities. With free trade, the gross gains are greater than the gross losses, and it is possible for the gainers to compensate the losers. However, compensation seldom occurs, so potential losers from freer trade often lobby for continued protection. Similarly, when an externality is internalized, the gross gains are such that the gainers should be able to compensate the losers. Again, compensation seldom occurs—so agents with the potential to lose when environmental regulations are applied are likely to be active participants in the political process.

In the literature that examines the effects of environmental policy on trade (and production), most empirical results suggest that there is much ado about nothing. The effects on production and trade have been small (Gardner and Gruenspecht, this volume). However, it is clear that the few losers have been effective in slowing the reform process. Rent-seeking theory provides an explanation for why this is not surprising.

## Greater Incorporation of the Spatial Nature of the Environment

If you asked someone on the street to define the environment, the answer would undoubtedly include a reference to location. Whether we think of aquifers, ecosystems, or the atmosphere, spatial orientation of the resource is key. Yet, in most of the economic literature on the environment, location is not part of the analysis.

The absence of space as part of the analysis of environmental problems arises in part because economists have traditionally left such work to geographers. Current models tend to use national boundaries (or the world for global climate models) as the region of analysis. The recent work by Krugman (1994) on the importance of location will undoubtedly raise the visibility of spatial issues in the economics profession. In addition, the development of spatial econometric techniques and tools by Anselin (1988) and others, software to manipulate spatial data (GIS systems), and inexpensive computing resources suggest a rapid expansion of research in this area.

## Greater Attention Paid to Data Needs

Everyone agrees that economic analysis of environmental problems has been hindered by lack of data. The conference paper by Lucas on international environmental indicators (appearing as a chapter in this book) stretches the limits of what can be done with existing data on environmental problems. But what kinds of data would be better? Data development can be an expensive and time-consuming process. It would be desirable if old data sources could be repurposed, perhaps with incremental efforts to collect new data.

As research in this area continues, three organizing themes might be used to guide data collection and reporting. First, since externalities are the essence of environmental problems, data collection efforts might be categorized by externality with priority given to problems likely to have the highest external costs. Rather than a taxonomy based on consumption or production, a taxonomy based on environmental resource might be used. Second, concerted efforts should be made to retain spatial characteristics of data already being collected, and new data collection efforts should ensure that spatial components of data are obtained. Third, development of "environmental indicators" can reduce the data collection needs. An ideal environmental indicator would capture the existence and severity of an externality without requiring a complete accounting of the external costs. Several national and international agencies are making substantial efforts to define and collect "environmental indicators." An example is work being conducted within the Resource and Technology Division of the Economic Research Service to develop indicators of the environmental impact of changes in the U.S. Conservation Reserve Program.[1] These efforts should be encouraged where they promise the ability to contribute to analysis and policy making. Care needs to be taken that a consistent framework underlies the indicators.

New data sources need to be exploited. Satellite images provide a potentially rich source for economic analysis of the environment. They have the advantages of providing data from the early 1970s to the present, and being geo-referenced. They have the disadvantage of taxing the data storage and processing capacities of today's computers (file sizes of 80 megabytes are common). However, as software becomes more sophisticated and hardware becomes cheaper, this data source holds rich potential for the analysis of environmental problems.

Finally, more attention needs to be directed to estimating the benefits of resolving environmental problems. For example, Gardner (this volume) focuses entirely on the costs associated with environmental regulations affecting agriculture. Yet his empirical results suggest that environmental regulations have had little effect on productivity while ending a forty-year growth in the use of farm chemicals. The beneficiaries of environmental regulation are diffuse and diverse, while the costs of regulation fall on a small, well-organized group. Rent-seeking theory suggests that in this situation, the existing regulations would be expected to leave the marginal external costs from the externality greater than the private costs to producers.

In part, the relative dearth of empirical estimates of benefits is due to the history of the agricultural economics profession. A well-developed literature and numerous models exist to measure the costs to producers and consumers of shifting production functions and supply curves with regulation. But the literature on measuring benefits of addressing externalities is much smaller. Furthermore, there has been a tendency in the literature to theorize about existence and site values rather than to use accepted social cost-benefit techniques to quantify more readily measurable and less controversial external costs.

## Note

1. The original CRP program was targeted to highly erodible land. Specifically, the issue for the RTD analysis is: If other environmental problems are to be addressed, how would the distribution of CRP land change? Environmental indicators of ground and surface water quality, habitat and biodiversity preservation, and air pollution from dust were developed. They were then estimated for cropland identified in the 1982 National Resources Inventory (323,000 points). A preliminary result is that addressing additional environmental problems would shift some CRP enrollment from the center of the U.S. to the coasts. Furthermore, such a change might use CRP resources more efficiently in addressing the environmental problems.

## References

Anselin, L. *Spatial Econometrics: Methods and Models.* Dordrecht: Kluwer Academic Publishers, 1988.

Grossman, G.M., and A.B. Krueger. "Environmental Impacts of a North American Free Trade Agreement." Working Paper No. 3914, National Bureau of Economic Research, Washington, DC, 1991.

Krugman, P. "Urban Concentration: The Role of Increasing Returns and Transport Costs." Paper presented at World Bank Conference on Development Economics, Washington, DC, 1994.

Nelson, G.C. "Trade Agreements, Structural Adjustment Programs, and the Environment." Paper presented at the May, 1994 Meeting of the Resource Policy Consortium, D. Ervin, ed. Washington, DC.

# 19

# Reflections on Research Needs

*Cathy Roheim Wessells*

## Introduction

The Trade and Environment conference assembled a distinguished and knowledgeable set of speakers. The papers presented a significant amount of valuable research on the various aspects of the interactions between environmental policy and international trade. The increasingly frequent calls for the next General Agreement on Tariffs and Trade (GATT) round to be a "green" round mean much more research must to be done to diffuse the often highly emotional rhetoric emphasizing the incompatibilities of free trade goals and environmental protection.

It is useful to return to the goals of the conference to evaluate its success. Although the conference was intended to be agriculturally oriented, the larger issues related to the general environment quickly emerged as the focus. Thus, it is appropriate to examine these goals with a broader view, rather than specifically in the context of agricultural trade. Four conference goals were established: 1) to identify dimensions of the problem and issues, 2) to develop an understanding of the other point of view, 3) to generate an appreciation of the political agenda, 4) to define a research agenda. Certainly these goals are ambitious; however, given the complex and intensely debated nature of the issues at hand, they also seem eminently appropriate. In the remainder of this discussion, each of the four conference goals will be examined, and comments will be offered as to the extent these goals were achieved.

The first goal set was to *identify the dimension of the problem and its related issues*. In his discussion on critical linkages, Dr. Bhagwati divided an array of problems between those intrinsically domestic and those intrinsically international because they involve transboundary spillovers. Dr. Heal added to the discussion of those problems which are inherently global, and thus requiring multinational cooperation for successful solutions.

The first grouping includes several issues affecting internationally traded goods, including those related to divergent environmental policies among nations, and differing product and production process standards. For example, differences in the use of pesticides and their impacts on food safety standards fall into this grouping. Likewise, national policies related to acceptable levels of incidental mortality of dolphins in tuna harvesting also fall into this group.

The second area of concern involves issues of, for example, water pollution which moves in a river across national boundaries. Another example, chosen from the list enumerated by Dr. Gruenspecht, is acid rain. Dr. Gruenspecht identified several additional issues falling under each of the three problem categories, including the multinational problem of global warming discussed in more detail by Dr. Heal.

The dimensions of the problem and the related issues were exemplified repeatedly throughout the conference, with alternative issues highlighted by each individual speaker. Thus the first goal appears to have been admirably accomplished. Indeed, it may be the case that in achieving this goal, many of the conference attendees were overcome by the scale and scope of the issues involving trade and the environment. The reaction on the part of some of the participants was a call for a more narrowly defined taxonomy of issues. This proposed taxonomy would aid in clarifying and focusing a research agenda.

The second goal was specified as *developing an understanding of the other point of view*. The definition of "other" seemed to be somewhat unclear; however, it primarily referred to the community of individuals and institutions who believe that, among other things, liberalization of trade is a detriment to environmental protection and that it is appropriate to use trade mechanisms in protection of the world's resources. This goal was not successfully achieved; rather, throughout the conference there was a distinct "us" versus "them" flavor to the discussions.

In part, this was due to a lack of representation of those on the "other" side, although Drs. Ballenger and Krissoff provided an intriguing and informative representation of the positions of nongovernmental organizations on the issues, such as the Audobon Society, Sierra Club, Defenders of Wildlife, Greenpeace, and others. In the Ballenger-Krissoff paper, some of the environmental groups surveyed were against the North American Free Trade Agreement (NAFTA). Their opposition, as well as that of many other individuals who do not necessarily consider themselves "environmentalists," in part stems from skepticism of the theories and views of economists. Members of the "other" side often suspect economists' arguments of costs versus benefits in presenting the inefficiency of trade-distorting environmental polices. In their calculations, economists attempt to place monetary value on environmental resources, some of which many noneconomists wholeheartedly believe are infinitely valuable. The objective focus on economic efficiency rather than on the subjective issue of equity is also contentious to the "other" side. The distribution of costs and benefits across groups of people are a concern. Appreciating their point of view requires further dialogue between "us" and "them."

The need for understanding the other point of view is necessary partly to *understand and appreciate the political agenda,* the fourth goal of the conference. (I will leave the third goal for last.) It was evident after the discussion by Ambassador Smith (if not before) that the political agenda is complicated. This is true for most environmental issues because of the well-organized and vocal special interest groups involved. The tuna/dolphin case and the controversy over the NAFTA illustrate this point quite well.

Some fear the new World Trade Organization (WTO) is a threat to national sovereignty. They argue that each nation must be allowed to set strict environmental standards if it wishes to do so. Trade in goods from nations with more lax standards should be discouraged, or prohibited, through trade barriers. Policy makers are bound by a need to find compromise policies which will satisfy the various groups of constituents. In so doing, policies most often fully satisfy no one. A case in point is typified by the difficult process of drafting the latest Clean Air Act. Resulting environmental policies created by the political process are in all likelihood not the least trade distorting in their range of possibilities. Given the amount of intensive and expensive effort expended through the political process, it is not surprising that individuals involved in this process are dismayed with the potential that the GATT may rule that a national environmental policy contradicts the trading obligations of its members. The world's best interests are served by a GATT that continues to play a role of pushing nations to strive for policies which achieve desired environmental goals in the least trade-distorting manner. However, the political agenda in which the GATT finds itself entangled may continue to give the appearance of a *non-green* GATT. Thus, under the weight of the political agenda, the GATT itself (or the new WTO) may be in danger of becoming an extinct species.

An avalanche of confrontations appears to be developing between the GATT and interest groups opposed to GATT interference in environmental policy. Before the tuna/dolphin case, there were a few cases where resource management policies and free trade agreements were in apparent conflict—for example, the lobster and the unprocessed salmon and herring disputes between the United States and Canada. However, these cases attracted relatively little popular attention. The tuna/dolphin case captured the public's attention, in large part because of the focus on dolphins (some cynically call it the "Flipper Syndrome"). Once the implications of this case on other production standards issues became apparent, the GATT rapidly became the "enemy" and the politics of negotiating trade agreements were altered. Many additional disputes appear on the horizon.

An example of a potential issue which could be even more politically contentious than the tuna/dolphin controversy lies in the possible use of trade sanctions by the United States against Norway for its resumption of commercial whaling. As with the tuna/dolphin case, commercial whaling is a highly emotionally charged issue. In an October 4, 1993 letter to the U.S. Congress, President Clinton stated that the U.S. would refrain from imposing any trade sanctions on Norway, for the time being, as efforts toward finding alternative means might be successful in persuading Norway to discontinue commercial whaling. In the interim, the Department of Commerce was directed to compile a list of seafood products which could be embargoed should these alternatives fail.

In this case, the resource is migratory in national and international waters. Some individual species of whales are endangered or threatened, while others are not. In 1986, the International Whaling Commission (IWC) declared a five-year moratorium on commercial whaling until population assessments could be completed. While population estimates are difficult to obtain given the migratory nature of whales and their wide geographic distribution, in 1992 the scientific committee of the IWC determined that the population of minke whales is large enough to allow for a sustainable harvest, given strict harvest quotas. Although the scientific committee made this recommendation to the full IWC, the membership of the IWC elected to continue the moratorium on commercial whaling. Norway, as a member of the IWC, has the right to formally object to conservation measures adopted by the IWC, and under the rules of the IWC is not bound by those measures. Norway did object, and initiated a limited commercial harvest of minke whales in the spring of 1993, without the approval of the IWC.

The U.S. Secretary of Commerce is required to certify nations which are "diminishing the effectiveness of an international conservation program," including the IWC, according to the 1971 Pelly Amendment and the 1979 Packwood-Magnusen Amendments. The President must then report the action taken, or reasons for not taking action, to Congress within sixty days of certification. Due to Norway's objection to the continued moratorium on minke whale harvests, and subsequent commercial harvests,

Secretary Brown was legally bound to certify Norway. This eventually led to the letter from President Clinton to Congress. In sum, even when Norway is exercising rights granted by the IWC, the U.S. is required, at minimum, to contemplate the use of trade sanctions.

Environmental special interests will be able to generate enough authority, through political pressure or through the courts (as in the case of the dolphin measures), to gain trade sanctions against Norwegian seafood. If so the GATT panel ruling on the tuna/dolphin case, could conceivably lead Norway to approach the GATT for a ruling on any trade sanctions imposed by the U.S. over the whaling issue. If such a case were to go to a WTO panel, and the panel ruled against the United States, the public outcry against the WTO would likely be thunderous. As a result, political support for the WTO might drop off precipitously.

This example, perhaps exaggerated scenario, illustrates the difficult circumstances for the organizations attempting to promote free and fair trade. Moreover, it illustrates the lack of understanding of the "other" point of view on the part of both "us" and "them," and the political reality of the trade and environment issue. This leads to the final goal of the conference, the research agenda.

*Defining a research agenda* is far from simple when there are so many diverse and difficult issues to be addressed. However, the papers presented at this conference indicate that a research agenda is emerging. Research is proceeding in each of the problem areas defined by Drs. Bhagwati, Heal, and Gruenspecht. The research agenda includes topics related to the impacts of trade liberalization on resource use, and changes in environmental regulations and resource management on comparative advantage and trade. The chapters by Gardner and Blom highlighted topics where research is necessary to estimate the impacts of environmental policies on comparative advantages in the United States and European Union. The papers by Anderson and Strutt, and by Antle and Crissman further illustrate measurement of those impacts.

As Dr. Antle pointed out, environmental and trade issues must be measured at both the micro and macro levels to contribute meaningfully to the analysis of the economic effects, such as those on income levels and income distribution between and within countries. Microeconomic analyses (such as that of Antle, et. al.) cannot be feasibly conducted for every industry in every part of the world. However, these analyses cannot be overlooked because they are critical to understanding the breadth of the possible costs and benefits of trade and environmental policies on international and domestic markets for goods and the use of resources in the production of these goods.

As an example, little if any economic analysis was completed on the costs and benefits of moving toward zero mortality of dolphins from tuna harvesting. While there remains little quantitative analysis of the costs and benefits of this policy, some observations can be made regarding the types of costs incurred. It is apparent that costs did accrue to both the tuna industry and tuna consumers in a variety of ways—some anticipated and some unanticipated.

Production sites and trade flow patterns among nations have shifted. Changes in fishing techniques increased harvests of juvenile tuna, particularly in Mexico, which may reduce future stocks of tuna in the Eastern Tropical Pacific. In addition to increasing the costs of production as stocks are depleted, there presumably are also costs to those who value the existence of tuna. Thus, the benefits of saving dolphins must be weighed against the costs of a decrease in tuna stocks through both production costs and the environmental cost.

Some of these higher production costs are ultimately passed on to consumers. In addition, some consumers were impacted in other ways. According to industry sources, when confronted with a "dolphin-safe" label on cans of tuna, some confused U.S. consumers wondered if tuna they had consumed prior to the labeling had also contained dolphin meat. A micro-oriented approach toward the problem exposes facets of the distribution of costs and benefits that a more macro-oriented approach might not.

An additional step in further developing the research agenda is to expand the multi-disciplinary approach into the research agenda. As Dr. Gardner pointed out in his discussion, adding an environmental damage function and the costs of damage to an international trade model is not simple. An environmental damage function is often nontransferable from resource to resource, or even site to site. Referring to the above example, biological models of population dynamics must be incorporated into the economic analysis. Biological models are different between species and geographical location. Estimating these models requires physical data. Finally, the valuation of damage is very difficult and often controversial, even within the profession, as exemplified by the environmental damage assessment research done on the Exxon *Valdez* oil spill.

As a final note, the International Agricultural Trade Consortium is a logical group to further this research agenda by focusing on agricultural trade issues and their relationships to environmental issues. This research agenda would benefit from a workshop made up of a group of agricultural trade and development economists and a group of resource and environ-mental economists. Although there have been workshops of this nature in the past, given the growing importance of the topic, it is vital to have repeated and continuous dialogue within the profession. Due to their appropriateness, the same four goals used in this conference should be submitted to such a workshop, where the "other" point of view is defined as the sometimes opposing viewpoints of the two economics subdisciplines, and as the viewpoint of opposing noneconomists.

Benefits could be gained by segregating the focus of the proposed workshop into three problem areas: those related to intrinsically domestic issues, those involving transborder issues, and those which are inherently global. For example, intrinsically domestic issues might include the effects on international food trade of differing product, production process, and labor standards among nations. Transborder issues might consist of studies of nonpoint source pollution from fertilizers and other nutrients contaminating surface or ground water which moves across borders. Inherently global issues might include agriculture's effect on species diversity and agriculture's contribution to global warming. Using this as an initial taxonomy of issues, the research agenda may mature to further stages.

# About the Contributors and Editors

**Kym Anderson**, Professor and Director, Centre for International Economic Studies, University of Adelaide, Australia

**John M. Antle**, Professor, Department of Agricultural Economics and Economics, Montana State University

**Nicole Ballenger**, Economist, Economic Research Service, U.S. Department of Agriculture

**Jagdish Bhagwati**, Professor, Department of Economics, Columbia University

**Jan C. Blom**, Deputy Director and Head, Agricultural Economics Research Institute, The Hague, the Netherlands

**Maury E. Bredahl**, Professor of Agricultural Economics and Director of the Center for International Trade Expansion at the University of Missouri at Columbia.

**Steve Charnovitz**, Policy Director, U.S. Competitiveness Policy Council, Washington, DC

**Graciela Chichilnisky**, Professor, Department of Economics, Columbia University

**Charles C. Crissman**, Economist, International Potato Center, Quito, Ecuador

**Xinshen Diao**, PhD candidate, Department of Agriculture and Applied Economics, University of Minnesota

**John Dunmore**, Deputy Director, Commercial Agriculture Division, Economic Research Service, U.S. Department of Agriculture.

**David E. Ervin**, Professor, Oregon State University and Visiting Senior Analyst, Office of Technology Assessment, U.S. Congress, Washington, DC

**Bruce L. Gardner**, Professor, Department of Agricultural and Resource Economics, University of Maryland

**Howard K. Gruenspecht**, Director, Office of Economic Analysis and Competition, Office of Policy, U.S. Department of Energy

**Stephen Haley**, Agricultural Economist, Commercial Agriculture Division, Economic Research Service, U.S. Department of Agriculture

**Geoffrey Heal**, Professor of Economics and Finance, Program on Information and Resources and Graduate School of Business, Columbia University

**John L. Hutson**, Senior Research Associate, Department of Soil, Crop and Atmospheric Science, Cornell University

**Vivian Noble Keller**, Research Analyst, Office of Technology Assesssment, U.S. Congress, Washington, DC

**Barry Krissoff**, Agricutlural Economist, Economic Research Service, U.S. Department of Agriculture

**Dale Leuck**, Agricultural Economist, Natural Resources and Environmental Division, Economic Research Service, U.S. Department of Agriculture

**Robert E. B. Lucas**, Professor, Department of Economics, Boston University

**Gerald C. Nelson**, Associate Professor, Department of Agricultural and Consumer Economics, University of Illinois

**Terry L. Roe**, Professor, Department of Agriculture and Applied Economics, University of Minnesota

**Ambassador Michael B. Smith**, President, SJS Advanced Strategies, Washington, DC

**Anna Strutt**, Department of Economics and Centre for International Economic Studies, University of Adelaide, Australia

**R.J. Wagenet**, Professor, Department of Soil, Crop and Atmoshperic Sciences, Cornell University

**Cathy Roheim Wessells**, Assistant Professor, Department of Resource Economics, University of Rhode Island

**John Whalley**, Professor, Department of Economics, University of Western Ontario, Canada

# About the Book

In this timely volume, an international group of economists, trade negotiators, and environmentalists brings diverse perspectives to bear on the contentious issue of international trade and the environment. Providing a conceptual framework to help assess the issues, the contributors discuss three themes: the dimensions of the economic and political linkages of trade and the environment, economic and political linkages in developed countries—as well as the impact of environmental regulations on agricultural competitiveness, and the linkages between trade, economic growth, and the environment in developing nations.